D1526774

DENIAL AND REPRESSION OF ANTISEMITISM

DENIAL AND REPRESSION OF ANTISEMITISM

Post-Communist Remembrance of the Serbian Bishop Nikolaj Velimirović

Jovan Byford

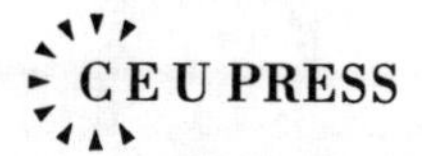

Central European University Press
Budapest New York

Published in 2008 by
Central European University Press

An imprint of the
Central European University Share Company
Nádor utca 11, H-1051 Budapest, Hungary
Tel: +36-1-327-3138 or 327-3000
Fax: +36-1-327-3183
E-mail: ceupress@ceu.hu
Website: www.ceupress.com

400 West 59th Street, New York NY 10019, USA
Tel: +1-212-547-6932
Fax: +1-646-557-2416
E-mail: mgreenwald@sorosny.org

ISBN 978-963-9776-15-9 cloth

LIBRARY OF CONGRESS CATALOGING-IN-PUBLICATION DATA

Byford, Jovan.
Denial and repression of anti-semitism : post-communist remembrance of the Serbian Bishop Nikolaj Velimirovic / Jovan Byford.
p. cm.
Includes bibliographical references.
ISBN 978-9639776159 (cloth : alk. paper)
1. Velimirovic, Nikolaj, 1880-1956. 2. Srpska pravoslavna crkva—Bishops—Biography. 3. Orthodox Eastern Church—Serbia—Bishops—Biography. 4. Christian saints—Serbia—Biography. I. Title.

BX719.V45B93 2008 2004
281.9092—dc22
[B]

2008001194

Printed in Hungary by
Akadémia Nyomda, Martonvásár

Table of Contents

Acknowledgments

My thanks are due first to the Hebrew University's Sassoon International Centre for the Study of Antisemitism (SICSA) for providing financial support for the research project that resulted in this book. I am especially grateful to Prof. Robert Wistrich, director of the Vidal Sassoon Centre, and to Dr. Leon Volovici, Head of Research, for giving my proposal serious consideration and for their encouragement. My gratitude goes also to Michael Billig and Filip David for their friendship, advice and support.

I am grateful to the following journals for their permission to include in the book portions of the articles previously published under their auspices: *Analysis of Current Trends in Antisemitism* (published by the SICSA) for "From Traitor to Saint: Bishop Nikolaj Velimirović in Serbian public memory" (2004) ACTA, no. 22, 1–41; *Patterns of Prejudice* (Routledge), for "'Serbs never hated the Jews': the denial of antisemitism in contemporary Serbian Orthodox Christian culture", 40 (2), 2006, 159–180; *State, Religion and Society* (Routledge) for "Distinguishing 'Anti-Judaism' From 'Antisemitism': Recent championing of the Serbian Bishop Nikolaj Velimirović", 34 (1), 2006, 7–31; and *East European Perspectives* (published online by Radio Free Europe) for "Canonizing the 'Prophet' of anti-Semitism: The apotheosis of Bishop Nikolaj Velimirović and the legitimisation of religious anti-Semitism in contemporary Serbian society" (March 2004).

I would also like to thank the Editorial Board of Central European University Press and Linda Kunos for their efficient management of the editorial and publication process, and Réka Benczes for her meticulous copy-editing.

Finally, I would like to thank my family and especially my partner Sabina Mihelj, for being there for me.

Chapter One
Introduction

Recent years have seen a rise in interest in the topic of "collective memory" among historians, sociologists, political scientists, and psychologists (Irwin-Zarecka, 1994; Kansteiner, 2002; Maier 1997; Middleton & Edwards, 1990; Misztal, 2003; Olick, 1999; Wertsch, 2002). Although the precise meaning and the scope of terms, such as "collective memory," "social memory," "social remembering," and "national" or "public" memory, remain a matter of debate (Wood, 1999), there appears to be agreement among scholars on the subject that shared, non-consensual, and frequently contested representations of the past, which define social identities and delineate boundaries between social groups, constitute a topic worthy of academic consideration.

One factor which contributed to the renewed interest in collective memory in the past fifteen or twenty years was the number of radical changes in the representations of the past which accompanied, and were in many ways constitutive of, the post-communist transition in Eastern Europe (Jedlicki, 1999; Muller, 2002; Todorova, 2004; Verdery, 1999; Wertsch, 2002). The fall of communism in the region was accompanied by extensive rewriting of history aimed at overturning communist interpretations of the past, which had dominated national historiographies and collective memory since the end of World War II. In many cases, this process led to misguided instances of revisionism and the rehabilitation of a number of contentious historical figures, some of whom, forty years earlier, had attained notoriety for their antisemitism and fascist and pro-Nazi leanings. Since the late 1980s, biographies of the likes of Ante Pavelić in Croatia, General Ion Antonescu in Romania, Jozef Tiso in Slovakia, and Miklós Horthy in Hungary were subjected to a comprehensive makeover, as attempts were made to transform their status from villains to heroes, perpetrators to victims (Ramet, 1999; Shafir, 2002; Volovici, 1994).

The rewriting of the past in Eastern Europe went hand in hand with religious revival across former communist lands and the return of organized religion into public life. One way in which resurgent Christian churches sought to establish authority in the ideological vacuum left behind by the decline of communism was through participation in the re-evaluation of national history. Ecclesiastical establishments aligned themselves with nationalist forces in the attempt to weave religion into the narratives of the national past and position the church at the core of national identity. As a result, in much of post-1989 Eastern Europe, confessional affiliation came to be regarded as an important marker of national belongingness; religious rites were a ubiquitous ingredient of nationalist commemorative rituals; while in some instances (such as in the case of the Romanov imperial family in Russia or Bishop Alojzije Stepinac in Croatia), canonization emerged as the appropriate symbolic act through which political rehabilitation could be signified.

The reinterpretation of the national past which swept Eastern Europe after the fall of the Berlin Wall did not bypass Serbian society (see Kuljić, 2002; Popov, 1993). For the duration of Milošević's quasi-socialist regime, revisionism was by and large devoid of official backing from the state, and remained the provenance of influential national(ist) institutions, such as the Serbian Academy of Arts and Sciences and the Serbian Union of Writers, who were aided in their endeavors by numerous public figures, right-wing political organizations, and publishers. As a result of their combined efforts over the years, the country witnessed a significant change in the understanding of the nation's history, especially in relation to World War II. The Serbian Orthodox Church—the largest and the most influential religious institution in the land and the self-professed guardian of the nation's values and main interpreter of its past—played a significant role in facilitating these changes. The much publicized exhumation and religious burial of Serbian victims of the Ustasha regime in Bosnia and Croatia, which the Serbian Orthodox Church organized in 1991, reflected the desire to reconfigure public memory and popularize the martyrological interpretation of Serbian history which had been articulated by the 1987 memorandum of the Serbian Academy of Arts and Sciences and which was being instrumentalized by the up-and-coming nationalist political elite. The Serbian Orthodox Church also helped to revise the popular perceptions of collaboration during the Nazi occupation of Serbia (1941–1944) and enhance the public image of a number of collaborators and World War II nationalist leaders such as Generals Draža Mihailović and Milan Nedić or Dimitrije Ljotić (Popov, 1993). In 1994, at the religious service in honor of the head of the Serbian collaborationist government, General Milan Nedić, Patriarch Pavle of the Serbian Orthodox Church hailed Nedić as a "savior of the Serbian people" (Torov, 1994). In doing so he affirmed, from the position of highest spiritual authority in the land, the apologist interpretation of collaboration which continues to be advanced by the political far-right to the present day, and which in 2003 even made it into the school curriculum (see Byford, 2007). Similarly, the longstanding positive stance towards General Draža Mihailović in the religious press in Serbia—which dates back to the late 1980s—culminated in 2004 when Father Miodrag Popović, editor-in-chief of the country's main Christian publication *Pravoslavlje*, suggested that Mihailović (who was tried for treason and executed as a Nazi collaborator by the Yugoslav communists in 1946) was not only a "Serb who genuinely believed in God," but also a "confessor and martyr who died for Christ's faith" and therefore nothing less than a "saint" (M. Popović, 2005, p. 55).

The present book examines a specific example of collective memory transformation in post-communist Serbian society, one in which the Serbian Orthodox Church played a central role. It explores the changing representation, over the past twenty or so years of the recently canonized Bishop Nikolaj Velimirović (1881–1956), a controversial early 20th century Serbian Orthodox Christian philosopher who, having been vilified by communist authorities as a traitor and a fascist, is today widely revered in Serbia as a saint and the greatest national religious figure since medieval times. As we will see in the next chapter, in Tito's Yugoslavia, Nikolaj Velimirović was the embodiment of the reactionary forces within the Serbian Orthodox Church. He was disparaged as an agent of imperialism, an antisemite, a "lackey of the Germans" even a "war criminal." These evaluations of Velimirović's personal history, although often exaggerated and tendentious, were nonetheless based on a number of controversies surrounding his life and work, which remain a topic of public contention even today. And yet, in spite of the ongoing controversy, in present day Serbia, the unprecedented greatness of "the Holy Bishop Nikolaj" and his unique contribution to Orthodox Christianity are routinely lauded in both mainstream and ecclesiastical press. His place in the history of the Christian Church is seen as being right next to St Sava and St John Chrysostom. He is hailed by the Serbian Orthodox Church as a martyr, a prophet, and a saint. In the days preceding the canonization ceremony in May 2003, more than ten thousand faithful queued for hours to worship Velimirović's "holy remains," displayed in an open casket. What is more, in recent years a score of public figures in Serbia, including a number of prominent politicians, have cited the once reviled Serbian bishop as an unquestionable spiritual and intellectual authority. The aim of the forthcoming chapters is to examine the transformation in Velimirović's public standing over the past two decades and shed light on the dynamics of social remembering and forgetting which enabled the now prevailing affirmative representations of his life and legacy to emerge from behind forty years of vilification and marginalization, and transform the controversial bishop into a central figure of contemporary Serbian Orthodox Christian culture.

In examining the shift in Velimirović's public image since the 1980s, the book focuses on collective memory. Subsequent chapters explore public memorial discourse, including representations of Bishop Velimirović in the media, at commemorative ceremonies, in political and ecclesiastical discourses, in books and pamphlets, in religious art, and in other aspects of Serbian Orthodox Christian culture. Remembering in the context of spoken dialogue is also examined, which includes the analysis of thirteen interviews—conducted specifically for the purposes of the present study—with public figures that have been actively involved in Velimirović's rehabilitation over the past two decades. Because of the focus on social remembering, rather than on accounts of Velimirović's life found in official and institutionalized historical writing, the temptation to look at the subject matter as an instance of "historical revisionism" will be resisted. Although the relationship between "history" and "memory" is a complex and controversial one, it can nonetheless be suggested that important differences exist in institutional, epistemological, and rhetorical dynamics between historiography as an academic discipline, and everyday social remembering (e.g., Kansteiner, 2002; Misztal, 2003). Peter Novick (2001) even argues that collective memory is not just "ahistorical" but "antihistorical." Contrary to what history at least ought to be like, memory is always simplistic, ideologically committed, "impatient with ambiguities," and prone to reducing events to "mythic archetypes" (pp. 4–5). This will be shown to be apparent in the memory of Nikolaj Velimirović. Public remembrance of Velimirović's life in Serbian Orthodox culture is fragmented and patchy. The spotlight of memory is focused on selected snapshots, singular episodes, and vivid images without sufficient regard for sequential chronological ordering or narrative coherence characteristic of historical accounts. The concept of "historical revisionism" is also inadequate because it implies that there is an official view of history or the past that is, or ought to be, the subject of revision (White, 2000). In the realm of collective memory there are no unitary, hegemonic representations of the past. Instead of a "mnemonic consensus," there are multiple memories engaged in a conflict for supremacy and social influence (Olick and Robbins, 1998). Memory is inherently tied in with the concept of social identity. Political, religious, national, ethnic, or gender divisions delineate "memory communities," whose conflicting representations of the past reflect diverse identities, motives, and ideological commitments. In the pluralist world of multiple memories, collective memory is not a consensual view of the past, but a field of contestation, a symbolic space where different perspectives compete over the "possession and interpretation of memory" (Thelen, 1989).

The assumption regarding the plurality of memory calls for the recognition of the inherently argumentative nature of remembering. To remember is not merely to recall the past, but to recall it in a way that undermines the alternative "counter-memories." As well as simply "telling a story," remembering seeks to actively "forget" potentially embarrassing or threatening aspects of the past, to undermine the credibility of the creators of alternative perspectives, or to "reify" one's own interpretation by presenting it as an indisputable aspect of empirical reality and a collection of "historical facts." According to Gur-Ze'ev and Pappé (2003), remembering involves "symbolic violence": its rhetorical dynamic aims to "[position] more effectively one's own narrative, interests, values, symbols, goals and criteria, while at the same time ensuring that those of the Other are marginalized excluded or destroyed" (p. 93). Also, the argumentative context, consisting of the nexus of publicly available "counter memories," determines what topics are worth remembering and how they are to be remembered

(Schudson, 1989). As the forthcoming chapters will show, the way in which supporters remember Bishop Nikolaj Velimirović is very much driven by the nature of the controversy surrounding his writing. Favorable accounts of the bishop's life and achievements orient towards, and attempt to undermine and sideline the alternative, less complimentary interpretations of his personal history, be it the remnants of the older communist critique or the more contemporary unsympathetic appraisals popularized in recent years by the liberal public opinion in Serbia.

The principal contention surrounding Velimirović's life and work—over which there is conflict among different "memory communities" in Serbia, and which determines the discourse of his remembrance—is antisemitism. The disagreement over the memory of Nikolaj Velimirović is a dispute over whether he should be remembered as a Man of God and the greatest Serbian religious persona since the medieval Serbian St Sava, or as a thinker and a writer whose status in Serbian history and the history of the Serbian Orthodox Church is compromised by a radical nationalist outlook rooted in the ideological context of the 1930s, and by the presence, in his writing, of an unpardonable contempt for Jews deeply reminiscent of the European fascist tradition.

In the forthcoming chapters, the public remembrance of Nikolaj Velimirović within Serbian Orthodox Christian culture will be shown to have been guided by the overwhelming concern with making him not appear antisemitic. This continuous effort to repress, undermine, deny, or justify Velimirović's contempt for Jews, to cleanse his biography of all controversy and popularize a sanitized version of his life—which is the principle topic of this book—exposes as the fundamental preoccupation, among Velimirović's supporters, what in discursive and rhetorical psychology is called "moral accountability management." Discourse analytic research has shown that individuals and groups participate in social interaction as actors in a moral universe, operating within a culturally specific set of rules regarding what is right or wrong, acceptable or unacceptable. Much of everyday interaction, including remembering, is spent accounting for one's beliefs and conduct within the salient framework of values, and negotiating for oneself a credible position within the moral universe (Burr, 2003). Crucially for the present discussion, the issue of moral accountability lies at the core of political debate on inter-racial, inter-ethnic, inter-religious, and other forms of community relations (see Augoustinos et al. 2002; Billig, 1990; LeCouteur & Augoustinos 2001; Rapley, 2001; Van Dijk, 1984, 1987, 1992, 1993; Wetherell and Potter, 1992; Wodak, 1991; etc.). When articulating views on what are widely perceived as controversial matters on race, ethnicity, and religion, speakers go to considerable lengths to deny that they are being prejudiced, presenting their beliefs and actions as compliant with the powerful social norm against public display of intolerance.

The willful forgetting or repression of Velimirović's antisemitism, as well the rhetoric of denial, which are constitutive of the way in which the bishop's followers recall their hero, both endeavor to give Velimirović and his ideological position credibility, authority, and integrity in a broader social context where some of his ideas might be seen as violating prevailing norms of ethnic and racial tolerance, and where his reputation is constantly brought into question by rival memory communities. As well as protecting the reputation of Nikolaj Velimirović, repression and denial of his antisemitism safeguard the public image and the social influence of his supporters and admirers, whose group identity is defined by their allegiance to the controversial bishop and by their shared favorable representations of his legacy.

Repression and denial of antisemitism in the remembrance of Nikolaj Velimirović have an additional broader dimension. In the aftermath of World War II, Christian churches found themselves under pressure to eradicate from their doctrines and religious life what Jules Isaac (1964) aptly referred to as the Christian "teaching of contempt" for Jews. The pressure on churches has been underpinned by the recognition of a historical and ideological link between the longstanding tradition of Christian anti-Judaism and modern variants of secular antisemitism (see Chapter 5 for a more detailed examination of this link). The response of different Christian denominations to the changing moral environment since 1945 has been varied. In the Protestant churches negative conceptions of Jews and Judaism have been mostly confined to the margins. The Catholic Church, on which much of the critical attention had been focused, formally distanced itself from the tradition of Christian anti-Judaism in a series of statements that built on the Nostra Aetate document adopted by the Second Vatican Council in 1965. Although it is often argued that efforts of the Catholic Church have been slow and in many ways inadequate (e.g., Carrol, 2002; Goldhagen, 2002), there appears to be agreement that the

Vatican has taken significant steps towards improving Catholic–Jewish relations.

Efforts to meet the standards of what Jocelyn Hellig (2002) calls "responsible theology," apparent in western Christendom since the Holocaust, have largely bypassed the Orthodox world. Eastern churches, including the Serbian Orthodox Church, have not as yet formally addressed, from a doctrinal or ecclesiastical perspective, the problem of Christian anti-Judaism (M. Đorđević, 1998; Gurevich, 1995; Hackel, 1998; Rudnev, 1995; Tabak, 2000). Dogged traditionalism and staunch belief in the immutability of the Holy Tradition ensures the persistence of "mediaeval preconceptions" of Jews in contemporary Orthodox theology (Tabak, 2000). Although Christian anti-Judaism is for the most part implicit, and thus cannot be said to play a significant part in the everyday religious life of the Orthodox faithful, the outdated and lamentable view of Jews as reprobate Christ-killers persists in Orthodox Christianity's official religious doctrine and liturgical practice. The failure of the eastern churches to follow in the footsteps of their western counterparts puts them in somewhat of a dilemma *vis-à-vis* contemporary mainstream political morality. When dealing with the issue of Christian–Jewish relations, Orthodox religious authorities must articulate their stance in a way that preserves the Church's traditionalist and reactionary anti-Judaic official dogma without blatantly contravening the prevailing secular norms of ethnic and religious tolerance. This "ideological dilemma" (Billig et al., 1988) imposes considerable rhetorical demands on the followers of Nikolaj Velimirović. The remembrance of the controversial bishop must be articulated not just in a way that makes the bishop's views appear non-antisemitic, but also in a manner that would not undermine in any way the Church's traditionalist ideological position on Jews. As we will see, the required ideological balancing act plays a role in determining the nature and the function of both repression and denial.

The remembrance of Nikolaj Velimirović is not the only arena in which the Serbian Orthodox Church manages its moral accountability *vis-à-vis* its position on Jews and Judaism. On several occasions over the past two decades, the Church found itself under pressure to distance itself from expressions of antisemitism within its ranks. In 1992 the magazine *Pravoslavlje*, the official publication of the patriarchate of the Serbian Orthodox Church, published an openly antisemitic text that alleged the persecution of Christians by Jews in Israel ("Jevreji ponovo raspinju Hrista," 1992). Following protests from the country's Jewish community, the synod of the Serbian Church dismissed the magazine's editor-in-chief and apologized for the incident (Synod of the Serbian Orthodox Church, 1992). Three years later the synod publicly condemned the publishing activity of Ratibor Đurđević, Serbia's most prolific writer and distributor of antisemitic material, whose anti-Jewish diatribes are steeped in Orthodox Christian rhetoric (see Sekelj, 1997). In 2002, the same body distanced itself from Father Žarko Gavrilović, after this notoriously antisemitic priest made unacceptable claims about the Jewish community in a television show. These instances of public distancing are a testimony to the desire of the Serbian Orthodox Church to maintain cordial relations with the local Jewish communal bodies, and build on a much longer tradition of amiable Christian–Jewish relations in Serbia (see Freidenreich, 1979; Gordiejew, 1999; Ž. Lebl, 2001). And yet, as we will show in Chapter 4, the condemnation of antisemitic outbursts tends to be articulated in a way that preserves the Serbian Orthodox Church's egalitarian and tolerant self-image, while at the same time warding off any substantive examination of the root causes of these recurring and discomforting (albeit rare) incidents.

Just like any representation of the life and the writings of Nikolaj Velimirović, this book is situated within the argumentative context at the centre of which is the controversy surrounding his legacy. For this reason, it may be beneficial to declare at the outset the author's stance on this matter. While reserving judgment on Nikolaj Velimirović's overall contribution to Orthodox theology and spirituality or the artistic merit of his extensive literary output, this book takes an unequivocally critical stance towards his position on Jews, which it regards as lamentable and indefensible. Forthcoming chapters are equally critical of the unwillingness and inability of the Serbian Orthodox Church—a prominent mainstream institution whose moral influence in Serbian society is steadily growing—to adequately distance itself from Velimirović's controversial writings and recognize that many of the views which "the greatest Serb since St Sava" held on society, history, and politics belong to an obsolete and discredited ideological tradition of 1930s conservative thought. What is more, one of the main argument of the book is that in an attempt to exonerate him from criticism and rescue his reputation from the marginal place in history allocated to it in communist versions of the past, Velimirović's supporters have gone as far as to present their hero's most controversial views not only as unproblematic, but sometimes also as a legitimate aspect of Orthodox Christian religious identity. By suppressing, justifying, excusing, minimizing and trivializing Velimirović's antisemitic writings, the dynamics of repression and denial have transformed his contempt for Jews into a satisfactory, acceptable and within some circles of Serbian Orthodox culture, even normative stance towards Jews.

A number of studies on antisemitism in Serbia published in the past fifteen years (Helsinki Committee for Human Rights in Serbia, 2001, 2003a, 2003b; Sekelj, 1995, 1997) have made a connection between the rise in antisemism in Serbia since the 1990s and Velimirović's return to the mainstream of Serbian Orthodox Christian culture. This link has been the focus of particular attention since the year 2000 when a number of often militant Christian right-wing organizations, which espouse antisemitic ideas, emerged on Serbia's political landscape (see Chapter 4). And yet, while accurately identifying Nikolaj Velimirović as the main ideological authority of the emerging Christian Right in Serbia, studies published to date have not explored in adequate detail *how* Velimirović's rehabilitation over the past twenty years contributed to the reappearance of antisemitism in Serbia. The forthcoming chapters address this question directly and explore specifically how the management of Velimirović's moral credibility and the failure by the Serbian Church to adequately tackle the issue of his anti-Jewish diatribes legitimized antisemitism and enabled it to emerge out of the woodwork within a society without an established antisemitic political tradition and within which anti-Jewish prejudice had hitherto had a negligible presence.

The present work is also the first detailed analysis of the post-communist remembrance of Nikolaj Velimirović and the first comprehensive exploration of the controversy surrounding his life and work. A critical examination of Velimirović's legacy is important because he is held in high regard not just in Serbia, but also within theological circles in Western Europe and the United States, where there appears to be a widespread unawareness of the controversy surrounding his views. As we will see, this lack of knowledge is caused mainly by the fact that much of the literature in the West relies on the very same sanitized interpretations of Velimirović's life which the present book aims to expose.

The following chapter (Chapter 2) provides an outline of Velimirović's biography, with particular focus on the controversy surrounding his life and work. Also, it examines the campaign against Nikolaj Velimirović during the communist era and situates it in the broader context of church–state relations in the former Yugoslavia. The marginal position which the controversial bishop occupied in public memory in the post-war period is then contrasted with the widespread popularity he is enjoying in Serbia today. This chapter sets the scene for the four empirical or analytical chapters, which examine discursive and rhetorical processes underpinning the transformation in Velimirović's public image.

Chapter 3 explores the dynamic of forgetting, or social repression. The rehabilitation of Nikolaj Velimirović—especially in the late 1980s and early 1990s—is shown to have involved continuous suppression and sidelining of the controversial aspects of his biography. Drawing on the work of Iwona Irwin-Zarecka (1994) and Michael Billig (1997a, 1999a, 1999b), this chapter suggests that embarrassing aspects of the bishop's life were "repressed" by being substituted with a suitable "replacement myth," namely the portrayal of Velimirović as a martyr and a victim of Nazi persecution. The chapter explores the dynamic by means of which the emphasis on the bishop's alleged martyrdom helped to maintain the controversy away from social remembrance.

Chapters 4 and 5 focus on the strategies of denial of antisemitism which have played a more prominent role in the memory of Nikolaj Velimirović since 2000, when his uncritical adulation within the Serbian Orthodox culture came under closer scrutiny and criticism from liberal public opinion and representatives of the country's Jewish community. Chapter 4 examines the responses to criticism and focuses on the rhetoric of social denial, namely the frequently articulated claim that there has never been any antisemitism in Serbian society and especially not within the Serbian Orthodox Church. By exploring the rhetorical construction of this general myth of national and confessional self-glorification and by examining its various components (e.g., literal and comparative denial, use of offensive rhetoric, and the strategy of reversal), this chapter reveals how social denial diverts attention from the specific controversy surrounding Nikolaj Velimirović's life and helps to undermine the credibility of memory communities that propagate a more critical stance towards his reputation. Most importantly, as well as shielding the bishop's reputation from criticism, the perpetuation of the myth about the inherent tolerance of Serbs keeps the topic of antisemitism off the public agenda and facilitates the refusal to recognize it as a social problem that warrants attention and action.

Chapter 5 explores in more detail the ways in which accusations of antisemitism directed at Velimirović personally are dealt with among his supporters. The chapter examines a variety of rhetorical strategies, the most important of which is the rhetoric of "interpretative denial," namely the construction of Velimirović's stance towards Jews as an acceptable form of "theological" or "Biblical" antisemitism, the roots of which are to be found in the Christian Bible. By exploring and scrutinizing this argument, Chapter 5 shows how this type of rhetoric enables Christian antisemitism, as well as to other forms of anti-Jewish prejudice, to be perceived as a normal and even normative aspect of contemporary Orthodox Christian identity.

Finally, Chapter 6 examines the campaign for Velimirović's canonization that began in the late 1980s and ended in May 2003, when the bishop was formally included in the Diptych of Serbian Saints. In exploring the construction of Velimirović's sanctity, it is argued that while the campaign tended to sidestep the controversy surrounding his antisemitism, certain constructions of the bishop's holiness were fundamentally linked to the controversy surrounding his earthly existence. Moreover, the social construction of Velimirović's sanctity will be shown to have endowed the antisemitic aspect of his ideology with almost divine authority, ensuring its persistence in the discourse of his celebration as a national saint.

What follows is a brief outline of the written materials used in the study and details of the interviews conducted for the purposes of this research.

Materials Used in the Study

PRINTED MATERIAL

The present research project is based on detailed analysis of representations of Nikolaj Velimirović in a wide range of texts ranging from the mainstream press and scholarly writings (Bigović, 1998; Janić,

1994; Janković, 2002a, 2002b, 2003; Jevtić, 2003a; Samardžić, 2004; Saramandić, 2004; etc.), through popular hagiographic booklets (e.g., Janković, 2004; Najdanović, 2001; A. Radosavljević, 1986; etc.) and the ecclesiastical press, all the way to representations found in books and magazines published by the extreme right in Serbia (magazines such as *Dveri*, *Novine Srpsko Ogledalo*, *Pogledi*, etc.; also Đurđević, 1997, 2002, 2003; Gavrilović, 1998; Krstić, 2002; etc.). The Christian press examined in the study includes *Pravoslavlje* (Orthodoxy), the official publication of the patriarchate of the Serbian Orthodox Church; *Glas Crkve* (Voice of the Church), published by the diocese of Šabac and Valjevo, which was instrumental in the popularization of Velimirović's work in the late 1980s and early 1990s; *Hrišćanska Misao* (Christian Thought), published by the Orthodox Theological Faculty in Belgrade; *Svetigora* (Holy Mountain), published by the Metropolitanate of Montenegro and the Littoral; *Žički Blagovesnik* (Žiča Herald), published by the diocese of Žiča; *Sveti Knez Lazar* (Holy Prince Lazar), published by the diocese of Raška and Prizren; and *Jefimija*, an independent publication from the city of Trstenik. The study also examines portrayals of Nikolaj Velimirović in the mainstream press, especially in dailies such as *Blic, Danas*, *Ekspress Politika*, *Glas Javnosti*, *Politika*, and *Večernje Novosti*; and weekly publications including *Blic News*, *NIN*, *Vreme*, and others.

In the examination of the press, special attention has been paid to reports and transcripts of commemorative ceremonies devoted to Nikolaj Velimirović. Speeches and sermons delivered by high church officials at such ceremonies were often reported, in the 1980s and 1990s in the ecclesiastical press (above all in *Glas Crkve* and *Pravoslavlje*), and more recently also in independent media, such as *Vreme*, *Radio B92* and *Radio Free Europe*, albeit in a more critical context.

Besides looking at media representations of Nikolaj Velimirović in the past two decades, the study briefly examines depictions during the communist era (between 1946 and the mid-1980s). Material pertaining to this period consists mainly of debates in the mainstream press about the merits of Bishop Nikolaj's philosophy and the nature of his political stance during World War II. The most significant debates took place in 1948–1950, 1968, 1972, 1981, and 1986. The outline in Chapter 2 of these early disputes about Velimirović's credibility offers insight into the background to the controversy and the argumentative context within which the subsequent rehabilitation had to be realized. The analysis of the material published since 1986 is more detailed, and focuses on the rhetorical and discursive dynamics by the means of which Nikolaj Velimirović gradually became reinstated in the roll call of Serbian national heroes.

Interviewees

While the bulk of the project examines textual material and speeches and sermons reported in the media, the analysis is supplemented with additional interview data. This data consists of recorded conversations with individuals from different political and occupational backgrounds who have an interest in Nikolaj Velimirović and who have played a role in the popularization of his views. Twelve interviews were conducted in July and August 2003 with members of the Serbian Orthodox Church, intellectuals, men of letters, and activists of Christian right-wing political organizations. The aim of the interviews was to examine the ways in which the management of the controversy surrounding Velimirović's work, which is apparent in the media, manifests itself and is played out in the context of spoken dialogue. These interviews also enabled the author to question many of the protagonists of Velimirović's rehabilitation who featured in the media, on issues specifically related to the project at hand. Interviews were recorded and subsequently transcribed by professional transcribers based in Belgrade. The details of the interviews and interviewees are listed below:

Milan Bates

Bates was interviewed as the leader of the now defunct Udruženje studenata Sv. Justin Filozof (St Justin the Philosopher Association of Students), popularly known as "Justin," founded in 2001. In the early days of its existence, "Justin" was as an extremist nationalist student organization, which openly espoused the ideology of Orthodox Christian far-right. However, by 2003 the organization's leadership sought to shed its extremist image and toned down its rhetoric. For a while it operated as a formal student organization with offices at the Philosophical Faculty in Belgrade. Nikolaj Velimirović was the organization's main spiritual and ideological authority. The conversation with Bates, which was held in Belgrade, lasted approximately 120 minutes.

MATIJA BEĆKOVIĆ

Bećković is one of Serbia's leading poets and public figures. In the early days of the campaign for Velimirović's rehabilitation, in the late 1980s, Bećković was a regular participant in commemorative ceremonies which were organized in the diocese of Šabac and Valjevo. He continues to perform this function to the present day: in 2002, Bećković delivered a speech at the unveiling of the statue of Velimirović at the Soko Monastery in central Serbia. Matija Bećković is thought to be close to Velimirović's followers within the Church, especially the Bishop of Montenegro Amfilohije Radović. The conversation held in Belgrade lasted approximately 75 minutes.

PROTOPRESBYTER RADOVAN BIGOVIĆ

Radovan Bigović is a priest at the Monastery St Archangel Michael in Zemun near Belgrade and lecturer in comparative theology at the Orthodox Theological Faculty in Belgrade. He is considered to be one of the leading experts on the work of Bishop Nikolaj Velimirović. His doctoral thesis on Velimirović, subsequently published as the book entitled *From All-Man to the Man of God: The Christian Philosophy of Bishop Nikolaj Velimirović* (1998) is one of the most comprehensive studies of Velimirović's life and work to date. Bigović is also a well-known and respected public figure who frequently appears in the media and comments on religious matters. The conversation with Bigović lasted approximately 45 minutes.

VUK DRAŠKOVIĆ

Drašković is a popular Serbian writer and politician. In the late 1980s and early 1990s, as leader of the right-wing Serbian Renewal Movement, Drašković was one of the leading opponents of Slobodan Milošević. He was also one of the main advocates of the rehabilitation of the Chetnik movement. In the late 1980s, he regularly attended commemorative ceremonies organized in Velimirović's honor and made a significant contribution to the popularization of the bishop's work. Following the electoral success at parliamentary elections held in December 2003, Drašković's party entered Serbia's ruling coalition, a move which earned him the post of Foreign Minister first in the federal government of Serbia and Montenegro, and later (after the secession of Montenegro in 2006) in the government of Serbia. At the January 2007 elections, Drašković's party failed to win any parliamentary seats, which marked the end of his ministerial career. The interview with Drašković lasted approximately 60 minutes.

PROTOPRESBYTER MILAN JANKOVIĆ

Janković is Secretary of the Holy Synod of the Serbian Orthodox Church and editor of an extensive three-volume collection of documents about Nikolaj Velimirović published in 2002 (vols. 1 and 2) and 2003 (vol. 3) under the title *Bishop Nikolaj: His Life, Thought, and Work*. Janković declined the offer of an interview, but agreed to provide a written answer to five questions, which were submitted to his office at the patriarchate by post. The answers, produced in the form of a six-page document, were returned to the author with the understanding that they represent Janković's personal opinion rather than the official stance of the Serbian Orthodox Church. During the brief encounter with the author at the headquarters of the patriarchate, Janković expressed the intention to publish his response in the near future in one of the publications of the Serbian Orthodox Church.

SLOBODAN MILEUSNIĆ (1947–2005)

Mileusnić, an art historian and theologian, was one of the leading experts on Serbian religious art and the curator of the Museum of the Serbian Orthodox Church, located in the building of the patriarchate in Belgrade. Between 1989 and 1992 Mileusnić was the editor-in-chief of *Pravoslavlje*. He was sacked in February 1992, following the publication of an antisemitic article (see above). Mileusnić was also an expert on Serbian saints and the canonization process in the Serbian Orthodox Church. The third and updated edition of Mileusnić's book, *Holy Serbs*, published in 2003, includes an entry on Nikolaj Velimirović. The conversation lasted approximately 45 minutes.

DEACON RADOŠ MLADENOVIĆ

Mladenović is the founder of the Bishop Nikolaj Velimirović Orthodox Spiritual Centre, located in the town of Kraljevo. The interview took place at the Centre, which is located in the house where Velimirović lived between 1936 and 1941, while bishop of Žiča. Until recently Mladenović was a lecturer in Philosophy at the University of Nikšić,

Montenegro and deacon to the now retired Bishop Atanasije Jevtić, one of the leading advocates of Velimirović's religious philosophy within the Serbian Orthodox Church. The conversation with Mladenović lasted approximately 180 minutes.

BRANIMIR NEŠIĆ

Nešić is the leader of the Srpski Sabor Dveri (Dveri Serbian Assembly), another Christian right-wing youth organization consisting mainly of students from the University of Belgrade. At the university, Dveri regularly arranges public debates and seminars devoted to the popularization of Velimirović's clerical-nationalist philosophy. The organization publishes a quarterly magazine, *Dveri Srpske,* of which Nešić is editor. In the autumn of 2004 he was instated as the executive editor of *Pravoslavlje.* The conversation with Nešić took place in Belgrade, and lasted approximately 220 minutes.

MLADEN OBRADOVIĆ

At the time of the interview, Obradović was the leader of Otačastveni pokret Obraz (Patriotic Movement Dignity), one of the leading right-wing youth organizations in Serbia founded in the mid-1990s, which cites Nikolaj Velimirović as the principal authority (see Byford 2002, 2006). Obradović took over the leadership of Obraz in 2001, following the death of the organization's founder, the theologian Nebojša Krstić. Obradović resigned in 2006, although he remains an active member of the organization. The conversation with Obradović lasted approximately 90 minutes.

ARCHIMANDRITE JOVAN RADOSAVLJEVIĆ

Archimandrite Jovan Radosavljević is one of a few remaining living associates of Nikolaj Velimirović. In the 1930s, Radosavljević obtained employment at Velimirović's episcopate and became one of his protégés. In 1991 Radosavljević wrote the book *Life and Suffering of Monasteries Žiča and Studenica Before, During and After the Occupation (1938–1945),* which contains a detailed account of Bishop Nikolaj's life during the Second World War. A second edition of this book was published in 2003 (J. Radosavljević, 2003). The conversation with Radosavljević lasted approximately 45 minutes.

DEACON LJUBOMIR RANKOVIĆ

Deacon Ljubomir Ranković is the director of Glas Crkve, one of the leading publishers of religious literature in Serbia, based in the Serbian town of Valjevo. Between 1974 and 1989 Ranković was deacon to Bishop of Šabac and Valjevo Jovan Velimirović, nephew of Bishop Nikolaj. Bishop Jovan and Deacon Ranković were the leading figures in the campaign for Nikolaj Velimirović's rehabilitation in the late 80s and early 90s. The two clerics publicized Velimirović's work in the journal *Glas Crkve* which they founded, and were the first to publish his books in post-communist Serbia. In 1996 Ranković founded *Radio Glas Crkve*, Serbia's first Christian radio station on which he presented a daily show until the station lost its broadcasting license in 2007. The conversation with Ranković, which took place in the offices of *Glas Crkve* in Valjevo, lasted approximately 180 minutes.

PROTOPRESBYTER LJUBIVOJE STOJANOVIĆ, PHD

Stojanović is an Orthodox priest officiating at the Sveta Petka Monastery in Belgrade. He is also lecturer in Pastoral theology with Homiletics at the Orthodox Theological Faculty in Belgrade. At the time of the interview, Stojanović was also editor-in-chief of *Pravoslavlje*, the official publication of the patriarchate of the Serbian Orthodox Church. Stojanović is considered to be a progressive voice within the Serbian Orthodox Church. He occasionally appears in national and local media where he comments on religious and ecclesiastical matters. The interview, which lasted approximately 120 minutes, was held in Stojanović's offices at the monastery.

Chapter Two

The Life of Nikolaj Velimirović and His Changing Public Image, 1945–2003

Nikolaj Velimirović was born on January 5, 1881 (December 23, 1880, according to the Julian calendar still used by the Serbian Orthodox Church) in the small village of Lelić, located outside the western Serbian town of Valjevo. Nikolaj was the first of nine children born to the modest and devout peasant couple Dragomir and Katarina Velimirović.

Accounts of Velimirović's childhood indicate that from a very early age little Nikola (who changed his name to the more archaic sounding Nikolaj after becoming a monk at the age of twenty-eight) showed "above average intellectual ability and great devotion to learning and acquiring knowledge" (Bigović, 1998, p. 27). A local priest and teacher, Mihajlo Stuparević, who took the youngster under his wing, cultivated his academic potential and encouraged him to attend school. After successfully graduating from high school in Valjevo, and having failed to join the military academy for reasons of poor health, Velimirović enrolled at the Orthodox seminary in the Serbian capital Belgrade.

In Belgrade Velimirović enjoyed the patronage of Fr. Aleksa Ilić, a well-situated Orthodox priest, who founded and edited the religious publication *Hrišćanski Vesnik* (The Christian Messenger). Ilić described Nikola Velimirović as "one of the most gifted and hard working pupils at the seminary, much loved and admired by friends and the tutors alike" (A. Ilić, 1938, p. 6). Shortly after Velimirović arrived at the seminary in 1898, Ilić recruited him to join the editors of *Hrišćanski Vesnik* and help out with "administrative duties." In 1902, Velimirović started to write for the journal, mainly on issues related to student life and conditions at the seminary. In the summer of that year, *Hrišćanski Vesnik* published Velimirović's speech delivered at the graduation picnic, which the rector of the seminary, Steva Veselinović, described as the "best speech ever." In the address entitled "At the top of the educational ladder—what next?" which offered the first glimpse of Velimirović's oratorical skills for which he was later to become famous, the young theologian called for the creation of a spiritually strong and lively ecclesiastical cadre which would "lead the Church on the path of national, religious, and moral revival" (Velimirović, 1902a). In line with the non-conformist stance adopted by the editors of *Hrišćanski Vesnik*, this speech, as well as other texts which he published at that time, criticized the "backwardness of the system" which operated within the church hierarchy (Velimirović 1902b, p. 590), and the inability of the ecclesiastical authorities to deal with the crisis of faith in the Orthodox world.

In the first decade of the 20th century, as part of a government-led drive to improve literacy and the general level of education in Serbia, all recent graduates were obliged to spend a period of time as school teachers, often in remote rural areas. Velimirović was sent to the small village of Dračić near Valjevo, although his mission there was brought to an abrupt end by a bout of *škofule*, tuberculosis of the lymph nodes in the neck, which he contracted a couple of years earlier while living in squalid conditions at the seminary. Velimirović returned to Belgrade from where he was sent to the bay of Boka Kotorska on the Montenegrin coast (which was under Austro-Hungarian administration at the time) in the hope that that milder climate and sea air would help him recover from his predicament. At the picturesque Savina Monastery where he stayed, Velimirović wrote a series of short reflections on life on the "Serbian coast," which was published in 1904 as his first book, *Souvenirs from Boka*.

After he returned from Montenegro and completed another short spell as a teacher, this time in the village of Leskovice near his native Lelić, Velimirović was awarded a scholarship to study at the Department of Old Catholic Theology at the University of Bern in Switzerland. His studies were funded by the newly crowned King Petar I Karađorđević, who was eager to invest in the education of promising young theologians and prospective Serbian Orthodox bishops. In 1908 Velimirović was awarded a doctorate in theology for the thesis entitled "Faith in the Resurrection of Christ as the Foundation of the Dogma of the Apostolic Church" (Velimirović, 1908), which he wrote and defended in German. During the stay in Switzerland, he completed a second thesis, a historical treatise on the battles between "Slavs" and Napoleon's army in Boka Kotorska between 1806 and 1814 (Velimirović, 1910). For this work he was awarded a second doctorate from the University in Bern in 1910.

Upon his return to Serbia in 1908, Velimirović sought to extend the state scholarship and continue his studies in England. After the Ministry of Education refused to fund this trip, he sought the help of his mentor and benefactor priest Aleksa Ilić, who agreed to loan him the money. Velimirović traveled to Britain, where he researched the philosophy of George Berkeley. In accounts of Velimirović's life there is considerable disagreement regarding his activities in England. Some of Velimirović's followers claim that he was based in Oxford and that he was awarded a second doctorate there, an impossibility given that apart from the honorary Doctorate of Divinity awarded exclusively to Anglican clergy, Oxford University did not award doctorates until 1917. Others claim that his work at Oxford formed the basis for a doctoral thesis which he later defended at the University of Geneva (Bigović, 1998; Janković, 2002a) or the University of Halle in Germany (Stanišić, 1977), or that he had not been at Oxford at all, but at Cambridge (Synod of the Serbian Orthodox Church, 1971, p. 514; "Dr Nikolaj Velimirović: episkop Žički," 1940, p. 17). This uncertainty surrounding his whereabouts in England dates back to 1909, when, shortly before he returned to Belgrade, a number of church publications reported, inaccurately, that Velimirović obtained a second doctorate ("Dva doktorata," 1909, p. 720). An article published in the daily *Večernje Novosti* in 1909 mocked the exaggerations surrounding Velimirović's educational attainment by suggesting ironically that if church publications are to be believed, Nikola Velimirović "possesses legendary capabilities and has seven doctorates, he taught at a German university, invented a *perpetum mobile* and has three hundred additional divine qualities and doctoral achievements" (cited in Janković, 2002b, p. 605). In any case, there is no evidence that Velimirović was ever registered at a British university or that he completed his study on Berkeley, and he certainly never published any work on the topic. It is most likely that he abandoned this project due to lack of income and returned early to Serbia (see the memoirs of Aleksa Ilić, 1938, for an account of Nikolaj's financial troubles in England). Given that Velimirović received his second doctorate from Bern a year after returning from England, it is not impossible that this qualification came to be associated with his stay in England, although both the timeline and the discrepancy in the topic of his research (Napoleonic wars in Boka Kotorska as opposed to the philosophy of George Berkeley) suggest that such connection is unfounded.

Following his return to Serbia in August 1909, Velimirović once again fell ill, this time with dysentery. During a six-week-long period of hospitalization he is said to have made a vow that should he survive the potentially lethal illness, he would enter a monastic order and devote his life to the church. In December 1909, at Rakovica Monastery near Belgrade, the fully recovered Nikola Velimirović was ordained as a hieromonk, and became Father Nikolaj. In taking his monastic vows, Nikolaj not only fulfilled the promise made to God from the hospital bed, but also laid the foundations for a rich and eventful episcopal career.

Shortly after his ordainment, Nikolaj once again left Serbia. This time he was sent to a Russian Orthodox seminary in St Petersburg. However, instead of spending time at the seminary, Nikolaj traveled around Russia, visiting monasteries and other holy places and acquainting himself with Russian culture and way of life. In Russia he came across the works of Fyodor Dostoyevsky, whose philosophical writings, as we shall see, made a lasting impression on his thinking.

In 1911, Velimirović returned to Belgrade as "one of the best educated young [Serbs] of his day" (Bigović, 1998, p. 30). He took up the position of tutor at the Orthodox Seminary in Belgrade, to which he had been appointed *in absentia* a year earlier. Velimirović's biographers repeatedly emphasize that "the classroom walls [at the seminary] were too narrow" for the hardworking and ambitious young cleric (A. Radosavljević, 1986, p. 8). By the age of thirty-five, Velmirović had already written a number of books on philosophy (*Njegoš's Religion* in 1911) and Orthodox spirituality (*Sermons under the Mountain* published in 1912 and *Above Sin and Death* in 1914) and had published extensively in religious magazines and theological journals. *Sermons under the Mountain* (a selection of sermons delivered between 1909 and 1912) is said to have been a bestseller, selling over 1800 copies in its first edition (Janković, 2003, p. 618). Also, Velimirović traveled regularly the length and breadth of Serbia and Bosnia, preaching to an increasingly enthusiastic public. His sermons were not just devoted to religious matters, but also advocated national and spiritual revival among Serbs, and promoted the idea of unity among south Slavic nations. He was especially popular in the Habsburg-occupied Bosnia, where he is said to have been influential among members of Mlada Bosna (Young Bosnia), the Serbian nationalist organization whose activists assassinated Archduke Ferdinand in Sarajevo in June 1914 (Bigović, 1998; A. Radosavljević, 1986).

The widespread respect and admiration which Velimirović commanded among the faithful in Serbia and beyond might be attributed to the fact that his broad education, oratorical skills, and personal charisma differentiated him from much of the rest of the Serbian Orthodox clergy, most of which was poorly educated and ineffectual in performing the church's social and spiritual functions. Writing on the state of Serbian Orthodoxy in the early decades of the 20th century, Milan Jovanović-Stojimirović (2003) notes that Velimirović came to the fore at a time when most Serbian clerics—who tended to be recruited from among the poor and the uneducated—had "very few manners and little worldly experience" (p. 12). Before Velimirović, Serbia had "very few priests who meant anything in an intellectual sense" (p. 11). The prevailing view of the clerical profession at the time was that it was a hotbed of provincialism, ignorance, and corruption, a stereotype that had been immortalized in the writings of two of Serbia's most popular comedy writers of that period, Branislav Nušić and Jovan Sterija Popović. A report on the state of the Serbian Church published in 1905 similarly concluded that "churches are empty and deserted, our clergy is way below modern educational and moral standards" (cited in Radić, 2003, p. 167). Velimirović, who belonged to the first generation of young, talented, and well-educated clerics, offered a promise of a better future for the Serbian Church and a break with the tradition of paucity of intellectual and spiritual leadership. What is more, at this early stage of his clerical career, Velimirović was widely perceived as a progressive young theologian and a liberal force within the Serbian Orthodox Church. For this reason, he appealed not just to the masses but also to the urban educated classes and the political elite which saw in him someone whose in-depth knowledge and enthusiasm for Western philosophy and theology might take the Serbian Church down a modernist path. He was believed to be an anglophile, with an affinity towards Protestantism acquired during his studies in the West. The renowned Serbian historian, literary critic, and a contemporary of Velimirović, Jovan Skerlić described the author of *Njegoš's Religion* as a "free thinker, a modernist who bears a mark of liberal protestant theology" and someone who is not ready to blindly follow "the sacred dogma and established canons" of the Orthodox Church (Skerlić, 1923, pp. 11–12).

In 1913, following the death of Bishop Domentijan of Niš during a typhoid epidemic, Velimirović was offered his first episcopal post. Much to everyone's astonishment he declined the honor. He justified this decision on the grounds that there is an "unhealthy climate in the Church" and that he would prefer to return to England and attend to some "unfinished business" (A. Ilić, 1938, p. 12) Such a response sparked speculation that Velimirović had a "wicked passion for adventure" and was more interested in seeing the world than in pursuing the mission of the Holy Orthodox Church. Fr. Aleksa Ilić warned him that malicious rumormongers were already interpreting his actions in the light of the "old French adage 'cherchez la femme'," and that this could irreparably damage his career in the Church (ibid., p. 13). However, Velimirović could not be persuaded to reverse his decision. The allusion to "unfinished business" in England may have been a reference to the scholarly work on George Berkeley which Velimirović abandoned four years earlier, and which he now wanted to resume. At the same time, it is also possible that his obstinacy was fuelled by vanity for which he was becoming notorious: two years earlier, in 1911, following the death of bishop Domentijan's predecessor Nikanor Ružičić, Nikolaj returned early from his travels in Russia, expecting to be ordained as the Bishop of Niš. However, Metropolitan of Serbia Dimitrije Pavlović had a last minute change of heart (probably on account of the candidate's young age and lack of experience) and instated Archimandrite Domentijan, whom Velimirović was now expected to succeed (Janković, 2002a, p. 27). Velimirović's steadfast rejection of the offer the second time round was a message to the authorities that would not be treated as second best.

With the advent of World War I, Velimirović was sent by the Serbian Prime Minister Nikola Pašić to England and the United States to promote the Serbian national cause. He was chosen to take part in this mission not only on account of his erudition, knowledge of the English language, and highly esteemed oratorical skills, but also because it was hoped that his reputation as an anglophile, admirer of Protestantism, and believer in ecumenical dialogue would facilitate contacts with the Anglican and Episcopalian churches in Britain and the United States. In addition, in *Above Sin and Death* Velimirović showed some enthusiasm for the idea of national and spiritual unity between South Slavic nations. This sentiment sat well with the Serbian government's drive to persuade western powers, and especially Britain, that a united Yugoslavia is the best post-war geo-political solution for the region.

In the summer of 1915, Velimirović first traveled to the United States. Together with Mihailo Pupin, professor of physics at Columbia University and Serbia's Consul General in New York, Nikolaj lectured and preached in New York, Chicago, Kansas City, and elsewhere. His audience consisted mainly of members of the Serbian diaspora, among whom the Serbian government sought to recruit volunteers and raise funds for the war effort (Dobrijević, 1982). Velimirović made a brief second visit to the United States in December 1917 before returning once again to London where he remained until 1919.

Supporters of Nikolaj Velimirović today frequently describe his activities in England and the United States as a "diplomatic mission" of singular importance to Serbia's war effort. One frequently encounters the quote, attributed to an unnamed senior British military official in London, in which he supposedly tells the Serbian General Milan Milovanović that Serbia has nothing to fear with "three armies on its side: the [Serbian] army, the Allies and a third army, father Nikolaj" (e.g., Janković, 2002a, p. 133). According to another anecdote, Nikola Pašić told King Aleksandar Karađorđević that Velimirović's activities in the United States and England "were worth to us as much as a whole division on the front line" (Janković, 2004, p. 20). And yet, even among Velimirović's admirers there are those prepared to admit that such claims exaggerate his achievements during the war (e.g., Bigović, 1998, p. 32). In historical literature devoted to the Yugoslav diplomatic mission in Britain during World War I, Velimirović is given at best a passing mention. This is not surprising given that he was not sent to London to transform western public opinion single handed: he was a cog in a complex, and not always well oiled public relations machine comprising the Yugoslav Committee (a group of pro-Yugoslav politicians and public figures mainly from South Slavic regions of Austro-Hungary), diplomats at the Serbian Legation in London, and the Serbian Relief Fund—a medley of pro-Serbian and pro-Yugoslav British nationals led by the historian R. W. Seton-Watson. These three bodies had a common aim: to influence public opinion in Britain and persuade the relevant power structures about the desirability of the dissolution of the Habsburg Empire and the creation of a viable Yugoslav state (Stokes, 1980; Wachtel, 1998). In spite of this shared goal, divisions existed among them regarding the character of the future state and how unification should be achieved. The Serbian Relief Fund, to which Velimirović was affiliated, promoted the cult of the Serbian soldier, drew parallels between the events in Serbia in 1915 and Serbian sacrifices in Kosovo in 1389, and endorsed the view that Serbs were destined to liberate their South Slavic brethren from under the Habsburg yoke. The Yugoslav Committee, which promoted a more inclusive Yugoslav identity, looked with suspicion at such tendencies towards "Serbian Orthodox exclusivism" (Stokes, 1980, p. 55), and distanced itself from rhetoric that would make it look like the extended arm of the Serbian government.

In the context of the mission in England, Velimirović's role was to propagate the Serbian government's agenda within the British ecclesiastical establishment. He formed a strong friendship with the bishop of Chichester, George Bell, and with Reverend H. J. Feyes-Clinton, who was affiliated with the Serbian Relief Fund. Velimirović was held in high esteem also by the archbishop of Canterbury, Randall Davidson, who assisted him in fundraising efforts and helped make arrangements for a group of Serbian Orthodox seminarians who escaped to England to continue their studies at British universities. Velimirović's links with the Anglican ecclesiastical establishment provided him with access to a broader British audience. He spent a substantial proportion of his time giving lectures on Serbia, South Slavic unification, and the Orthodox Church. His lectures were published in English as pamphlets, while some were also included in three larger edited collections, *The Soul of Serbia* (1916a), *Serbia in Light and Darkness* (1916b), and *The Agony of the Church* (1917). These works were published or at least funded by bodies affiliated with the Church of England (such as The Faith Press or the Student Christian Movement) and usually included a preface from the likes of R. W. Seton-Watson and the archbishop of Canterbury.

Apart from lecturing before secular audiences, at universities in Cambridge, London, Edinburgh, Birmingham, and elsewhere, Velimirović delivered sermons in Anglican churches across the country. He was generally not allowed to take part in religious service or address the audience from the pulpit, but was invited to speak (Heppell, 2001). On July 2, 1916, he accepted the invitation to address the congregation at St Margaret's Church in Westminster, the parish church of the British Houses of Parliament. Five days later he spoke at a memorial service for fallen British and Serbian servicemen, which was led by the archbishop of Canterbury at St Paul's Cathedral in London. This service was initially planned for 28 June, St Vitus' Day, the anniversary of the Battle of Kosovo in 1389. However, given that on that same day in 1914 Gavrilo Princip assassinated Archduke Ferdinand and his wife in Sarajevo, British authorities postponed the ceremony, lest it should offend Austrian sensitivities. Nikolaj took part in the procession after the service which, as one connoisseur of ecclesiastical protocol commented at the time, was the highest honor ever bestowed upon a foreign religious dignitary in St Paul's Cathedral in London (cited in Heppell, 2001, p. 7).

Velimirović's sermons in Britain were very well received. According to eyewitnesses and reports mainly in Church of England publications, eager crowds gathered readily to hear him speak. This is unsurprising, given that by 1916 the whole country was witnessing a wave of pro-Serbian euphoria. Cries of "To hell with Serbia!" with which the newspaper *John Bull* greeted the assassination of Archduke Ferdinand in 1914, gave way to a very different sentiment. In June 1916 British schools commemorated "Kossovo Day" in support of Serbia, in *The Daily News* the British writer G. K. Chesterton hailed Serbia as the "eldest brother of the Alliance," Prime Minister Lloyd George praised the "dignity" and "valor" of the small Balkan nation, while the *Daily Express* hailed it as the "shining tower of the east" (cited in Klimon, 1994). In such a context, Velimirović's exotic charm and personal charisma undoubtedly appealed to the British audience and made him a welcome guest in the salons of London's high society. In the 1930s Rebecca West described Velimirović as "the most remarkable man she had ever met," "a supreme magician," and someone who gave the impression that he could speak to "gods and men and beasts" (West 1994, p. 720). It is not unlikely that Velimirović made a similar impression on his hosts during the war. However, contrary to claims made by his followers,

Velimirović's "popularity" reflected, rather than initiated, the shift in British public opinion around that time. What is more, in terms of public appeal, Nikolaj was outshined by the famous Croatian sculptor and member of the Yugoslav Committee Ivan Meštrović, whose work still adorns the halls of the Tate Gallery in London. Meštrović was promoted during the war as the "national artist of Yugoslavia" and hailed as a symbol of the "civilizing capacities of the [South Slavic] race" (Wachtel, 1998, p. 64). An exhibition of Meštrović's sculptures in the Victoria and Albert Museum in London in 1915 was offered to the British public as proof that there was more to the South Slavs than the military reputation of the "Serbian soldier" (ibid.).

After the war, Velimirović's friends among the Anglican clergy (above all, Rev. H. J. Feyes-Clinton) wanted him to receive some form of formal recognition for his work on improving Orthodox-Anglican relations (Heppell, 2001). Velimirović was put forward for an honorary Lambeth Doctorate of Divinity, awarded by the archbishop of Canterbury, but was found to be ineligible on the grounds that he was not a British subject. Subsequent attempts to award him some form of honorary degree at Oxford also failed. The patronizing tone with which the Canon of Westminster, William Hartley Carnegie, responded to such a request reveals that in spite of all his efforts, Velimirović had still been unable to break the social barriers that guarded the British establishment from intruders and to soften the colonial attitude which the country's intelligentsia adopted towards those it saw as coming from "the Orient." Canon Carnegie wrote the following:

> The honour sought is a very considerable one, not to be lightly accorded. We know and appreciate Fr. Nikolai's merits and powers, but he still has to "make good" in the English academic world. Moreover, a consideration not to be overlooked, one has to be a little careful in one's dealings with these Orientals. They are, all of them, I find, a little apt to get above themselves, and to make larger claims for recognition than Englishmen of similar status would think of making... This is a lesson that Fr. Velimirović has not yet fully learnt, as Frere is just learning to his cost... (cited in Heppell, 2001, p. 14)

Velimirović left Britain without an honorary doctorate, although on St George's Day (23 April) in 1919 the archbishop of Canterbury awarded him a specially designed pectoral cross and chain, a symbol of personal friendship, shared commitment to ecumenical unity and common faith in Lord Jesus Christ.

Velimirović's writings in the English language published during his time in Britain do not occupy a prominent place in his opus. They are rarely flagged either by admirers or by critics as particularly noteworthy. And yet, these essays contain within them themes which continued to occupy Velimirović's thinking in subsequent years. Pieces such as "The Soul of Serbia," "Serbia's Place in Human History," or "Serbia's Tragedy" were mainly patriotic treatises in which Serbs are promoted as, on the one hand a "silent, melancholic and discreet" people who "[do] not impose [themselves] on anyone" and on the other hand as an uncompromising and heroic nation dedicated to the principle that "slavery is uglier than death" (e.g., Velimirović, 1916a, pp. 91–92). Both of these themes aimed to counter the stereotype common in the West after the Sarajevo assassination that Serbs were perennial troublemakers. In his patriotic speeches Velimirović also advanced what he later referred to as the "Kosovo creed": the claim that "beautiful" death, such as that achieved by the Serbian heroes at the battle of Kosovo in 1389, is "the very aim of life" (ibid., p. 24) and that the whole of Serbian "national philosophy is founded on the conception of suffering" (p. 94). This message was meant to create in the audience the feelings of sympathy and admiration, especially because in 1914, just like in 1389, Serbia supposedly "fought and died for Christianity and Civilization" (Velimirović's letter to Seton-Watson, cited in Trgovčević, 2003, p. 230).

In other speeches and essays attention often shifted away from Serbia towards "Jugoslavia." In "Religion and Nationality in Serbia," which was published both as a pamphlet (1915) and as part of the edited volume *The Soul of Serbia* (1916a), Velimirović expresses a strong pro-Yugoslav sentiment. He suggests that "Jugoslavs—Serbs, Croats, and Slovenes" are "one and the same nation in language, in blood, in destiny, and in their aspirations" (Velimirović, 1916a, p. 56). This stance was based above all on a Slavophile sentiment, which in this incarnation had strong regional and religious components. In Velimirović's speeches, the state for which he campaigned was one of Christian South Slav people, whose unity lay not just in "blood," language, or political interest, but also in Christ (see Trgovčević, 2003;

also Velimirović, 1914). He did not present confessional divisions and schisms of the past as insurmountable obstacles on the road to unification: Southern Slavs "have risen superior to all divergencies [*sic*] of creed between the Orthodox and Catholic churches, and have held fast only to that which unites, not to that which divides in religion" (Velimirović, 1916a, p. 57). Among Yugoslav nations "Orthodoxy and Catholicism were subordinate to the one name—Christianity, and contrasted under this single name with the cruel and bloodthirsty Islam" (ibid., p. 58). In particular, Velimirović praised the work of the Catholic bishop of Đakovo, Josip Juraj Strossmayer (1815–1905), as one of the pioneers of the Yugoslav idea and keen advocate of interfaith dialogue between Catholicism and Orthodoxy in the region. "Religion and nationality in Serbia" was specifically written in Strossmayer's memory on the centenary of his birth.

Significantly, however, the enthusiasm for Yugoslavia as a league of equal nations and faiths which Velimirović professed in his speeches reflected his role as the representative of the Serbian state, rather than his genuine political orientation. Behind the enthusiastic conciliatory rhetoric lay a profound suspicion towards Catholicism which he regarded as "the most conservative among western denominations" (see Bigović, 1998, p. 35). In public, Velimirović readily advocated the signing of a Concordat with the Vatican as a mark of Serbia's broadmindedness and tolerance. Also, he proclaimed that in Yugoslavia, once it was created, the Serbian Orthodox and the Roman Catholic churches would be on equal footing, with comparable rights and privileges (e.g., Velimirović, 1916a, pp. 70–71). In conversations with his associates, however, he endorsed the opposite view. He called for complete severance of ties with the Vatican and the creation of a national (Yugoslav) Catholic Church. Similarly, he maintained that following unification, Orthodox Christianity should not forfeit the status of state religion which it previously occupied in the Kingdom of Serbia (memoirs of Dr. Bogumil Bošnjak, cited in Janković, 2002a, p. 39). In other words, Velimirović's approach to the Yugoslav question bore all the hallmarks of "Serbian Orthodox exclusivism," which non-Serbian exponents of the Yugoslav idea feared at the time, and which subsequently plagued interethnic relations in the Kingdom of Serbs, Croats, and Slovenes.

A further interesting aspect of Velimirović's writing in the English language is the reference, in some his speeches and sermons, to the concept of "All-man" (*Svečovek*) which is sometimes referred to in English also as the "Omni-human." The idea of the "All-man" (which made an appearance in Velimirović's earlier work, including *Sermons under the Mount*) received the most detailed elaboration in one of his best-known books, *Words on the All-Man*, published in Serbia in 1920. Given that Velimirović wrote this book during his stay in Britain, it is not surprising that the "All-man" appears also in speeches delivered at the time.

The concept of "svečovek" or "svečoveštvo" (all-humanity) was borrowed from Fyodor Dostoyevsky, who mentions it (*vsechelovek* in Russian) in his famous "Pushkin speech" delivered in 1880. For Dostoyevsky, "vsechelovek" denotes the pan-humanist ideal of "final brotherly communion of all nations in accordance with the law of the gospel of Christ." In Velimirović's work, "svečoveštvo" is similarly conceived as an ethical ideal of universal humanism and unity in spirit achieved through faith in Jesus Christ. It is based on two basic Christian principles: "first—freedom, the second—love" and is the "only salutary philosophy for the soul and body of humankind. It will draw man nearer to man, nation to nation, state to state, one kingdom of God upon the earth" (Velimirović, 1916a, p. 36). Christianity's principal mission in this world is therefore to transform the human race into "All-men," thereby achieving unity of humanity in God. And yet, in spite of the pan-humanist overtones visible in their writing on the "All-man," both Dostoyevsky and Velimirović perceived "all-humanity" as an expression of the values of the Orthodox East. Dostoyevsky's "vsechelovek" represents an ideal emanating specifically from the "spirit of Russian nationality" and the "Russian soul" (Dostoyevsky, 1960). For Velimirović, "All-man" is the Slavic and Orthodox antidote to the selfish Nietzschean, Germanic, and pagan "superman." Velimirović first elaborated the opposition between Orthodox pan-humanism and Western secular individualism in the essay "Nietzsche and Dostoyevsky" (1912), where he suggested that the two figures represent "two irreconcilable worlds. They personify Judea and Rome, Christianity and paganism, the people and the despot, faith and atheism, hope and despair, Christ and antichrist" (Velimirović, 1912, p. 4). In "Serbia's place in human history," written in 1915, Nikolaj interpreted World War I in terms of this fundamental opposition: "Kaiser William" stood for the Nietzschean spirit, one whose aim was not just the creation of the "superman," but also of a "super-state" intent on destroying smaller nations. Within the same analogy, Orthodox Serbs were seen as "upholding" and symbolizing the noble Christian philosophy of the "All-man." Significantly, however, in Velimirović's view, although "All-man" is essentially a "Slavonic philosophy" epitomized by Orthodox nations, it is not exclusively so: its spirit has also been "carved in the ethical consciousness of European mankind" through the works of Hugo, Dickens, and Shakespeare (Velimirović, 1916a, p. 34).

The opposition between Dostoyevskyan "All-man" and Nietzschean "superman" as ultimate expressions of the tension between Eastern (Christian) and Western (secular) world-views is significant because this dichotomy would eventually become a central theme in Velimirović's writing. Already at this stage, Velimirović's stance towards the West was ambivalent: the admiration for its philosophical and cultural achievements of the past coexisted with the fear that individualism and materialism were driving the Western civilization away from God. Velimirović believed that religion is the fabric of society: the Church imbues the state with a "soul" and it constitutes a "spiritual medium" through which the "national ideal" can be expressed (Velimirović, 1916a, p. 56). The achievement of the pan-humanist ideal of "svečoveštvo" required for this particular view of church–state relations to become a universal principle, and yet he saw no evidence of it in the increasingly secular Western societies. In the 1920s and the 1930s Velimirović's ambivalence towards and growing disenchantment with the West became radicalized, setting him on the path of controversy which plagues his memory to the present day.

In May 1919, following his return from England, Nikolaj Velimirović was ordained as bishop in the ancient diocese of Žiča. This was a time of great change for the Serbian Orthodox Church. When the Kingdom of Serbs, Croats, and Slovenes was created in 1918, the Orthodox Church on its territory found itself divided into six separate church organizations. Five dioceses of the former Kingdom of Serbia were under the jurisdiction of the autocephalous Serbian Metropolitanate. Seven Orthodox dioceses in Vojvodina, Croatia, and Slavonia comprised the Karlovac Metropolitanate, which was also autocephalous, as was the Metropolitanate of Montenegro and the Littoral with three dioceses. Four dioceses in Bosnia and Herzegovina and two in Dalmatia were affiliated to the Ecumenical Patriarchate of Constantinople, while the status of the Orthodox Church in Macedonia (previously also under the jurisdiction of the Ecumenical Patriarchate) remained unresolved in the aftermath of the departure of Bulgarian and Greek bishops during the Balkan Wars of 1912–1913 (Gligorijević, 1997). In May 1919, following a series of discussions among representatives of the six regional church organizations, and with full support from Regent Aleksandar Karađorđević, the Archiereic Assembly of the Serbian Church consisting of all Orthodox bishops from the territory of the new state proclaimed the "spiritual, moral, and administrative unity of Serbian Orthodox regions" and announced unification. The administrative control of the Church was placed in the hands of the Central Archiereic Council, which was based in Belgrade and consisted of five bishops under the chairmanship of the Metropolitan of Montenegro, Mitrofan Ban. Almost a year later, in March 1920, following the resolution of a dispute concerning the jurisdiction over Macedonian dioceses, the Ecumenical Patriarchate of Constantinople recognized "the United Serbian Orthodox Church of the Kingdom of Serbs, Croats, and Slovenes" as a single autocephalous church (Gligorijević, 1997). Shortly afterwards its status was raised to that of a patriarchate, and in August 1920, Metropolitan of Serbia Dimitrije Pavlović was elected the patriarch of the Serbian Orthodox Church, the first since 1766 when the patriarchate of Peć, where the Serbian church had been based since medieval times, was abolished by Ottoman rulers.

One of the reasons why the (re-)unification of the Serbian Orthodox Church was conducted with such urgency is that many in Serbia, including the Regent Aleksandar Karađorđević, felt that in the aftermath of the Russian revolution, the Kingdom of Serbs, Croats, and Slovenes ought to become the new hub of the Orthodox world. To fulfill this new ambition, state authorities invited the Russian Orthodox Church in Exile (which had been based in Constantinople) to set up its headquarters in Serbia (first in Sremski Karlovci, 1921–1938, and later in Belgrade, 1938–1944; see Jovanović, 2005). Also the Czech Orthodox Church, founded by a group of reformist Czech Catholics, was established in the 1920s with the help of the Serbian Orthodox Church, and was placed under the jurisdiction of the Serbian patriarch (Radić, 1997).

Nikolaj Velimirović played an important role in the Church's activities on the international stage, which meant that he was frequently absent from his diocese at Žiča. He traveled to England, the United

States, Russia, and Greece, establishing links between the newly united Serbian Church and religious communities abroad. And then, less than eighteen months after he took over the position at Žiča, Patriarch Dimitrije made the decision to transfer him to Ohrid, one of the dioceses in the territory claimed during the Balkan Wars of 1912–1913. At the time, this small, isolated, and neglected diocese based in the city of Ohrid, on the shores of the beautiful lake of the same name, had only around thirty parishes under its administration and not a particularly active religious life. Ohrid seemed like a strange destination for someone with Velimirović's educational background and public profile, and the precise reasons why he was transferred there remain unknown. Some authors have suggested that Velimirović requested to be placed at Ohrid (e.g., P. Ilić, 2006), although his correspondence with Bishop George Bell indicates that he was initially unhappy there, and shocked by the "extreme poverty and primitive lifestyle" which dominated his new surroundings (Heppell, 2001, p. 19). What is more, within a year of his instatement at Ohrid, Nikolaj offered his resignation, which was rejected by the synod of the Serbian Church. He remained at Ohrid until 1936, when he was reinstated as the bishop of Žiča, a title which he retained until his death in 1956.

Before taking up his duties at the new diocese at Ohrid, Velimirović traveled once again to America where he was instructed to investigate the "moral and spiritual" situation within the local Serbian Orthodox parishes (which had hitherto been under the administration of the Russian Orthodox Church), and prepare the grounds for the creation of the American–Canadian diocese of the Serbian Orthodox Church (Đikanović, 2006; Dobrijević, 1982). This trip preceded his appointment in the spring of 1922 as the administrator of the Serbian Orthodox Church in America, a role which he performed simultaneously with duties at Ohrid. There is evidence which suggests that Nikolaj was very keen to be transferred to the United States permanently to take over the administration of the church there. However, by the end of 1923 he was relieved of all duties in North America, and the administrator's role was transferred to his assistant Archimandrite Mardarije Uskoković, who subsequently became the first bishop of the American–Canadian diocese. Velimirović had to wait until 1946 before taking permanent residence in the United States, in circumstances that he could not have foreseen in 1923.

In the early 1920s, Velimirović also became involved with Bogomoljački pokret, or the Devotionalist movement, a network of Orthodox Christian evangelists who became a focal point of his interest in the 1920s and 30s (Subotić, 1996; Vojinović, 1971). The Devotionalist movement emerged in the mid-19th century in Vojvodina, which was under Austro-Hungarian rule at the time. It consisted of informal groups or "brotherhoods" of pious young men and women who, as well as attending Orthodox Christian services on a regular basis, also congregated in homes for "prayer meetings"—during which they read passages from the New Testament—and organized regular pilgrimages to Vojlovica Monastery near the town of Pančevo (Vojinović, 1971, p. 346). These groups were strictly Serbian Orthodox, although their habits and rituals (including public readings from the scripture, something rarely practiced by Orthodox Christians) are believed to have been influenced by Baptist communities, which had a strong following among the local Hungarian population. After 1870, Devotionalist "brotherhoods" emerged also in south-eastern Serbia, although it remains unclear whether they were inspired by their counterparts in the north, or whether they developed spontaneously. By early 20th century the movement was fairly widespread, and the presence of groups of Devotionalists among conscripts in Serbian army camps during World War I was sufficiently noticeable to attract the attention of military authorities (Vojinović, 1971).

Many in the Serbian Orthodox Church, both among bishops and at grassroots levels, expressed suspicion towards the Devotionalists. Their practices seemed alien, even a bit "Catholic," and their piety was judged to be excessive (see Bremer, 1997). Parish priests, unused to any form of religious austerity, were unsettled by the presence, among their flock, of lay man and women who referred to each other as "brother" or "sister," and whose routine involved twice-daily prayers, regular church attendance and communion, fasting on Wednesdays and Fridays, and frequent and elaborate confessions. What is more, by holding informal religious services in their homes, the Devotionalists appeared to be distancing themselves from the official Church, provoking fear that they might even turn into a "sect." In order to prevent this, in its dealings with the movement, the Serbian Orthodox Church adopted a stance which Bishop of Bačka Irinej Ćirić described in 1931 as one of "benevolent neutrality" (cited in Vojinović, 1971, p. 356).

"Neutrality" implied that the Devotionalists were tolerated, occasionally encouraged, but without ever being recognized as an official movement within the Church.

The first formal contact between Velimirović and the Devotionalists was established in July 1920, during the First Assembly of Devotionalist Brotherhoods held near the town of Velika Plana. Velimirović attended this event in an official capacity, as the delegate of Patriarch Dimitrije. Unlike many of his fellow bishops, Nikolaj looked upon the movement with sympathies. Not only was he impressed by the genuine piety shown by the Devotionalists, but he also shared with them a sense of frustration at the inability of the Serbian Orthodox clergy to provide adequate spiritual and moral guidance to the faithful. In 1921, Velimirović published the article "Don't reject them—a note to the clergy," in which he defended the movement from critics (Velimirović, 1921). Devotionalists instantly recognized in him a powerful guardian and spiritual leader and chose him for their patron. The synod approved of Velimirović's involvement with the Devotionalists (it appointed him a permanent "delegate" to the movement), in the hope that patronage from a senior official of the Church would bring them closer to the mainstream of Serbian Orthodox Christian culture.

Under Velimirović's guidance, the Devotionalists went from strength to strength. A governing council known as the Central Office was elected and placed in charge of coordinating the activities of brotherhoods. The centralization resulted also in a name change, as the Devotionalists were given a more formal sounding title: Narodna hrišćanska zajednica (National Christian Association). Serbian expatriates in the United States donated a printing press, which allowed the Devotionalists to publish hundreds of pamphlets and to start their own journal *Hrišćanska Zajednica* (The Christian Community), renamed *Misionar* (The Missionary) in 1936. In 1924, the movement formed the Missionary Order, consisting of lay preachers and "promoters of Orthodoxy" whose role was to propagate the Orthodox faith among the people. The Missionary Order proved divisive, as lay preachers were accused of being disrespectful towards the clergy and of ignoring the jurisdiction and "canonical privileges" of parish priests. And yet, the Church continued to maintain a neutral stance towards the movement as a whole, if for no other reason than because Devotionalists constituted a rich source from which the Church recruited monks and nuns for its depleted monasteries. The overall success of the Devotionalists and their unwavering dedication to the evangelical mission impressed even visitors from abroad. In 1931, Donald A. Lowrie, an official of the YMCA who campaigned on behalf of the Russian Orthodox Church in Exile, wrote in one of his reports from Belgrade that the Devotionalists represent a welcome sign of "fresh life" in the Serbian Orthodox Church (cited in Latourette, 1973, p. 527).

The reason why the involvement with the Devotionalists constitutes an important episode in Velimirović's life is that it is often linked to the dramatic personal transformation which he is said to have undergone in the early 1920s (e.g., Jerotić, 2000; A. Radosavljević, 1986; Stanišić, 1977). Within a few years of his arrival at Ohrid, Velimirović, who had been known for his tidy hair, silk cassocks, and confidence that bordered on arrogance, became a recluse, ascetic, and conservative figure. In *Reflections on Good and Evil*, published in 1923, Velimirović provided an account of this transformation, describing it as a form of spiritual homecoming. He wrote that "we are sometimes drawn to and seduced by the great waters of this sensual world. And just as water from a spring is never as sweet as when we return to it burdened with disappointment, with throats sore from the salty and bitter waters we had to drink; so the Christian faith is never as dear to us as when we return to it from afar, as penitents, ashamed and disappointed..." (cited in Bigović, 1998, pp. 39–40).

Velimirović's return to the "spring" of authentic Christian faith provoked a change in the style and the focus of his writing. The somewhat pretentious tone of his earlier philosophical work (*Words on the All-man* were intended as a "response" to Nietzsche's *Thus Spoke Zarathustra*) gave way to simpler literary forms, mainly poems, homilies, pastoral letters, and instructional pieces on Orthodox Christian way of life (e.g., Velimirović, 1925, 1932). *Prayers by the Lake* (1922), the first book which Velimirović wrote at Ohrid, was a collection of religious poetry. *Ohrid Prologue* (1928a), one of his best known works, provided an accessible introduction, in encyclopedic form, to the lives of saints and the main events in the Church calendar. Between 1932 and 1934, Velimirović published thirty-eight pamphlets containing over three hundred "missionary letters," written as a fictional correspondence with members of the public, in which he offered simple guidance on a range of practical issues from how to raise children to how to deal with crisis of faith (Velimirović, 2005). These and other similar writings aimed at a wider readership had a clear missionary and evangelical purpose not apparent in Velimirović's earlier scholarly work.

Velimirović's followers today view this unexpected change of style and direction as an unequivocally positive development, which enabled their hero to emerge as the true representative of Serbian Orthodox religious spirit. In 1986, Archimandrite Artemije Radosavljević described the transition as follows:

> In this second period of his life, Nikolaj shunned all things foreign and rejected all forms of western superficiality. He became graced by the warm currents of Orthodoxy. He was enchanted and thrilled by the beautiful and salvationist image of Christ and inspired by the religious work of St Sava. Fame became unimportant to him. Compliments bored him. He rejected the excessively refined literary expression, and discarded earthly wisdom as a symptom of spiritual misery and desolation. However, the bishop did not become "vulgar." Rather, he became more spiritual and uncomplicated. Christ's words, "I am the way, the truth, and the life" became everything to him. (A. Radosavljević, 1986, p. 14)

Radosavljević (1986) sees this transformation as the moment when "Nikolaj the genius became Nikolaj the Saint" (p. 14). Similarly, Radovan Bigović (1998) describes Velimirović's new direction—which confirmed him as "an apostle and Christ's poet"—as marking a "Copernican turn" within Serbian religious thought (p. 380). It enabled Serbian Orthodox theology—which until then was a formal "religious and ethical system," a "doctrine" devoid of a visible spiritual dimension—to become truly "Christocentric" and representative of "a concrete life with Christ and in Christ" (pp. 25–26). On the other hand, for Velimirović's critics, the Ohrid period marks the bishop's demise as a religious thinker. In 1931, literary critic Milan Bogdanović noted that Velimirović had strayed off the progressive route and described his writing at that time as "nothing but aphoristic paraphrasing of the strictest canonical dogma" by a conservative who "glorifies the church as an institution, openly championing the Orthodox ceremonial" (Bogdanović, 1931, p. 78). More recently, Mirko Đorđević (1996) concluded that Velimirović's post-Ohrid writing brought nothing new to theology, but merely reproduced, and applied to the Serbian cultural context, the ideas of Russian slavophile thinkers, such as Dostoyevsky, Leontiyev, and Homyakov.

It is noteworthy that in the writing of Velimirović's followers, it is not just his "return" to Orthodoxy which is cited as the significant legacy of the conversion at Ohrid. More often than not, authors also emphasize what it is that Velimirović was returning *from.* Radosavljević noted, in the earlier quotation, that Velimirović's passage from "genius" to "Saint" involved the abandonment of the youthful attraction to "western superficiality." For Bishop Amfilohije Radović, Ohrid ended Velimirović's "enchantment with Europe, and the great ideas born in Europe." Velimirović started to "go deeper" in his theological and evangelical explorations only after he "experienced the tragedy of European thought, European culture, European civilization" (A. Radović, 1991, p. 41; see also A. Radović, 2003, p. 508). In other words, Velimirović's ascent as an "apostle" of the Orthodox faith is seen as causally linked to a shift in his stance away from Europe and its culture.

Indeed, by the mid-1920s, the admiration for Western Europe and the sympathies for the ecumenical movement which Velimirović harbored in his youth (and towards which he was becoming increasingly skeptical around the time of World War I) all but disappeared from his worldview. In some ways, Velimirović "gave up" on the West, which he believed has discarded God for the secular values of the French revolution. He abandoned hope that a new Christian civilization could be built on the pan-humanist principles which preoccupied him a decade earlier. In 1926 for instance, he bitterly criticized the formation of the League of Nations not because he disagreed with its agenda, but because he believed that a new world order built on secular, rather than on explicitly Christian values is destined to fail (Velimirović, 1926).

And yet, the thorough disenchantment with the West did not bring about a withdrawal into the sheltered and comforting world of his newly found spiritual enlightenment at Ohrid. The metaphorical "great waters of this sensual world" which Velimirović claimed to have "left behind" became an obsession. In "Godless Europe," which provoked such "disappointment," he saw a menacing deluge threatening to engulf the Orthodox world. Nietzsche (whom he had already identified in 1912 as the symbol of "atheism," "despair," and the "antichrist") was joined by Charles Darwin and Karl Marx to form the "three ghosts of European civilization" (Velimirović, 1940). Individualism, equality, religious tolerance, democracy, science, and other products of modernity and enlightenment which he associated with the godless spirit of Europe became an anathema to him, prompting a declaration of "an uncompromising war" against "all forms of culture, materialist science, atheistic philosophies, godless politics and various forms of pseudo-religiosity" (Bigović, 1998, p. 26). Also, Velimirović became disillusioned with Yugoslavia. The country which he once hoped would be built on Christian principles became in his eyes a structure erected "on the foundations of the metaphysics of Protestantism, French Enlightenment philosophy, English political economy, liberal thinking and utilitarian ethics," all of which he vehemently opposed (Bigović, 1998, p. 25).

Anti-westernism apparent in Velimirović's writing, which culminated in the 1930s, went hand in hand with a new and more "parochial" approach to the Christian mission. The realization that in Western Europe "Christianity is on its deathbed, destroyed and betrayed by Christians themselves" led him to become an "Orthodox Serbian patriot" (Jerotić, 2000, pp. 238–239). The pan-humanist ideal of the "All-man" retreated before an increasingly xenophobic strand of Serbian religious nationalism and populism (M. Đorđević, 1996; Popov, 1993). Velimirović came to regard the Serbs (exemplified by the pious Devotionalists) as a unique cultural, civilizational, and national entity, and the embodiment of the authentic Orthodox Christian spirit. In the essay "Above East and West" he went as far as to suggest that "Christian Serbia alone can fulfill the apostolic task to bring the [Far] East to Christ, and lead the West to repentance" (Velimirović, 1977, p. 807). The belief in the messianic role of the Serbs reflected the older slavophile tenet that the Orthodox East holds the key to the West's spiritual salvation, but in the aftermath of the Russian Revolution, in the bishop's writing this ideological motif acquired a more restricted interpretation and became confined to the Serbs and the Balkans. Velimirović believed that geographically Serbia stands between the East and the West, but that spiritually it is above such divisions, and closest to God.

The belief in the spiritual superiority of Serbs in relation to other Slavs reflected also the conviction that "Svetosavlje"—the uniquely Serbian brand of Christianity derived from the teachings of the medieval Serbian saint Sava—contains within it the blueprint for a truly

Christian society (see van Dartel, 1984). In Velimirović's interpretation of Serbia's national history (which was reflected also in the writing of a number of his contemporaries and followers, most notably theologians Justin Popović and Dimitrije Najdanović), St Sava was not just the founder of the autocephalous Serbian Orthodox Church, but also the father of the Serbian nation and the embodiment of the medieval Serbian Christian state. Consequently, Velimirović interpreted the legacy of the first Serbian archbishop as constituting more than just a Christian doctrine: it represents also the foundation of a unique "evangelical nationalism" and a specific theory of government. In the writing of Velimirović and other nationalist theologians in the 1930s, "Svetosavlje" was elevated to the status of a unifying principle that seamlessly binds together the church, the nation, and the state into an "organic," "undividable" whole. It obliterates the division between the sacred and the secular, and in doing so it paves the way for a society entirely devoted to God's work (Bremer, 1997; M. Đorđević, 2003). The ultimate expression of "Svetosavlje" is what Velimirović referred to as "Teodulija," a society in which God is the *raison d'être* of "the Church, the state, the schools and all national institutions," where "every dwelling is a monastery" and life is governed by four simple principles: "faith, honesty, obedience, and fortitude" (Velimirović, 2003). Velimirović believed that the medieval Serbian kingdom was a "Teodulija" and that Serbs, because of their innate ties "in blood and spirit" with St Sava, have the capacity to recreate it in the 20th century as the perfect antithesis to the Godless, modern, secular European state. Serbs were thus elevated to the status of "God's chosen people, a new Israel after the Jews, new chosen people in this world" (Jerotić, 2000, p. 241). What is more, in Velimirović's writing the importance which Christianity traditionally attributes to the notions of individual righteousness and personal salvation disappeared before the belief in collective salvation of Christian nations (Janić, 1994; Jerotić, 2000). For Velimirović, it is Serbia's history of collective suffering and martyrdom for Christ (whether in Kosovo in 1389, or during World War I) and the aspirations towards "Teodulija" that will earn the whole of the Serbian nation a place in heaven. This notion of collective salvation gave meaning to the idea of "Heavenly Serbia"—a space in Heaven reserved for the Serbian people—which Velimirović's followers revived so effectively in the 1980s and 1990s.

By the end of the 1930s, the view of the Serbian people as the symbol of the authentic, Christian view of the world attained disturbing racist overtones. In 1939, in the speech "Whose are you, little Serbian people," delivered at the ceremony commemorating the 550th anniversary of the Battle of Kosovo, Velimirović spoke of Serbs as "God's children and people of the Aryan race, who have been granted the honorable role of being the main pillar of Christianity in the world" (Velimirović, 2001, p. 40). He asserted that "we are Aryan by blood, Slavs by surname, Serbs by name, Christians in heart and spirit'" (ibid.).

As much as Velimirović believed in the chosenness of the Serbs and their messianic mission in this world, he at the same time despaired over their apparent feebleness before the temptations of modern, secular, European culture. The attitude towards his people fluctuated between adoration and revulsion: the more he idealized their spiritual potential, the less he could forgive the weaknesses that they exhibited. More importantly, the failure of the ambition to create a land founded on the principles of "organic, evangelical nationalism" was explained away by reference to a vast international conspiracy against his nation and its religion. In some sense, the appearance of conspiracy theory in Velimirović's writing is unsurprising, not just because in the 1920s and 1930s there were plenty of conspiracy theories around from which to draw inspiration (including those propagated by the reactionary Russian immigration which settled in Serbia after 1917, see Timotijević, forthcoming) but because, as Karl Popper (1972) noted, such explanations are characteristic of those worldviews or ideologies which are concerned with the implementation of fundamental truth, or with the creation of "heaven on earth." The unavoidable failure of projects such as "Teodulija" can only be explained by reference to an evil force which has a "vested interest in thwarting this illustrious endeavour" (Popper, 1972). Importantly for the present discussion, the conspiracy theory which Velimirović propagated saw at the hub of the alleged anti-Serbian and anti-Orthodox plot the same secret force which dominated conspiratorial thinking in early 20th century, namely the Jews (see Cohn, 1957). The broader anti-western and anti-modernist perspective which dominated Velimirović's thinking in the late 1920s and the 1930s became infused with anti-Jewish slurs, which consisted of a blend of Christian antisemitism and Jewish conspiracy theory typical of the era in which he lived and worked.

The first instance of antisemitism in Velimirović's writing can be found in the sermon "A Story about the wolf and the lamb," which he delivered during a trip to the United States in the autumn of 1927. In January 1928, several mainstream Serbian newspapers (including *Politika* and *Vreme*) published extracts from this sermon, while the official publication of the diocese of Žiča, *Pregled crkve eparhije žičke* (Review of the diocese of Žiča) published it in its entirety. In his take on the well known Christian parable about the wolf and the lamb, Velimirović referred to "Jewish leaders in Jerusalem" at the time of the crucifixion as "wolves," whose thirst for blood of the Lamb of God was motivated by their "god-hating nationalism." He explicitly stated that the deicidal actions of Caiaphas were not attributable to "individual depravity," but that, in plotting to kill Christ, he and other Jewish leaders "represented the Semitic race" and acted "in the interest of their nation" (Velimirović, 1928b, pp. 6–9). What is significant, however, is that the parable was not just a regurgitation of the old Christian deicide accusation against Jews. The motif of Jewish responsibility for the crucifixion also informed Velimirović's perspective on contemporary political reality. Caiaphas, along with Herod and Pontius Pilate, was put forward as the embodiment of the anti-Christian, deicidal "spirit" which endures to the present day. Velimirović warned his audience that the world will eventually have to chose between the spirit of Christ and that of his murderers, and that should they opt for the latter (including the spirit of Caiaphas, or rather of "Judaism"), the outcome will be war, death, and destruction. This sermon provoked a bitter reaction from the Belgrade Rabbi Dr. Isak Alkalaj, who saw in Velimirović's words a reiteration of the medieval blood libel against the Jews, and a potential incitement to violence against the followers of Mosaic faith in Serbia (Alkalaj, 1928, p. 3). Velimirović responded to the rabbi's protest, but without recanting the claims that crucifixion was a manifestation of an enduring anti-Christian tendency among the Jewish "race" and that the spirit of Judaism remains a threat to the future of humanity (Velimirović, 1928c, see also Chapter 5, below).

A similar portrayal of Judaism as an inherently anti-Christian and dangerous creed is to be found in a speech which Velimirović delivered in 1936, shortly after he once again took over the diocese of Žiča. In this speech, delivered before an audience which included the Yugoslav prime minister Milan Stojadinović, Nikolaj explicitly warned that among the "dangers that loom over our internal and external lives" are not just the "clericalism" of the Catholic Church—a topic salient in Velimirović's mind at the time given his opposition to the planned Concordat between Yugoslavia and the Vatican, see below—but also "the bloody Jewish Judaism, because Jews are working slyly and cleverly on the destruction of faith—faith in real God" ("Zapisnik XVII redovne skupštine sveštenstva eparhije žičke oržane na dan 16/3 jula u manastiru žiči," 1936, p. 23; see Velimirović, 1940 for similar claims). In the same issue of *Pregled crkve eparhije žičke* in which this speech was reported, another contributor, evidently inspired by the "words of the bishop of Žiča, Dr. Nikolaj," elaborated further on the danger posed by "Jewish Judaism." He described Jews as "ideologues of freemasonry," "servants of Satan" who "rule with money," "control the media," and use "socialism to destroy Christianity and Christian culture." Like much of conspiratorial literature of that era, the author of this text identified freemasonry, capitalism, and socialism as "three heads of a hydra" that is "world Jewry" (Pašić, 1936, pp. 3–6).

It appears, therefore, that for Velimirović and a sizable number of his followers, behind modernity and secular European values which were an anathema to them at the time, laid a Satanic, Jewish conspiracy dating back to the crucifixion. In Velimirović's subsequent writing, Jews reappear, time and time again as a satanic people who tried and murdered Christ "inspired by the stinking breath of Satan." In his most controversial work, *Words to the Serbian People Through the Dungeon Window*, written in 1944, Velimirović writes that Jews

> [s]howed themselves to be worse enemies of God than the godless Pilate, because in the fury of their malice, they uttered those terrible words: Let his blood be on us and on our children! So innocent blood became the whip that drove them like cattle through the centuries, from land to land, like fire that burns their repository of schemes against Christ. Because that is what their father, the Devil teaches them; the Devil taught them how to stand against the Son of God, Jesus Christ. The Devil taught them through the centuries how to fight against the sons of Christ, against the children of Light, against the followers of the Gospel and eternal life. (Velimirović, 1998; p. 193)

The same murderous and Satanic "spirit" is manifested in the secular values of contemporary, Godless Europe:

> Europe knows nothing other than what Jews serve up as knowledge. It believes nothing other than what Jews order it to believe. It knows the value of nothing until Jews impose their own measure of values [...] all modern ideas including democracy, and strikes, and socialism, and atheism, and religious tolerance, and pacifism, and global revolution, and capitalism, and communism are the inventions of Jews, or rather their father, the Devil. (Velimirović, 1998, p.194)

Similarly, in the book *Indian Letters*, which Velimirović wrote sometime between July 1941 and December 1942, there is an allegorical story in which "Satan" is portrayed as an evil Jewish woman, "Rebeka Natan," a seductress and leader of a communist uprising. Velimirović describes Rebeka Natan, "whose name reveals her stock," as a member of "all destructive and secret associations plotting against Christianity, religion, and the state." She is a "mistress of disguise," an illusionist and hypnotist who "weaves a web of deceit" around the Earth. She is the "moving force" behind world affairs: she provokes assassinations, revolutions, and disorder wherever she appears (Velimirović, 2000). In other words, a Jewish woman is offered as the embodiment of what Velimirović saw as the destructive, immoral, anti-religious, and revolutionary aspects of European culture and civilization.

In the context of the Serbian Orthodox Christian culture of the 1920s and 1930s, the presence of conspiratorial antisemitism in Velimirović's writing should not be viewed as an isolated incident. The antisemitic dimension of his Manichean perspective on the contemporary historical moment was a reflection of a broader milieu in which this now discredited tradition of political explanation was becoming regarded as increasingly acceptable. In the early 1920s, antisemitic interpretations of the revolutionary changes in Russia (namely the assumption that behind the Bolshevik revolution lay a sinister plot by international Jewry), which the Russian political immigration promoted at the time throughout Europe and the United States (see Poliakov, 1987), did not bypass elements within the Russian Orthodox Church in Exile, which had its headquarters in Serbia (Timotijević, forthcoming). The links between the expatriate Russian clergy and the Serbian Orthodox Church enabled such ideas to penetrate Serbian religious publications, where anti-Jewish themes of this kind have hitherto been uncommon. As early as in 1923, *Pregled crkve eparhije žičke* serialized over the period of three months the article "Russian Golgotha," penned by the former Russian army chaplain, Priest Mihailo Spiridonovich Peleh. In the article, Lenin and Trotsky were described as "servants of western Jewish capital" engaged in "devil's work" against Orthodox Russia, and followers of an evil Jewish plan concocted in 1897, the aim of which was "the destruction of Christianity in the whole world" and the creation of "Satan's kingdom" (Peleh, 1923). In subsequent years, the theme of Jewish conspiracy gradually gained momentum of its own. The Jewish origins of communism remained a dominant theme, although other more generalized claims about the pervasive and decisive role of Jews in history and world politics were also to be found in Church publications. In 1927, the voice of the Devotionalist movement, *Hrišćanska zajednica*, featured extracts from Henry Ford's *The International Jew*, in which communism and freemasonry were identified as two "darlings of the Jew" ("Neprijatelji Hrišćanstva po Henriu Fordu," 1927, p. 7). A year earlier, the same journal published extracts from *Protocols of the Elders of Zion* ("Krvave Osnove ili Protokoli sionskih mudraca," 1926) and the 19th century German pamphlet *Religious Teaching of the Talmud, or the Mirror of Kike Honesty*, which was first translated into Serbian in 1882 by the well-known publicist Vasa Pelagić ("Verozakonsko učenje Talmuda ili ogledalo čivutskog poštenja," 1926). The latter two texts appeared also in *Pregled crkve eparhije žičke* (see Timotijević, forthcoming). Extracts from the *Protocols* were printed in these journals eight years before the first full Serbian translation of this book was published (and subsequently banned by the authorities), which suggests that the reactionary, nationalist stream within the Church played an important role in introducing the Serbian public to antisemitic conspiracy theory. Also, the Devotionalists often defined their struggle for the hearts and minds of the Serbian people in explicitly antisemitic terms, as a war against Jewish power. Their battle against the influence of smaller religious communities in Serbia (above all, the Adventist Church), whom they saw as promoting heresy, was defined as resistance against "the fruit of Judeo–masonry within Christianity" (cited in Subotić, 1996, p. 40).

As was already noted in the Introduction, antisemitism in Velimirović's writing is the major controversy of his life, one that in recent decades dominated the argumentative context surrounding his remembrance. However, the negative stance towards Jews is by no means the only contentious aspect of the bishop's biography which casts a shadow on his legacy. In the attempt to undermine Velimirović's credibility, detractors after the war regularly cited three further issues: a medal which he received from Hitler in 1934, an affirmative reference to the German Fuhrer which can be found in one of his speeches, and his association with Dimitrije Ljotić, a Nazi collaborator and the leader of the fascist movement Zbor (Rally).

In 1934, Nazi Germany awarded the bishop of Ohrid a civilian medal for his contribution to the restoration, in 1926, of a World War I German military cemetery in the Macedonian town of Bitolj. As Velimirović's supporters rightly point out, the medal does not in itself demonstrate an ideological or political affiliation between the bishop and the Nazis. After all, it was awarded for an "honorable" deed and an act of Christian charity which Velimirović undertook eight years before the Nazi state came into being (e.g., Jevtić, 1986a). However, in the attempt to play down the significance of this potentially compromising episode, supporters have also suggested that Velimirović was profoundly embarrassed by this decoration and that he never showed it to anybody (Skrobonja, 2002). What this version of events overlooks, however, is that Velimirović received the medal at a high-profile ceremony at the German Embassy in Belgrade, which was attended by representatives of the Yugoslav government and the Patriarch Varnava Rosić. What is more, a speech which Velimirović delivered shortly after receiving the award suggests that, at the time, he did not feel that the attention conferred upon him by Hitler was anything to be particularly "embarrassed" about. In the spring of 1935, during a manifestation entitled "Orthodox Week," Velimirović gave a lecture on the "nationalism of St Sava." This speech, which was meant to be just another homage to St Sava, became one of his most regrettable public appearances. At the very end of the speech, in which he lamented Europe's "rejection of Christ" in the name of "progress" and glorified the idea of "evangelical nationalism," Velimirović's uttered the following words:

> One must commend the current German Leader, who, as a simple craftsman and a common man, realized that nationalism without faith is an anomaly, a cold and insecure mechanism. In the 20th century he arrived at the idea first introduced by St Sava, and although a layman, he took upon himself that most important of all missions, one that is only worthy of a saint, a genius, a hero. (Velimirović, 1935, p. 28)

After World War II, Velimirović tried to defend this speech, suggesting that rather than praising Hitler for his endeavor to form a national German church and create a faith-based nationalist creed, he was in fact criticizing the "German Leader" for apparently taking upon himself a task worthy only of a saint (Velimirović, 1983, p. 704). And yet, both the precise wording of the speech and the context in which Hitler was mentioned (as a positive development in otherwise godless Europe) suggest that Velimirović may in fact have been seduced, at least momentarily, by the Nazi political project. Given the timing of Velimirović's lecture, the reference to the "current German Leader" may also have been a subtle sign of gratitude for the honor bestowed upon him by Hitler a few months earlier (Tomanić, 2001).

Velimirović's followers today have been eager to point out that the praise for Hitler occurred in the mid-1930s, when the murderous nature of the Nazi regime was not yet fully apparent, and at a time when other notable personalities in Europe and beyond harbored similar illusions about the Fuhrer's place in history. For this reason, they suggest, the worst thing that Velimirović can be accused of is a lack of political judgment and foresight. This assessment of the speech is not without foundation, given that the allusion to the Fuhrer in the 1935 lecture was the only occasion where Velimirović publicly paid tribute to Hitler in this way. What is more, by the late 1930s, Velimirović adopted a more critical stance towards the Third Reich. In April 1939 he wrote in *Žički Blagovesnik*:

> In the West there is a dream about a great western empire. About the great Reich. The first was founded by Napoleon. It lasted 8 years, and then it fell [...] the Second Reich was founded half a century after the fall of the first. The Second Reich was founded by Prussia, Austria, and Italy, in the hope that they would come out of World War I with the basis of a new empire called "Mittel Europa." Fortunately this

> idea remained—Utopia. The First Reich provoked a world war and those who caused it were destroyed. The Second Reich provoked a world war and those who caused it were destroyed. The Third Reich will also end in a world war, and its fate can be gleaned from the fate of the first two... (Velimirović, 1939)

Over the following year, the same journal, whose editorial policy was under Velimirović's influence, published a series of articles in which Nazism was described as a "Satanic evil" (cited in Timotijević, forthcoming). Also, in 1940, Mihailo Konstantinović, a minister in the government of Dragiša Cvetković, noted in his diary that during a meeting with Velimirović in Kraljevo, the bishop "spoke against Hitler, the 'Viennese decorator,' and his brutal politics. He spoke resolutely against 'emperor' Hitler... against Hitlerism" (Konstantinović, 1998, p. 200). And yet, even if Velimirović's ill-advised comments in the 1935 speech are seen as a sign of political naivety, rather than an indication of definitive political allegiances, it appears that the bishop's stance towards Hitler remained in some respects ambivalent. In the years subsequent to the controversial speech, even at the time when Velimirović was becoming more critical of the Nazis, Hitler's failure to give German nationalism a sound Christian underpinning continued to be regarded in ecclesiastical circles close to the bishop of Žiča as a regrettable development and a lost opportunity. In 1939, only two months before Velimirović prophesized the destruction of the Third Reich, an editorial published in *Žički Blagovesnik* protested against the arrest by the Nazis of a German Protestant pastor, but at the same time bemoaned the fact that "the leader of the German people did not succeed in his attempt to unite German religious communities into a single national church" ("Hrabri pastor," 1939, p. 57). Also, although today Velimirović's speech on the "Nationalism of St Sava" seems uniquely misguided, comparably flattering evaluations of the Fuhrer could be heard from other Church dignitaries in Serbia at that time, who saw in Hitler a barrier against communist expansion. In 1937, Patriarch Varnava Rosić gave an interview to a German newspaper in which he defended Hitler from accusations of imperialism, portraying him as a warrior against Bolshevism, and a savior of Slavs (cited in M. Đorđević, 2003, p. 21).

A few months before Velimirović delivered his controversial speech on the "nationalism of St Sava," Dimitrije Ljotić, a politician from the town of Smederevo and former minister in the government of Petar Živković, founded a political movement called Zbor (Rally). Although Zbor was a profoundly unpopular organization in Serbia—it had fewer than ten thousand active members and in two parliamentary elections, in 1935 and 1938, it won 0.84% and 1% of the votes respectively—it made a mark in history as Serbia's only notable pre-war fascist organization. What is more, following the German invasion of Yugoslavia in April 1941, its leader, Dimitrije Ljotić, became the *eminence grise* of the collaborationist establishment, which was composed almost entirely of current or former members of Zbor. At the same time, the organization's grassroots members formed the mainstay of the Serbian Volunteer Corps (Srpski Dobrovoljački Korpus, SDK), Serbia's most zealous collaborationist paramilitary organization, which fought alongside the German army against Partisan and Chetnik insurgents (Martić, 1980; Stefanović, 1984).

Before the war, Dimitrije Ljotić, who was deeply religious and well connected within the Serbian Orthodox Church (he was the representative of the Braničevo diocese at the Patriarchical Council of the Serbian Orthodox Church), maintained close links with Nikolaj Velimirović and the Devotionalists. This was reflected in one of Ljotić's nicknames, which was "Mita Bogomoljac" or "Devotionalist Mita." There is strong evidence to suggest that Velimirović approved of Zbor and encouraged his followers to join this organization. His disciple, the theologian Dimitrije Najdanović states in his autobiography that he joined Zbor in 1936 on the instruction of his mentor (Najdanović, 2001, p. 108). Najdanović eventually became one of Zbor's main ideologues, and a senior official in the Ministry of Education in the collaborationist government of Milan Nedić (1941–1944). Priest Aleksa Todorović, one of the leaders of the Devotionalists and for a while editor of their publication *Hrišćanska Zajednica*, was also closely affiliated with Zbor. After Ljotić formed the Volunteer Corps in 1941, Todorović was instated as their chaplain and spiritual guide. The significant overlap between the membership of Zbor and that of the Devotionalists has led to suggestions that from 1935 onwards, members of Zbor gradually infiltrated the Devotionalists and became the "backbone" of the movement (Subotić, 1996, p. 195), while according to others, it was the Devotionalists who collectively joined Ljotić's organization in the late 1930s (Stefanović, 1984). In a signed statement which he gave to the Yugoslav security services shortly after the end of World War II, Patriarch Gavrilo Dožić—head of the Serbian Orthodox Church between 1938 and 1950—went as far as to suggest that Ljotić was "brought up and encouraged" by Velimirović, whose ambition was to use Zbor to draw the Serbian Orthodox Church into the sphere of politics (cited in P. Ilić, 2006, p. 100).

In the autumn of 1940, when Yugoslav authorities outlawed Zbor, incarcerated a number of its prominent members (including Dimitrije Najdanović), and issued an arrest warrant for Ljotić (who went into hiding), Velimirović was one of a very few public figures in Serbia who protested on their behalf. He wrote a letter to the Serbian prime minister Dragiša Cvetković, in which he demanded Najdanović's release, and praised Ljotić's "faith in God" and his "good character" (cited in Janković, 2003, p. 217). Also, although the relations between the two figures soured during the Nazi occupation (mainly because Velimirović did not share Ljotić's collaborationist zeal), Velimirović delivered a eulogy at Ljotić's funeral in Slovenia in April 1945, in which he spoke of the deceased—by that time an undisputed Nazi collaborator—as "a politician bearing a cross," and an "ideologue of religious nationalism" whose importance "transcends the boundaries of Serbian politics" (Velimirović, 2001, p. 58).

The lasting affinity between Ljotić and Velimirović can be attributed to the fact that Zbor's political program was influenced by Velimirović's perspective on "evangelical nationalism" and his views on history, politics, and society. Ljotić, just like Velimirović, advocated the abandonment of individualism and parliamentary democracy, and believed that the Serbian nation must return to its religious and cultural traditions. Also, Ljotić shared with Velimirović the belief in a sinister anti-Serbian conspiracy. He alleged that behind the world's problems lies the "Great Director" (as in theatre director), a "collective personality" which consists of "a people without land, language, a stable religion, a people without roots, the Jews" (Ljotić, 1940a, pp. 9–11). Jews were portrayed in Zbor's propaganda as the force behind liberal democracy, Freemasonry, and communism, and therefore as the movement's (and by extension the nation's) principal enemy. Ljotić saw "liquidating the influence of Masons, Jews, and every other spiritual progeny of Jews" as the only way of saving Yugoslavia from the threat of war (Ljotić, 1940b).

In spite of the evident similarities between Velimirović's and Ljotić's political outlooks, an important difference persisted throughout the late 1930s and 1940s. Whereas Velimirović was becoming increasingly critical of Hitler's imperialism, Ljotić remained an unrepentant admirer of Nazi ideology in which he saw a welcome form of resistance against Bolshevism and global Jewish control. And yet, Velimirović never publicly denounced the leader of Zbor for his pro-Nazi stance, and their difference of opinion did not prevent him from speaking at Ljotić's funeral in Slovenia in 1945. Even after the war, Velimirović maintained that in the 1930s, he and Ljotić pursued a common ideological agenda. In an interview to a Serbian newspaper published in the United States in the 1950s, he stated that in his overall Serbian Christian nationalist project, Ljotić—his "pupil and faithful follower in Christ"—was "passing the incense burner" (cited in Popov, 1993).

In the latter part of the 1930s, at the time when his views were becoming radicalized and the involvement with Zbor intensified, Velimirović came into open conflict with the Yugoslav government and found himself increasingly isolated within the ecclesiastical establishment in Serbia. In 1936 he took a leading role in the fight against the signing of the Concordat between Yugoslavia and the Vatican, which many in Serbia saw as a threat to the primacy of the Serbian Orthodox Church in the Kingdom of Yugoslavia (see Mišović, 1983; Radić, 2002a). The opposition to the Concordat amounted, in Velimirović's view, to "defending his people" from the proselytizing ambitions of the "heretical bishop of Rome" (letter to the synod dated June 16, 1938, cited in Janković 2003, p. 246). In July 1937, the "Concordat crisis" reached its climax. A standoff between armed gendarmes and a street procession led by the bishops of the Serbian Orthodox Church (in which Velimirović did not partake) ended in a riot. On the same day the synod of the Serbian Orthodox Church announced that Serbian parliamentarians who offer their support to the Concordat would be excommunicated from the Church. Shortly afterwards Patriarch Varnava Rosić suddenly died, which led to rumors (which persist to the present day) that he had been poisoned because of his opposition to the foreign policy of the Prime Minister Milan Stojadinović. In the end, in response to public pressure, the government took the Concordat off the agenda. Following the election of Gavrilo Dožić as the new patriarch, relations between state authorities and the Serbian Orthodox Church were restored. Velimirović, however, offended by attacks on him in government controlled press during the crisis, opposed any reconciliation between the Church and the state. He even proposed that the Church should demand the resignation of the Prime Minister Milan Stojadinović. After this directly political initiative was rejected by the other bishops, Velimirović embarked on a protest. For almost three years he boycotted the sessions of the Synod and the Assembly of Bishops, and refused all contact with state officials in his diocese. Only in 1940, after a meeting at Kalenić Monastery in central Serbia, Velimirović made peace with Patriarch Gavrilo Dožić and resumed normal relations with other bishops and with secular authorities.

After World War II, Yugoslav authorities frequently accused Velimirović of "Nazi collaboration," mainly on account of his pre-war association with Dimitrije Ljotić and his speech at the latter's funeral in 1945. And yet Velimirović's actions before and during World War II appear to go against these grave accusations. Velimirović's whereabouts during the war will be examined in more detail in the next chapter, as they are closely linked to the process of his rehabilitation, so only the essential facts will be provided here. In March 1941, together with a number of prominent members of the Serbian Orthodox Church (including Patriarch Gavrilo Dožić), Bishop Nikolaj came out in support of the putsch which deposed the Yugoslav regent Pavle Karađorđević and annulled the treaty between Yugoslavia and the Axis Forces which the regent signed a few days earlier. The putsch, which attracted considerable public support in Serbia, provoked the invasion of Yugoslavia by Nazi Germany ten days later. The famous patriotic speech in favor of the putsch, which Serbian Patriarch Gavrilo Dožić read out on national radio shortly after the fall of Pavle Karađorđević, is widely believed to have been written, or at least inspired by Nikolaj Velimirović (Jevtić, 1988; A. Radosavljević, 2003).

In April 1941, only eleven days after the surprise bombing raid on Belgrade on Easter Sunday (April 6), Nazi Germany completed its invasion of Yugoslavia. The ensuing partition of the country left a large part of Serbia under direct occupation by Nazi Germany. One of the first steps undertaken by German authorities in Belgrade was to isolate influential public figures whom they believed might become a source of instability in the country. Because of their support for the coup of March 1941, both Velimirović and Patriarch Gavrilo Dožić were treated with suspicion. There are indications that before the war, German authorities considered Velimirović—as a committed nationalist and anticommunist—a potential candidate for collaboration. In January 1969 *Politika*'s Bonn correspondent reported on a trial, which took place in Germany at the time, in which Eugen Gerstenmaier, the former head of the German Evangelical Church's Office for External Relations (Kirchlichen Aussenamt) testified how Velimirović was Germany's favorite candidate to take over leadership of the Serbian Orthodox Church following the German occupation of Serbia ("Kako je Gerstenmajer vrbovao Nikolaja Žičkog," 1969, p. 4). However, after the events of March 1941 Velimirović was identified as "pro-British" and, therefore, as a potential threat to Germany's interests. And yet, in contrast to Patriarch Gavrilo Dožić, who was immediately arrested by the Nazis and incarcerated in the Gestapo prison in Belgrade, Velimirović remained at liberty, possibly because Ljotić and other collaborators managed to convince the Germans that he might yet be persuaded to offer support to the puppet "Commissars' Administration" led at that time by two notorious Nazi sympathizers, Milan Aćimović and Dragi Jovanović (P. Ilić, 2006).

Velimirović was eventually arrested in July 1941 on suspicion of links with the Chetnik insurgents who fought against the German troops at the time. However, he was promptly released, on condition that he would suspend his activities as the bishop of Žiča and remain under German surveillance at Ljubostinja Monastery (P. Ilić, 2006). The decision to let Velimirović go was at least partly influenced by the fact that his associates showed the interrogating officer the medal which he received from Hitler seven years earlier, as well as by a series of letters which Dimitrije Ljotić sent to German officials in the spring and summer of 1941, in which he informed them that the bishop had "praised Hitler" before the war and should therefore not be regarded as an enemy of the Reich (cited in Subotić, 2004, pp. 442–446). At Ljubostinja, Velimirović was frequently visited by German officials and representatives of the collaborationist administration who wanted him to denounce the partisan insurgency in Serbia. Although Velimirović delivered a number of anti-communist speeches at the time, he nonetheless refused to sign any form of written proclamation to that effect (P. Ilić, 2006; Radić, 2002a). In December 1942, after a search of Ljubostinja Monastery uncovered an illegal radio transmitter, Velimirović was arrested for a second time and transferred to another monastery, in Vojlovica near Belgrade. He was kept there, together with Serbian patriarch Gavrilo Dožić, under house arrest for eighteen months. Both Velimirović and Dožić resisted further pressure to collaborate with the Germans and refused to partake in the planned pro-German "government of national salvation" with which Nazis intended to replace the quisling administration of General Milan Nedić (Džomić, 2003; J. Radosavljević, 2003).

In September 1944, as German troops began to loose ground in the war against the partisans and the Red Army, Velimirović and Dožić were transferred to Germany, via Budapest and Vienna. Eventually, they ended up at the notorious concentration camp at Dachau where they were held as "honorary prisoners" (*Ehrenhafling*) for just over two months. The reason behind Velimirović's and Dožić's release in November 1944 remains a matter of controversy, although historical evidence strongly suggests that their freedom was part of a deal struck between Serbian collaborators and the German envoy in the Balkans, Hermann Neubacher (P. Ilić, 2006; see also B. Kostić, 1991; Parežanin, 1971; Petranović, 1983).

Upon their release from Dachau, Velimirović and Gavrilo Dožić were sent, under German escort, to recuperate at the Bavarian lake resort Schliersee (P. Ilić, 2006), before being transferred to Vienna, where they remained until March 1945. From Vienna they traveled to Slovenia, where Ljotić and other Serbian nationalist warlords were fighting Slovenian partisans under the command of the notorious SS official Odilo Globocnik, and were preparing a final mass offensive against Tito's army. During the stay in Slovenia, Velimirović gave his blessing to Ljotić's volunteers, as well to other collaborators, such as the Chetniks of Momčilo Đujić and Dobroslav Jevđević (B. Kostić, 1991; Parežanin, 1971).

Velimirović left Slovenia after Ljotić's death in a car crash in April 1945. A year later he emigrated to the United States, where he hoped to become actively engaged with local dissident *émigré* organizations in a propaganda campaign against the communist authorities in Yugoslavia. He believed that he would serve his country better from abroad, in accordance with the old proverb that he often quoted at the time, namely that "if a house is burning, the best way to put out the fire is from the outside." However, disenchanted with the divisions within the Serbian diaspora in North America and aware of his diminishing influence in the homeland, Velimirović soon withdrew form public life and retreated to the Russian St Tikhon's Monastery in South Canaan, Pennsylvania. There he taught at the local seminary and lived a solitary existence until his death on March 18, 1956, at the age of 76. An official report sent to the patriarchate in Belgrade shortly after Velimirović's death stated that he died of heart failure during the night, with a rosary still in his hands (cited in Janković, 2003, p. 484). His death did not attract much publicity in Belgrade, for reasons which will become apparent shortly, although in his eulogy to Velimirović, the Anglican bishop of Chichester, George Bell, mentioned that, when the news of his death reached Belgrade, church bells in the city tolled simultaneously in his honor (cited in Heppell, 2001, p. 87).

Following a dispute within the Serbian community in the United States about where Velimirović should be buried, it was decided that his remains would be interred in the gardens of the Serbian St Sava Monastery in Libertyville, Illinois, a monastery which he helped to build in the 1920s. Before the funeral, Velimirović's body was displayed in the Serbian Orthodox churches in New York, Chicago, and Lackawanna (New York state) where it was worshiped by local faithful. He was buried on March 27, 1956, in the presence of forty-two Serbian priests and prominent members of the Serbian diaspora. As we will see in the next chapter, the serene surroundings of St Sava Monastery, which became a place of pilgrimage for the Serbian diaspora in the United States and the occasional visitor from Serbia, proved to be only a temporary resting place. In May 1991, among considerable pomp and ceremony, Velimirović's remains were brought back to Serbia and laid to rest in a chapel in his native village of Lelić.

Denigration and marginalization: Velimirović's status in post-war Yugoslavia

Within the Serbian Orthodox Church today, the time under communist rule is often portrayed as one of great misery and oppression. Priest Savo Jović, author of the book bearing the indicative title *Incarcerated Church* (2002) describes the period as one of "greatest suffering" (p. 44), stating that "never in peacetime were we [the Church] persecuted, arrested, and murdered as frequently as between 1945 and 1985" (p. 11). Communist Yugoslavia was, according to this author, built on the "blood of Orthodox clergy," which it sought to destroy with "mallet, knife, red hot iron, saw, rocks, and firearms." In the hands of "Satanic killers," Serbian priests, "shepherds of Christ's flock" and "Christ bearers," were elevated to "Golgothic heights" of martyrdom (p. 12). Priest Velibor Džomić, author of the five-volume work *The Suffering of the Serbian Church under Communism* stated recently that the fate of the Church under Tito "is more moving, more painful, and more terrifying and tragic" than that endured under Turkish yoke (2005, p. 46). On a previous occasion, he too drew a direct parallel between "crucified Christ" and the "crucified people" under communism, namely "Serbs and their Serbian Orthodox Church" (Džomić, 2000). In most instances, the alleged murderous actions of Yugoslav communists are attributed to militant secularism of the Yugoslav state and its "godless ideology" concocted by the "disturbed psyche of Soviet revolutionaries" (Đurić, 2002, p. 8).

These and similar dramatic portrayals of what are said to have been "the most painful and the bloodiest pages in the history of the Serbian people" (Džomić, 2005, p. 46) in fact conceal a more complicated story of church–state relations in post-Word War II Yugoslavia, which were marked by a mixture of pragmatism, mutual suspicion, and political gamesmanship. While the Yugoslav constitution guaranteed the freedom of religious belief and allowed the churches the freedom to regulate matters of faith, secular authorities in socialist Yugoslavia sought to exclude churches from public life and confine religion to the domain of the private. For the Serbian Orthodox Church, life under communist rule was a lengthy exercise in damage limitation. Its stance towards the authorities was driven by the quest for the right balance between cooperation and resistance, all with the aim of keeping afloat an institution decimated by war and demoralized by the loss of privileges which it enjoyed in the past.

From the early days of the Partisan uprising, the firm anti-religious stance which the Communist Party of Yugoslavia adopted before the war, gave way to a more pragmatic and liberal approach to religion. In order to make their movement acceptable to the rural population steeped in religious traditions, the Partisans promoted the fundamental right to religious belief and preached tolerance and interfaith understanding. In line with this more inclusive stance, Partisan units had "referents for religious affairs," who catered for the spiritual needs of the fighters, while clergy who joined the movement were promoted into army chaplains who performed christenings and burials, and held religious services in liberated territories. Chaplains wore on their uniforms a badge bearing a curious combination of a cross superimposed over the usual red star (Alexander, 1979). The accommodating stance of the authorities towards religion was apparent also in the fact that in 1944, a liturgy was held in Belgrade for the fallen Yugoslav and Russian soldiers who perished during the liberation of the city. At the liturgy, Dr. Ivan Ribar, the President of Antifascist Council of the National Liberation of Yugoslavia (the temporary ruling body of the emerging socialist federation), and a number of other high-ranking state officials received communion and kissed the cross (Lilly, 1991). In the post-war years, the state controlled press regularly acknowledged the principal Christian holidays, such as Christmas or Easter, although in a way that advanced the cause of the regime. The Easter edition of *Politika* in 1945 stated for instance that Tito was "sent by God" and that the liberation from Nazism represented a form of resurrection (cited in Lilly, 1991). Furthermore, a directive issued by the authorities after the liberation promoted the annual celebration of St Sava's Day, which included a reception in the building of the state assembly attended by Tito and other government officials (Radić, 2002a). This tolerant stance towards religion, which emphasized the equality of nations and faiths, was consistent with the rhetoric of "brotherhood and unity" on which the new multi-ethnic state was being founded. In line with this drive towards reconciliation among Yugoslav nations, state authorities annulled all acts of forceful religious conversion to Catholicism of the Serbian Orthodox population in Croatia and Bosnia which was carried out by the Ustasha during the war, a move that received support from the leadership of the Orthodox Church (Alexander, 1979).

The liberal approach to religion by Yugoslav authorities at the early stage of post-war consolidation of power was motivated also by fear that radical measures against religious organizations might turn them into centers of opposition activism. Furthermore, Tito was trying to build a reputation for Yugoslavia as a tolerant and progressive state, an image that would have been undermined by rumors of religious oppression. The aim of the authorities was therefore to tolerate religion, while gradually driving the church away from public life and keeping as much of it as possible under state control (Radić, 2002a). As Tito acknowledged in a speech delivered in 1947, religion cannot be "eliminated by decree," but it can be put "in the service of the people" and turned into a contributor to the building of socialist society (Lilly, 1991, p. 180). Placing the church "in the service of the people" was a euphemism for marginalization and the demand for unquestioned compliance.

In the eyes of the Yugoslav authorities, the Churches were unquestionably a latent source of instability. This was not just because their dogma threatened to the materialist and secular philosophy promoted by the ideologues of the League of Communists, but also because in multi-ethnic and multi-confessional Yugoslavia national and religious boundaries often ran along the same lines. Confessional divisions (especially between Serbs and Croats as the two largest ethnic groups) were seen as a potential obstacle to a unified Yugoslav identity. Hence, religious communities were treated as a potential hotbed of nationalism and chauvinism. The Serbian Orthodox Church was viewed with particular suspicion, mainly because it traditionally defines itself as more than a religious institution: it is also the "authorised interpreter" for the Serbian national interests, a "symbol of the venerated traditions, the embodiment of a past both glorious and painful" (Pavlowitch, 1988, p. 96). Given that Serbian hegemonism and "Greater Serbian nationalism" were perceived as the greatest threat to "brotherhood and unity" among Yugoslav nations, the Serbian Orthodox Church was treated as an especially seditious organization, in whose activity it would be the hardest to differentiate religion from what was known at the time as the "misuse of the church for political purposes" (Radić, 2002a).

The attempts to sideline religious institutions in Yugoslavia inevitably provoked resistance from within the churches, to which the authorities responded with uncompromising determination. As Stevan Pavlowitch (1988) put it, "it was necessary to make [the churches] harmless before they could be tolerated, and since their hierarchies did not want to understand that they had to change their ways, they would be made to understand—by obstruction, by attacks, by trials, by imprisonment" (p. 102). Overall, the Serbian Orthodox church adopted a more compromising stance towards the new authorities, compared to the Catholic Church, which bore the brunt of state oppression (Lilly, 1991; Pavlowitch, 1988). While the patriarchate in Belgrade frequently protested against government measures (see Živojinović, 1998), instances of public defiance were sporadic and localized, and in most instances swiftly quashed by the authorities. Nevertheless, the clergy was regularly subjected to intimidation and harassment by local party officials, especially in rural areas. Although persecution of the clergy was not a deliberate state policy towards the Church, the authorities for the most part turned a blind eye to these incidents, which was in itself a source of encouragement to eager local apparatchiks (Ramet, 2002).

The first step towards the weakening of the Serbian Orthodox Church was taken during the war, in 1942, when the state-sponsored Union of Associations of Orthodox Priests of the Federal People's Republic of Yugoslavia was founded. The Union (which began to operate in earnest in 1949) consisted of Orthodox clergy sympathetic to the new regime, and was formally the successor to the Association of Orthodox Clergy, which existed in Serbia since 1889. Before World War II, the Association had a long history of conflict with Church hierarchy, mainly over the rights of the junior clergy to form a professional organization that was not directly accountable to the Synod and the Assembly of Bishops. By reviving an association with a history of dissidence, and by strengthening its influence through state sponsorship, the authorities endeavored to set up a parallel source of authority within the Church and in doing so create internal divisions.

The most effective way in which the state endeavored to weaken the church's influence was by removing its economic base. Land reform and the nationalization of church-owned property resulted in churches loosing eighty-five per cent of their assets (Lilly, 1991). What is more, land previously owned by the church was given to poor peasantry, which drove a wedge between the church and its flock, who suddenly became competitors over land and real estate. As a consequence of these reforms, the Serbian Orthodox Church became increasingly dependant for its existence on state subsidies, which were discretional and had to be negotiated every year. State donations depended on the regime's good will and the assessment of the churches' contribution to the building of "socialist society."

The state also tried to minimize the presence of the Church in public life. Constitutional measures introduced in 1946, which heralded the arrival of a truly secular state, stripped the churches of their jurisdiction over the registration of births, deaths, and marriages. Religious instruction was gradually phased out from school curricula. *Litije*, religious street processions, which were common before the war and which were often the central events in the religious life of parish communities, were outlawed. The Church was excluded even from the celebrations of supposedly "religious" holidays (such as St Sava's Day) as the organization was placed in the hands of local party organizations (Lilly, 1991; Radić, 2002a). All of these measures meant that by 1980s the socialist Yugoslavia brought up a whole generation of citizens for whom religion was not a significant part of everyday life (Ramet, 2002).

Most importantly for the present discussion, another means by which the authorities sought to undermine the influence of the Serbian Orthodox Church was by drawing the public's attention to those segments of the clergy whose wartime record was compromised by the involvement with Nazi collaborators, or who emigrated to the West after the war. Selected representatives of the higher echelons of the Orthodox Clergy against whom the authorities felt that they could build a case were subjected to an orchestrated campaign of vilification, all with the aim of popularizing the image of the Church as an inherently backward-looking institution, "whose gospel was the dispensation of depraved reactionaries" (Ramet, 2002, p. 100). Because of his public image and widespread popularity before the war, Nikolaj Velimirović was instantly placed at the top of the list of "traitors": his citizenship was revoked, his name was included on an unofficial list of authors whose work could not be openly published, and his reputation was subjected to public disparagement.

In order to increase the effectiveness of such campaigns, especially in the early days, while Velimirović was still alive, the criticism of the reactionary clergy was presented as coming not from the secular authorities, but from the Church itself. The campaign against Velimirović was fronted by the Union of Associations of Orthodox Priests, whose statute specifically stated, as one of the organization's main tasks, "leading the Battle [*sic*] against the Church's most reactionary bishops" (Radić, 2002a, p. 321). The Union's fortnightly publication, *Vesnik*, provided the medium through which this "battle" was waged.

On the pages of *Vesnik* Velimirović, along with two other exiled bishops, Dionisije Milivojević and Irinej Đorđević, was routinely dismissed as a "clerical-nationalist," a "traitor," and an "enemy of the socialist revolution." In the early stages of post-war transition, the bishop's biggest fault in the eyes of the authorities and numerous critics from within the ruling establishment was not the association with Zbor in the 1930s, or his activities in Slovenia in the spring of 1945, or even his antisemitism. Rather, Nikolaj was criticized above all for emigrating to the United States and for siding with the "imperialists." At the first convention of the Union of Associations of Orthodox Priests held in 1949, the delegates issued a statement proclaiming that "we condemn and distance ourselves from the workings of Bishop Nikolaj Velimirović [...] who, after the liberation of our country remained in the camp of the imperialist countries, and together with the imperialists is plotting new slavery for our people, and is sowing lies, darkness, and ignorance" ("Osnovan je savez udruženja pravoslavnog sveštenstva FNRJ," 1949, p. 1). Velimirović and other exiled bishops were branded "deserters, traitors of their country and their church, and mercenaries of foreign capital." Velimirović, who was still officially the bishop of Žiča, was singled out as a "servant of American imperialism," an "enemy of all the values of the fight for national liberation of the Yugoslav nations," and "a warmonger and an inciter of unrest in our country" ("Sa skupštine sveštenstva NR Srbije," 1949). He was dismissed as a "cancerous wound on the body of our Serbian Orthodox Church" (Jelić, 1950, p. 2) and conspirator "against the interests of his country" (Đorđević, 1950, p. 2). He was accused of "placing our faith in the service of imperialism" and "serving the dollar, rather than God and his people" (Ž. Kostić, 1949, p. 3). Only occasionally were readers reminded of the deeper origins of the bishop's credentials as a "traitor," when Velimirović's association with nationalists during World War II was mentioned in passing: "In the war we had four bishops who were traitors, of which three are today in the U.S.: Nikolaj Velimirović, Irinej Đorđević, and Dionisije Milivojević. A sad state of affairs, brothers. Three bishops who can't return to their land because of their treason" (J. Radović, 1950, p. 9). In another editorial in the same publication, Velimirović was dismissed as "lackey of the Germans" ("Kome ne ide u račun da Srpska pravoslavna crkva nađe svoj pravi put," 1950, p. 4).

The likely reason why criticisms of Velimirović in the late 1940s and the early 1950s focused on his status as a dissident and a stooge of imperialist powers—rather than as a fascist or Nazi collaborator—

is that the emphasis on the bishop's current "sins" was more in line with the overall ideological context defined by the emerging Cold War divisions. Also, at the time, both secular and ecclesiastical authorities hailed Patriarch Gavrilo Dožić—who returned to Serbia in 1946 and remained head of the Church until 1950—as the wartime hero of the Serbian Orthodox Church. In 1946 the publication *Glasnik Srpske Pavoslavne Crkve* portrayed Patriarch Gavrilo as the organizer of protests that followed the coup in 1941, the champion of anti-German resistance, and a victim of Nazi persecution. The issue of the same periodical published on the occasion of the patriarch's death in 1950 made identical claims about Dožić's patriotic credentials. Given that Dožić and Velimirović spent much of World War II (between 1942 and 1945) in each other's company, interned in Vojlovica Monastery, in Dachau, or with Ljotić in Slovenia, references, in a negative context, to Velimirović's activity during World War II inevitably would have undermined Patriarch Gavrilo's emerging credibility as a patriot. In fact, in accounts of Dožić's life in ecclesiastical press in the 1940s and 1950s, Velimirović's companionship during the war is hardly ever mentioned. His name is routinely omitted from accounts of the patriarch's patriotism and incarceration by the Nazis. Thus, the narrative of the bishop's "treachery" was formulated in a way that emphasized, as much as possible, the differences between him and Dožić, while carefully omitting the commonalities. According to Radmila Radić (2002a), one of the reasons why Tito invited the patriarch to return to Serbia in the first place, was because he anticipated that the homecoming of a Church leader with strong anti-fascist and patriotic credentials, and his reinstatement as the leader of the Church could be used to further marginalize and undermine the reactionary Serbian clergy whom Dožić left behind in the West (Radić, 2002a). The emphasis on the contrast between Velimirović and Dožić initiated at that time persisted until the 1980s. In one article published in the daily *Večernje Novosti*, the "traitor" Velimirović was denounced through comparison with "the illustrious figure of Patriarch Gavrilo," claiming that the two individuals were '"antipodes" (P. Simić, 1986b, p. 8).

With the passage of time, and especially after Velimirović's death in 1956, the forceful public campaign against him in the regime-controlled media gave way to a different strategy, that of marginalization. Apart from periodical instances of public criticism which are examined below, Velimirović was by and large confined to oblivion. His contribution to theology was ignored and his work was excluded from the teaching programs at Orthodox seminaries. His legacy was kept alive surreptitiously among only a small circle of admirers on the fringes of the Serbian Orthodox Church, who were gathered around Velimirović's former associate and disciple, the dissident monk Father Justin Popović. Velimirović's supporters in the church, apart from Justin Popović, included four of Justin's disciples: Atanasije Jevtić, Artemije Radosavljevic, Amfilohije Radović, and Irinej Bulović, as well as Velimirović's nephew, Jovan Velimirović, who was bishop of Šabac and Valjevo between 1960 and 1989 (Tomanić, 2001). Also, Velimirović had considerable support among the nationalist organizations in the diaspora, both in Western Europe and the United States. In the 1960s and 1970s the Munich-based publishing companies Iskra and Svečanik, run by Velimirović's disciples Dimitrije Najdanović and Aleksa Todorović and by the historian Đoko Slijepčević, occasionally published Velimirović's work. Back in Serbia, however, except amongst his fan base on the margins of the Serbian Church, Velimirović was for the most part forgotten by the largely secularized Yugoslav public. Post-war generations knew little about Velimirović's life or his religious philosophy, other than what was said about him in the sporadic attacks in the national media.

The 1960s in Yugoslavia was a period of relative liberalization of church–state relations. In 1958 the League of Communists of Yugoslavia adopted a new program which took a more liberal stance towards the public presence of religious communities, as long as it remained under close scrutiny of the regime-controlled Socialist Alliance of Working People of Yugoslavia. Churches were given greater freedom to (re)build temples and monasteries, the number of religious publications increased (the first issue of *Pravoslavlje* was published in 1967), as did the number of educational institutions, such as seminaries and theological schools. The rapprochement between the Serbian Church and the state was facilitated by the election, in 1958, of the moderate Bishop German Đorić (who succeeded Velimirović as the bishop of Žiča in 1956) as the Patriarch of the Serbian Orthodox Church. Patriarch German, who is today often criticized within the church for his proximity to the authorities, took a pragmatic stance in his dealings with the state, realizing that public endorsement of Tito's domestic and foreign political agenda resulted in more generous state subsidies and greater freedom for the institution which he headed (Perica, 2002; Ramet, 2002).

By the end of the 1960s, however, secular authorities in Yugoslavia were somewhat taken aback by a number of unwelcome consequences of its more liberal stance towards religious life. Ecclesiastical establishments in Yugoslavia showed a surprising eagerness to test the boundaries of "religious freedom" and the readiness of the League of Communists to tolerate challenges to its authority (Radić, 2002a). A government report issued in 1969 stated that the desire by the state to avoid "anti-religious and anti-church campaigns" was being brought into question by the tendencies within the churches towards "nationalism and chauvinism." Stricter boundaries needed to be set between "strictly religious and therefore legal, and political, that is illegal, activity of the churches" (cited in Perica, 2002, p. 36). In Serbia in the late 1960s and the 1970s, the Church's "political ambitions," which the state feared, manifested themselves most evidently in the rising concerns about the state of the Serbian population in Kosovo, in the aftermath of the nationalist mobilization among the province's Albanian population. By 1968, the Church protested regularly at what it saw as the failure of the federal authorities to deal with the emerging crisis, while *Pravoslavlje* occasionally published reports of intimidation and violence against clergy and the Orthodox faithful in Kosovo. In May 1968, senior Orthodox clergy, led by Patriarch German, defied a longstanding ban on all forms of public processions of a religious nature and carried, through the streets of the capital, the relics of the medieval emperor Dušan, the founder of the first Serbian patriarchate in the Kosovo town of Peć. Emperor Dušan was hailed as "defender of Orthodox faith and our national identity," and his body symbolized the Serbian Orthodox Church's claim over the province of Kosovo which it saw as the spiritual cradle of the Serbian nation. The Church's actions were quickly condemned by the authorities as a "nationalistic provocation" and a threat to the idea of "brotherhood and unity" (see Perica, 2002).

The relations between the Serbian Orthodox Church and the state deteriorated in the aftermath of these events, although never to the point that would necessitate the reintroduction of repressive measures that marked the late 1940s and the early 1950s. This was mainly because the Serbian Orthodox Church was aware of its financial dependence on government donations, but also because, as an institution which traditionally maintained strong links with the state, opposition was not its natural stance *vis-à-vis* secular authorities (Radić, 2002a). Nonetheless, in the early 1970s, state authorities saw the Serbian Church as the hub of nationalist opposition, which led to a renewal of verbal attacks on what were seen as reactionary trends within the Serbian Church (Pavlowitch, 1988). Censors became increasingly attentive to the goings on in religious publications and reacted more forcefully to the slightest "nationalist provocation," mainly through public condemnation, although on two occasions between 1971 and 1973, issues of *Pravoslavlje* were banned for allegedly inciting "ethnic and religious hatred" (see Perica, 2002).

The campaign against Nikolaj Velimirović in state controlled media during this period was inherently tied up with the broader context of the strained relations between the Serbian Church and the state. Attacks on the former Bishop of Žiča tended to occur in response to attempts by the nationalist elements within the church to bring the maligned bishop back into the public domain, or violate the informal but nonetheless strict ban on the promotion his work. These "provocations," most of which occurred around the time of the 1968 crisis, were in some sense a mark of the Church's newly discovered assertiveness and deliberate (although arguably counterproductive) attempts to test the patience of communist censors.

In June 1968, *Pravoslavlje* printed extracts from Velimirović's controversial 1939 speech, "Whose are you, little Serbian people," in which Serbs are referred to as "a people of Aryan race." The publication of this speech, which was originally delivered as part of the commemorations of the 550th anniversary of the Battle of Kosovo, reflected the Church's increasing preoccupation at the time with events in the province, and its desire to popularize the battle of 1389 as a seminal event in Serbian national history. Within a matter of days, editors of the regime controlled daily *Politika* reacted. In the publication of the extracts from the controversial essay they saw an expression of "political ambitions of the highest circles of the Serbian Orthodox Church" who remain "prisoners of the idea of Greater Serbia" and who continue to play with the "fire of nationalism" ("Čiji si ti mali srpski narode?," 1968, p. 7). The article in *Politika* went on to remind the public that the author of the controversial text was a "pre-war nationalist mystic, post-war political emigrant, and the unwavering enemy of socialist Yugoslavia," whose writing consists of a mixture of "medieval mysticism, chauvinistic exaltation, and racist, or rather fascist, intolerance" (ibid.). Velimirović was dismissed as the sympathizer of Ljotić, a "protégé of Milan Nedić," and the propagator of the "idea of Greater Serbia among the most aggressive émigré groups in America." In subsequent weeks, *Politika* published two further articles on Velimirović, in which it drew attention to the praise of Hitler in the 1935 speech and the affirmative references to the Chetnik leader Draža Mihailović, which appear in some of Velimirović's post-war writings. His "émigré activity in the post-war period" was flagged as directed at the "unification of all reactionary refugee communities for the purpose of inciting enemy activity against Yugoslavia" ("Ipak, ton i gest šovinistički," 1968; "Šta je u emigraciji govorio i radio Episkop Nikolaj," 1968). Thus, once again Velimirović's controversial biography proved a useful tool to draw the public's attention to the Serbian Church's inherently nationalistic and reactionary tendencies.

In 1969, another article in *Pravoslavlje*, penned by the magazine's editor-in-chief, Milisav Protić, referred to Velimirović's uncontroversial work *Njegoš's Religion* as a "work of genius." The Sunday edition of the daily *Večernje Novosti* promptly published an article in which Velimirović was portrayed as an advocate of "Serbian hegemonism, racism, and anti-communism," and *Pravoslavlje* dismissed as a journal prone to anti-socialist and nationalist outbursts (Glišić, 1969, p. 6). Three years later, a text published in the weekly magazine *NIN*, which—just like the 1968 campaign in *Politika*—explicitly targeted what it saw as the continuing nationalistic and counterrevolutionary tendencies within the Serbian Orthodox Church, singled out Nikolaj Velimirović, the "fascist and until his dying day sworn enemy of this society," as the embodiment of the unwelcome developments in Serbia's largest religious institution (Miletić, 1972).

The controversy surrounding Nikolaj Velimirović was revived in 1976, when a group of Orthodox clerics, including Nikolaj's nephew and bishop of Šabac and Valjevo, Jovan Velimirović, organized a memorial sermon in the village of Lelić to commemorate the twentieth anniversary of Velimirović's death. This event was attended among others by Father Justin Popović, the dissident monk and disciple of

Velimirović, who spent much of his post-war existence in isolation in Ćelije Monastery, near Valjevo. Ever since the early 1960s Popović had been organizing, at Ćelije, regular semi-clandestine annual commemorative services devoted to his mentor, which were attended by a clique of Velimirović's admirers in the Church. However, the 1976 memorial, which endeavored to take this commemorative ritual out of Ćelije and into a more public domain of the village church in Lelić, provoked a critical commentary in the Sunday edition of the daily *Večernje Novosti* (Đonović, 1976). The main object of criticism was Justin Popović, whom the authorities regarded as a troublesome nationalist dissident. In his sermon Popović hailed Velimirović as an "apostle" and a "martyr," dismissed the "suicidal culture of modern Europe," and alluded to contemporary (Yugoslav) society as "sinful" and "rotten." In the article in *Večernje Novosti*, the criticism of Popović's nationalism soon turned to a denouncement of his mentor. The former bishop of Žiča was dismissed for offering his blessing to collaborators in Slovenia, an indictment which was illustrated with a photo taken in 1945, which shows Velimirović in the company of the Chetnik commander Priest Momčilo Đujić. In addition to his alleged collaborationist links, Velimirović was said also to be "propagating a fratricidal crusade against his own people, thus placing himself among the conspirators against his native land, all to the benefit of some foreign intelligence agencies" (ibid.).

In the aftermath of Tito's death in 1980, the ruling League of Communists of Yugoslavia feared a nationalist revival in the country, and were concerned that ecclesiastical establishments (Orthodox, Catholic, and Muslim) might become the main source of nationalist opposition and therefore a threat to the ideology of "brotherhood and unity," which formed the hub of socialist Yugoslavia's symbolic order (see Pavlowitch, 1988). These fears were most apparent in Bosnia, because of its multiethnic and multi-confessional composition. In July 1981, Branko Mikulić, Bosnia's representative in the Central Committee of Yugoslavia's League of Communists, delivered a speech dismissing emerging "clerical-nationalist" tendencies within the three largest religious communities in Bosnia. When referring to the Serbian Orthodox Church, Mikulić singled out the attempts by the clergy in the diocese of Zvornik and Tuzla to recreate the Devotionalist movement, a development which he saw as nationalist and "counter-revolutionary"

("Slobodom ponosni-jedinstvom snažni," 1981). Shortly afterwards, the Sarajevo daily *Oslobođenje* elaborated on the themes touched upon in Mikulić's speech and went as far as to accuse the reformed Devotionalists of pursuing the "ideology of the war criminal, the bishop of Žiča, Nikola [*sic*] Velimirović," whose "career as a war criminal offers sufficient insight into the potential effects of this new movement among the Orthodox faithful, and the aims of the clerical nationalists among them" (Jakšić, 1981, p. 3). Unsurprisingly, Velimirović emerged as the embodiment of the Orthodox Church's emerging nationalist aspirations. Later that month, *Oslobođenje* featured a four-part article, entitled "Attempted abuse of Orthodoxy," which included further critique of the former bishop of Žiča (Kozar, 1981).

The concerns among the ruling establishment about the emergence of "clerical nationalism" within the Church were fuelled in part by the increased readiness of the representatives of the country's ecclesiastical institutions to respond to criticism and engage in a public debate with secular authorities. In August 1981, *Pravoslavlje* published the article "Who benefits from a level playing field?" by the then little known Orthodox monk Atanasije Jevtić. This article was a direct response to Mikulić's speech and the subsequent comments in *Oslobođenje* (Jevtić, 1981). Jevtić, who later became a principal protagonist of Velimirović's rehabilitation and remains one of his most vocal admirers in Serbia, objected to the allusion, apparent in the criticism of his bishop's legacy, that his wartime record was comparable to that of Alozije Stepinac, the Croatian Catholic archbishop who was closely affiliated with the leadership of the pro-Nazi Independent State of Croatia, and who was imprisoned by Tito's government after the war. More importantly, Jevtić's article constituted a direct challenge to the dominant and regime-enforced representation of Velimirović as a "Nazi collaborator" and sympathizer of Ljotić, and in that sense is widely regarded as the first significant step in the campaign for the re-evaluation of the bishop's legacy (Bigović, 1998).

One significant feature of the representations of Nikolaj Velimirović in the state controlled media up until the mid-1980s is the relative absence of references to the bishop's antisemitism. Most of the criticism between 1960 and 1985 focused on his associations with "enemies of the revolution" and the controversial speeches in 1935 and 1939 neither of which was antisemitic. The main reason behind the absence of references to antisemitism was that up until the mid-1980s, Velimirović's notoriously anti-Jewish writings were not particularly well-known either to admirers or to critics. The controversy surrounding Velimirović's "Story about the wolf and the lamb" seems to have been forgotten, as were antisemitic articles published before the war in church publications. The most controversial work, *Words to the Serbian People Through the Dungeon Window,* which as was quoted from earlier, was written during World War II and was unknown until the mid-1980s, when the bishop of Western Europe, Lavrentije Trifunović published it in Germany, as part of Velimirović's collected works. In fact, the appearance of the first edition of *Words to the Serbian People Through the Dungeon Window* in 1985 in many ways transformed the argumentative context surrounding the remembrance of Nikolaj Velimirović. This previously unknown work placed antisemitism at the centre of the controversy surrounding the bishop's legacy and credibility.

The first criticism of the *Words to the Serbian People Through the Dungeon Window,* and by extension of Velimirović's antisemitism, appeared in the Croatian magazine *Danas* in the article entitled "What is going on within the Serbian Orthodox Church?" (Ivanković, 1986). Shortly afterwards, another wave of attack on Velimirović appeared in the Belgrade daily *Večernje Novosti* (P. Simić, 1986a, 1986b, 1986c, 1986d). Criticism in the state controlled press now focused on the most controversial sections of *Words to the Serbian People Through the Dungeon Window,* which were quoted *verbatim.* The article in *Danas* began with the paragraph from the book in which Velimirović refers to Europe as knowing only that which "Jews serve up as knowledge." In antisemitism, critics saw "the thread that binds together all the elements of [Velimirović's] fascist ideology" (P. Simić, 1986a, p. 8). The stance on Jews was interpreted as a blemish on Velimirović's legacy that reinforces the claims about his "treachery" and "pro-Nazism." Velimirović became representative of "classic fascistoid anticommunism and antisemitism" (P. Simić, 1986a, p. 8), a "virulent antisemite," even "the darkest individual in the history of Serbian people" (P. Simić, 1986c, p. 8). Articles in *Danas* and *Večernje Novosti* provoked a series of responses from Atanasije Jevtić on the pages of *Pravoslavlje* (Jevtić, 1986a, 1986b, 1986c, 1986d), marking the beginning of "memory wars" over the bishop's reputation.

Fig. 1.
Nikolaj Velimirović shortly after graduation from the St Sava Orthodox Seminary in Belgrade in 1902. *(Source: Narodni muzej, Kraljevo)*

Fig. 2.
Nikolaj Velimirović following his ordainment as Bishop of Žiča in 1919. (*Source: Narodni muzej, Kraljevo)*

Fig. 3.
Nikolaj Velimirović (right) in the company of Mihajlo Pupin (left), the renowned physicist, Professor at Columbia University and Serbian Consul in New York. The young woman in the picture is most probably Pupin's daughter Varvara. The picture was taken during one of Velimirović's visits to the United States in the 1920s. *(Source:* Politika*)*

Fig. 4.
Nikolaj Velimirović attending a public function in Kraljevo in the late 1930s. *(Source: Narodni muzej,Kraljevo)*

Fig. 5.
Nikolaj Velimirović in Žiča in 1940. *(Source:* Politika*)*

Fig. 6.
Nikolaj blessing a young child during a visit to London in the early 1950s *(Source: Narodni muzej, Kraljevo)*

Fig. 7.
Velimirović's grave in Libertyville, Illinois, where his remains were buried between 1956 and 1991. It is at this site that Amfilohije Radović and Atanasije Jevtić are said to have experienced a 'miracle' in the 1970s, see Chapter 6. *(Source: Narodni muzej, Kraljevo)*

Fig. 8.
12 May 1991. Pilgrims worshiping Velimirović's remains prior to their reburial in his native village of Lelić. *(Source:* Politika*)*

Fig. 9.
Belgrade, 24 May 2003: Canonisation ceremony at the Cathedral of St Sava. (*Source:* Danas)

Fig. 10.
Belgrade, May 2003: Pilgrims worshiping Velimirović's holy remains at the Cathedral of St Sava. The remains were brought to Belgrade from Lelić for the canonisation ceremony. *(Source:* Danas*)*

Fig. 11.
The Orthodox Spiritual Centre Bishop Nikolaj Velimirović, Kraljevo, Serbia. The Centre is located in the house where Velimirović resided while Bishop of Žiča between 1934 and 1941. (Source: author's collection)

Fig. 12.
Statue of Nikolaj Velimirović unveiled in March 2002 at Soko Monastery in western Serbia. The statue, three meters high is the work of sculptor Darinka Radovanović. *(Source: magazine* Horizont, *www.casopishorizont.com*)

Fig. 13.
Fresco at the Church of St Constantine and St Jelena, Voždovac, Belgrade. Painted by Milić Stanković (aka Milić od Mačve), 1989. *(Source: author's collection).*

Fig. 14.
'The New Martyrs of Jasenovac and Glina, and Bishop Nikolaj at Dachau', Fresco at the Serbian Monastery Nova Gračanica, Grayslake, Illinois. Painted by Father Theodore Yurevitch, c.1997. *(Source: Nova Gračanica Monastery).*

Fig. 15.
'Bishop Nikolaj and German Soldier in Ljubostinja' *(Author unknown).*

The attacks on Velimirović in 1986 were published as part of broader drive against the "misuse of religion" for political purposes, which the authorities initiated in the mid-1980s (Pavlowitch, 1988). This move coincided with a more permissive overall stance towards religion. For instance, in the early 1980s the Serbian Orthodox Church was allowed to resume after almost 50 years the building of the large Cathedral of St Sava in central Belgrade and erect a new building for the Theological Faculty in Belgrade (Ramet, 2002). However, the efforts of the authorities to strike the balance between on the one hand the affirmative stance towards religion beliefs and legitimate spiritual needs of the faithful, and on the other hand the critique of the political endeavors of the nationalist clergy, proved increasingly difficult. Just like in the late 1960s, the gradual worsening of the ethnic relations in Kosovo meant that the resurgent Serbian Orthodox Church came forward as the principal articulator of "nationalist interests," and became the hub of nationalist opposition. This time around, however, the overall context was different. The iron curtain was hanging by a thread and the ruling elite's grip on power was gradually loosening. What is more, ethnic divisions within the Yugoslav federation were beginning to show, and the state built on the principles of "brotherhood and unity" was clearly tearing at the seams. Nationalist revival in Serbia seemed unstoppable, and the nationalists in the Church were eager to ensure that it was given a pronounced "Orthodox" dimension. This naturally called for the return, into the public domain, of the high priest of Serbian religious nationalism, the "Serbian apostle" Nikolaj Velimirović. As Archimandrite Jovan Radosavljević explained in a book first published in 1991, Velimirović was never just a notable theologian. He was also "the spiritual and national leader, and the true father of his nation" (J. Radosavljević, 2003, p. 116).

The start of the campaign for Velimirović's rehabilitation coincided therefore not only with the nationalist revival in Serbia, but also with the publication of the *Words to the Serbian People Through the Dungeon Window*, which propelled antisemitism into the centre of the debate surrounding his life's work. For this reason, bringing Velimirović into the public domain required for this controversy to be addressed and his moral accountability managed. The dynamics of remembering and forgetting through which this was accomplished are the main topic of subsequent chapters.

Apotheosis and widespread admiration: Velimirović's status today

The condemnations of Velimirović in the mainstream press during the Tito era, and his marginal status in Serbian society after World War II, stand in stark contrast to the bishop's reputation in present-day Serbian society. Today, Velimirović is widely regarded as the most respected Serbian religious figure since the medieval Serbian St Sava. In religious circles, Velimirović is routinely compared, in terms of importance, to St John the Baptist and St John Chrysostom. Reference to Nikolaj as "the thirteenth apostle, the fifth evangelist, doubtlessly the greatest Serb since St Sava," attributed to his disciple Father Justin Popović, is routinely quoted and repeated in church literature. Bishop Amfilohije Radović recently referred to Velimirović as a "prophet and missionary of the rarest kind" (cited in Kuburović, 2003, p. 21). Bishop of Šabac and Valjevo, Lavrentije Trifunović, called him "the greatest Serbian son, cleric, and thinker after St Sava" whose work is a "spiritual skyscraper, a mountain of natural wealth yet to be discovered and explored" (Trifunović, 2002, p. vii).

Significantly, Velimirović's popularity in Serbia today extends beyond the circles of the Serbian Orthodox Church. Multiple editions of Velimirović's books, including the controversial titles, such as *Words to the Serbian People Through the Dungeon Window* or the essay "Nationalism of St Sava," are widely available in Serbia's bookshops. Deacon Ljubomir Ranković, editor of Glas Crkve, a publishing house which has been publishing Velimirović's work since the early 1990s (and which today is only one of many publishers that have titles by Velimirović in their catalogue) claims to have sold over a million copies of his books over the years. Although this figure is likely to be an exaggeration, Velimirović is without a doubt the bestselling Serbian author of the past two decades. Velimirović's influence has even penetrated the traditionally cosmopolitan and progressive elements of Serbian culture, such as rock 'n' roll music. In 2001 the compilation album containing rock 'n' roll renditions of Velimirović's religious poetry, performed by some of Serbia's leading rock bands, was released by a state-owned record company, in collaboration with the Serbian Orthodox Church (Pesme Iznad Istoka i Zapada, PGP-RTS, 2001)

The regard for Velimirović extends also to members of the Serbian political establishment. In 2001, Vladan Batić who was at that time Serbia's Justice Minister and leader of the Christian Democratic Party of Serbia, asserted that Bishop Nikolaj was an indisputable moral and intellectual authority for Orthodox Serbs. His party's website included whole sections devoted to Velimirović's work. In the election campaign of 2000, material distributed even by the pro-western, liberal political party G17+ included an affirmative reference to "Bishop Nikolaj" ("Znaci zla kao simboli vremena," 2002). In January 2003 a favorable stance towards Velimirović was expressed on a popular television chat show by the historian Dušan Bataković, advisor to the current Serbian president Boris Tadić and member of the Serbian delegation at the negotiations on the future status of Kosovo ("Utisak Nedelje," Studio B, January 5, 2003). More importantly, in an open letter to the symposium on Velimirović held at Žiča Monastery in April 2003, the leader of the Democratic Party of Serbia and current Serbian Prime Minister Vojislav Koštunica referred to Velimirović as "our guide," "who is and forever will be among us," and cited the bishop's "real patriotism" as a suitable blueprint for the emerging post-Milošević version of Serbian nationalism (cited in Jevtić, 2003, pp. 321–322; see also "Rodoljublje nije mržnja," 2003, p. 3). During the election campaign in December 2003, speeches delivered by Koštunica at public rallies held throughout Serbia were interspersed with quotes from Velimirović's writings. Koštunica's admiration of Velimirović appears to be shared by Vojislav Šešelj, leader of the nationalist Radical Party and an indicted war criminal currently on trial in The Hague. In August 2003, Šešelj's wife, Jadranka, told the tabloid *Kurir* that her husband spends his prison days acquainting himself with the Statute of the Criminal Tribunal for the Former Yugoslavia and reading the collected works of Nikolaj Velimirović ("Šešelju prija Hag," 2003).

The widespread endorsement of Nikolaj Velimirović among the political elite is seldom counterbalanced by critical voices from among the liberal circles of the country's political establishment. It is as if there is widespread recognition among political parties in Serbia that criticizing Velimirović is politically damaging, in that it alienates the Serbian Church, an organization that stands firmly among the top three most influential institutions in the country. Criticisms of Velimirović are thus confined to the liberal media (*Danas*, *Vreme*,

Republika, Radio B-92), a relatively small circle of Serbian liberal intelligentsia (Nebojša Popov, Mirko Đorđević, Radmila Radić, Olivera Milosavljević, Filip David, and Ivan Čolović), representatives of the Jewish community (Aca Singer and Aleksandar Lebl) and a number of civil rights organizations, the most outspoken being the Helsinki Committee for Human Rights in Serbia.

In the 1990s, Velimirović's writing had also captured the imagination of representatives of another influential mainstream institution in Serbian society, namely the military (see Byford, 2002; HCHRS, 2003a). This popularity reached a climax at the time of the NATO bombing of Yugoslavia, when Velimirović's work became regarded by the ideologues of the Serbian Armed Forces as the bible of anti-westernism and nationalist self-aggrandizement (see Byford 2006). At the time, Velimirović's remembrance became a symbolic space, where different anti-western political options in Serbia, including those espoused by the Army and the Church, could converge. In the autumn of 1999, Serbia's main military journal, *Vojno Delo*, published the article "Philosophical thought of Bishop Nikolaj Velimirović on war and Europe," in which *Words to the Serbian People Through the Dungeon Window* was introduced as the bishop's "most important work on Europe." Velimirović's dictum that the Soviet Union is "Kyke Russia," which appears in his work *Serbian People as a Theodule* (2003), was cited without any critical reflection (M. Milošević, 1999, pp. 180–183). The influence of Velimirović's writing within the Army continued even after the fall of Milošević. In 2001, at the time when Serbia's new government sought to repair its ties with the West, Vojno-izdavački zavod, the Serbian military's official publishing house, published two books written or edited by officers of the Army's Morale and Propaganda Corps—*Army and Faith* (Grozdić and Marković, 2001) and *Orthodoxy and War* (Grozdić, 2001)—in which Velimirović's writings on the dangers posed by the west's continued "spiritual imperialism" are the most frequently cited works. The overtly anti-western collection of essays, *Army and Faith*, even contains contributions from several controversial right-wing antisemites, including Nebojša Krstić, a controversial young theologian and founder of the right-wing, nationalist, and antisemitic organization Obraz (see Byford, 2002) and the discredited priest Žarko Gavrilović. In 2001, the army magazine *Vojska*, which was distributed freely to all military personnel, published a series of articles on Bishop Nikolaj Velimirović, in which the readers were presented with a favorable interpretation of the bishop's views on the army, war and the west. These articles, which were part of a campaign aimed at the "spiritual revival" of the armed forces, were written by the aforementioned Nebojša Krstić ("Sveti Vladika Nikolaj Velimirović," February 15, 2001 – March 22, 2001). Furthermore, in March 2002, one of the central commemorative events marking the third anniversary of the NATO bombing of Yugoslavia was the unveiling of a statue of Nikolaj Velimirović at Soko Monastery, near the town of Šabac. Serbian Patriarch Pavle and the then head of the Yugoslav Army, General Nebojša Pavković, were the highest dignitaries present at the event. The mnemonic link between the remembrance of Nikolaj Velimirović and that of the NATO bombing, which was established on this occasion, confirmed the bishop's continuing status in Serbian nationalist rhetoric as the symbol of anti-westernism. Even today, when the Serbian army is preparing to join NATO, and when anti-westernist rhetoric is gradually being banished from military publications, Velimirović remains a relevant authority for the Army. In 2006, the new military magazine *Odbrana* (Defence), which replaced *Vojska* in 2005 as part of the drive to modernize all aspects of the military and give the Serbian armed forces a more liberal and progressive public image, carried an affirmative portrait of Velimirović. In the article bearing the indicative title "The blameless martyr," the magazine commemorated the fiftieth anniversary of Velimirović's death, without reflecting on any of the controversies surrounding his writing. What is more, it informed the reader that the "author of probably the prettiest verses in the history of religious poetry," the "successful preacher, philosopher, and prophet" also "rose up against westernism and western intelligentsia" (K. Milošević, 2006, p. 75).

Velimirović's popularity in Serbia reached its climax in May 2003, when the Assembly of Bishops of the Serbian Orthodox Church voted unanimously to canonize him, and include his name as the seventy-seventh entry in the roll call of Serbian national saints (see Chapter 6). Velimirović became entrenched in the Orthodox ceremonial, with prayers and hymns being written in his celebration. Icons with Velimirović's image have become a regular sight in churches, in the homes of the faithful, or even in taxis, where they are sometimes prominently displayed on the dashboard. The canonization has also sparked a noticeable merchandising industry: key rings, postcards, credit-card size laminated icons, and other memorabilia can now be bought in shops owned by the Church cooperative. In recent years, the Church has invested considerable funds, mainly obtained from private and corporate donations, on modernizing various shrines devoted to Velimirović. A chapel with an adjacent museum dedicated to Velimirović has been restored in his native village of Lelić. Soko Monastery, which houses the bishop's statue, also includes a large commemorative complex including several churches, large living quarters for up to 150 pilgrims, a library, a car park, and a spacious garden containing a mill and two fountains with water from a nearby mountain spring. On the grounds of the monastery, one can also find a gold-plated cross twelve meters in height. The route that leads from the monastery to this unusual shrine is lined with ten chapels, each devoted to one of the Ten Commandments. Finally, in the centre of the town of Kraljevo is the Orthodox Spiritual Centre Bishop Nikolaj Velimirović. The centre is located in the house where Velimirović resided while bishop of Žiča in the 1930s. It includes a room that has been converted into a chapel, dedicated to the "Holy Bishop Nikolaj." Kept at the chapel is a piece of Velimirović's holy remains: a finger, said to be from his right hand. This unusual relic is located behind the altar, in a small wooden box lined with cotton wool, and is worshipped by visitors to this institution.

It is difficult to determine the extent to which the proliferation of memorial artifacts and monuments devoted to Nikolaj Velimirović in recent years, and especially since his canonization, is the cause or the consequence of the bishop's wider popularity. Either way, there is no doubt that the Serbian Orthodox Church is determined to preserve the memory of the bishop as a holy man and Serbia's most important religious figure since the medieval St Sava. This determination is not surprising, given that Velimirović owes his current status to the success of almost twenty years of commemorative work by the Serbian Church that brought to an end forty years of marginalization and deprecation. The chapters that follow will endeavor to examine the ideological and discursive dynamic of remembering and forgetting that made the rehabilitation possible. In doing so, they will attempt to chart the posthumous passage of Nikolaj Velimirović from "traitor" to "Saint."

CHAPTER THREE

Collective Remembering and Collective Forgetting

Memory of Nikolaj Velimirović and the Repression of Controversy

> Ivan Kuzminović: "We have just canonized the famous Bishop Nikolaj. This is a man who writes in his book *Nationalism of St Sava* that Adolf Hitler is a man who will promote [the values of St Sava]... Do you want me to give you the exact quote? I can read it out, I have it here."
>
> Vladimir Đukanović: "You know, he was in Dachau. So, he was so in favor of Hitler that the latter then placed him in Dachau?"
>
> (Debate among students from the University of Belgrade in the documentary "Why People Whisper in Church?" ["Zašto se u crkvi šapuće?"] *Anem/TV B92,* May 19, 2005)

Bearing in mind the controversies surrounding the biography of Nikolaj Velimirović which were examined in the previous chapter, it might be argued that the maintenance of the positive memory of his life and legacy involves a significant amount of forgetting. The perpetuation of the representation of Velimirović as a positive historical figure and respectable authority can be said to be contingent upon a continuous process of not remembering things like his association with Nazi collaborators, his antisemitism, or the positive evaluation of Hitler which appears in one of his essays.

The emphasis on "forgetting" is not new in scholarly work on collective memory. Peter Burke (1989), for instance, argues that the study of social remembering necessitates the exploration of the "organisation of forgetting, the rules of exclusion, suppression and repression" (p. 108). The means by which uncomfortable, troubling, and traumatic episodes from the past can be kept away from popular consciousness is also considered by Henri Rousso's *Vichy Syndrome* (1991), Peter

Novick's *Holocaust Remembered* (2001), and Iwona Irwin-Zarecka's *Frames of Remembrance* (1994).

In literature on collective memory, the notion of social forgetting is frequently alluded to as "repression," drawing on the vocabulary of Freudian psychoanalysis. According to Freud, repression or "willed forgetting" (Bower, 1990) refers to the driving away of troubling thoughts and impulses from conscious awareness (e.g., Freud, 1914, 1916, 1933, 1940). It is a mechanism that protects the conscious part of the self, the ego, from threatening and potentially damaging unconscious drives and desires. The use of the concept of repression in literature on collective memory stems from the possibility that "groups, like individuals, may be able to suppress what is inconvenient to remember" (Burke, 1989, p. 109).

Recent years have seen a reaction against the reliance on psychological terminology in the study of social remembering (Kansteiner, 2002; Novick, 2001; Wertsch, 2002; Wood, 1999). Wulf Kansteiner (2002) for instance, argues that, when considering collective phenomena, psychological terminology—including words such as "repression," "amnesia," or "trauma"—is "at best metaphorical and at worst misleading" (p. 185). He contends that "we are best advised to keep psychological or psychoanalytical categories at bay and to focus, rather, on the social, political and cultural factors at work" (p. 186). The objection to the drawing of parallels between individual and collective memory rests on the belief that the former is regulated by various "laws of the unconscious" (Wood, 1999, p. 2) and specific mental processes (including repression), the ontology of which is in the human brain. Collective memory, on the other hand, is seen as "disembodied" and devoid of an "organic basis" and in that sense as more abstract and elusive. It consists of "texts" or representations originating from "shared communications about the meaning of the past that are anchored in the life of the world of individuals who partake in the communal life of the respective collective" (Kansteiner, 2002, p. 188).

Because of the assumed ontological difference between collective and individual memory, Iwona Irwin-Zarecka (1994) argues that, in the domain of social remembering, there can be no "unexpressed memories" stored in the unconscious, and therefore no "repression" as such. For aspects of the past to be preserved in the public consciousness, they must be continuously present in the life of the community through the "full information base of remembrance": commemorations, celebrations, monuments, museums, and publications (see also Terdiman, 1993). Put simply, only that which is "publicly known and spoken about" is committed to memory (Irwin-Zarecka, 1994, p. 195). Conversely, for something to be forgotten, its recollection in public discourse must be suspended. Memories are confined to oblivion by not being invoked, spoken about, and remembered in public.

In exploring what it is that determines what will and what will not be socially remembered, studies of collective memory often focus on the role of intentionality and power in the creation, maintenance, and transformation of shared representations of the past. Nancy Wood (1999) writes that collective memory always "testifies to a will or desire on the part of some social group or disposition of power to select and organize representations of the past" and as such it "[embodies] the intentionality—social, political, institutional, and so on—that promotes or authorises its entry [into the public domain]" (p. 2). Similarly, studies in the sociology of reputation often emphasize that a fundamental component of "reputational dynamics" is the "strategizing and political manoeuvring" by a figure's representatives through which his or her image is constructed and managed (Lang & Lang, 1988; Taylor, 1996). The focus on intentionality assumes that "memory enterpreneurship" always involves a manipulation of representations of the past by structures of power, for specific contemporary political and ideological purposes (Olick & Robbins, 1998, p. 126). Thus, a pertinent question in the study of collective memory is "who wants whom to remember what and why?" (Burke, 1989, p. 107).

The rehabilitation of Nikolaj Velimirović over the past two decades, and the transformation of his image from "traitor" to "saint" could indeed be explored from the perspective of intentionality and instrumentalism. In the late 1980s, as nationalism gradually began to replace communism as the dominant ideology of Serbian society, the previously marginal clique of Velimirović's supporters in the Serbian Orthodox Church became a prominent force within the ecclesiastical establishment. Riding on the waves of patriotic euphoria in Serbia, the likes of Amfilohije Radović, Artemije Radosavljević, Atanasije Jevtić, and Irinej Bulović emerged as front-runners in the campaign aimed at Serbia's national and spiritual revival (Perica, 2002; Radić, 2002b; Tomanić, 2001). Together with other nationalist institutions such as the Serbian Academy of Arts and Sciences and the Serbian Union of Writers, the four clerics became the principal voice of Serbian ethnic nationalism. The Metropolitan of Zagreb and Ljubljana, Jovan Pavlović, once lamented that the four "young professors, future episcopes [...] abandoned their theological work and embarked on a cheap political adventure" which helped drag the country into civil war (cited in Tomanić, 2001, p. 17). By 1991, Radović, Radosavljević, Jevtić, and Bulović had all been ordained by bishops, and since then have been wielding considerable influence in the Serbian Orthodox Church.

The newly acquired status of Velimirović's supporters within the Serbian Church enabled them to embark on an aggressive public campaign aimed at improving their hero's standing and ending almost forty years of vilification and marginalization. Moreover, the nationalist clique within the Church viewed Velimirović's return to public consciousness as a necessity, and a means of exorcising the ghost of communism from the Serbian national corpus. An editorial published in *Glas Crkve* in 1987 interpreted it as a manifestation of the "forthcoming revitalization of the whole of the Serbian people" and the rebirth of a nation that would once again be "deeply conscious of its ethnic and spiritual identity" ("Kandilo pred ikonom," 1987, p. 26). Nationalist politician and poet Milan Komnenić saw it as a way of "removing, from the spiritual horizon, all traces of the absurd, of things vulgar and anti-Serbian, of fraud and humiliation" (Komnenić, 1988, p. 30). For the priest Dragan Terzić, Velimirović's reinstatement in public memory was a way of "healing a huge wound on the Serbian Orthodox national body" (Terzić, 1991, p. 52).

The campaign aimed at restoring Velimirović's reputation consisted of different measures aimed at imposing positive interpretations of his life on public consciousness. In 1985, Velimirović's nephew, Bishop Jovan of Šabac and Valjevo, founded the journal *Glas Crkve* which was edited by his personal assistant, Deacon Ljubomir Ranković. The aim of this somewhat rebellious journal was to "write openly and freely about problems within the church, problems that often reflect the broader struggles of society" and "comment on the decisions and policies of the highest Church authorities and form its own judgment on these issues, a judgment that may be disputed in the context of democratic dialogue" ('Posle dve godine," 1987, p. 72). The journal's more specific aim however was to "offer its contribution to the objective evaluation of Bishop Nikolaj [Velimirović]'s character" and bring the "harmful campaign [against him] to an end" ("Žurnalistika—ili ????" 1987, p. 73). Its editors were engaged in a battle against the "dark forces of today, who seem to be bothered by [the bishop's] presence among the Serbian people and who are therefore resolute to ostracize him from the consciousness and memory of our contemporaries" (ibid.). The descriptions of the "dark forces" provided in the same editorial resembled something from Bishop Nikolaj's own writing: "mercenaries," "scribblers," "nameless epigones whose pamphlets reek of the wretched stench of Masonic–Vatican–Comintern rot, and whose lies poison the healthy minds of the people" (ibid.).

A considerable proportion of each issue of *Glas Crkve,* which had a circulation of some 10,000 copies, was devoted to the popularization of Velimirović's thought. Extracts from Bishop Nikolaj's writings regularly featured in the journal, accompanied by eulogistic appraisals of his work. One article, for instance, argued that "there are only a few texts written by Nikolaj that are not worthy of a place in any anthology of world literature. In his literary works there are no flaws or weaknesses [...] As a philosopher [Velimirović] is unsurpassed [...] as a poet he was a gift from God [...] as an orator he had no rivals" ("Mnogosvećnjak—Vladika Nikolaj," 1987, pp. 19–21).

By the end of the 1980s, *Glas Crkve* became also a publishing house, the first to publish Velimirović's books in postcommunist Serbia. In 1986 Archimandrite Atanasije Jevtić published, privately, the book *The New Chrysostom* by Artemije Radosavljević, the first affirmative biography of Velimirović (A. Radosavljević, 1986). Around the same time, at the theological faculty in Belgrade, the young scholar Radovan Bigović began his doctoral thesis on Velimirović, under the supervision of Bishop Amfilohije Radović.

In addition to its various publishing activities, the diocese of Šabac and Valjevo organized regular commemorative ceremonies dedicated to Velimirović which were endorsed, attended, and publicized by the likes of Jevtić, Radović, and Radosavljević, as well as by the country's nationalist elite, including writers Vuk Drasković and Danko Popović, poet Matija Bećković, painter Milić Stanković (better known by his artistic name Milić od Mačve), politician Radovan Karadžić, and others. On March 18, 1986, an icon bearing Velimirović's image was added to the altar of a church in Valjevo. A year later, editors of

Glas Crkve, in agreement with the local clergy and some influential Serbian bishops, informally canonized Velimirović and declared him the journal's patron saint (see Chapter 6 for a more detailed account of this event and its significance). Around the same time, 139 priests from the diocese (although *Glas Crkve* reported the number as over two hundred) signed an appeal to the Assembly of Bishops of the Serbian Orthodox Church, calling for an "ecclesiological and historical evaluation of the life and work of Bishop Nikolaj especially in the light of the continuing challenges to his integrity." The appeal, which received a favorable reaction from the Assembly of Bishops, stated that "in the lives of the pious Serbian people and all other Orthodox faithful, God's annunciator from Žiča already occupies the place that he deserves, that of a witness, someone chosen by God, a Teacher and Prophet, Archshepherd and Father of the all God-loving people" ("Priziv za zaštitu ličnosti i dela Vladike Nikolaja Žičkog," 1987, p. 19). The appeal was a reaction to the continued attacks on the bishop, which originate "not just from the Godless ruling ideologues and journalists at their service, but which are sometimes inspired and stirred up from within [the church], by some unshepherdly and unclerical forces and groups, hidden beneath someone else's umbrella, serving someone else's unchristian interests" (ibid).

In the spring of 1989, on the thirty-third anniversary of Velimirović's death, *Glas Crkve* organized a gathering during which a chapel dedicated to Velimirović's memory was formally consecrated by Bishop Danilo of Budim and Archimandrite Atanasije Jevtić. The building of the chapel, financed from private donations, had been commissioned several years earlier by Velimirović's nephew, Bishop Jovan, who died shortly before its completion. The consecration ceremony was followed by a literary evening dedicated to Velimirović, which featured members of the Serbian nationalist elite, such as Vuk Drašković, Milan Komnenić, and Danko Popović, all of whom paid tribute to the great Bishop Nikolaj. The event attracted publicity after the publication of the speech by Vuk Drašković—which was neither more nor less nationalistic or controversial that his other speeches of this era—was formally banned by authorities. In spite of the ban and in the desire to "push the boundaries of democracy in Serbia," *Glas Crkve* published Drašković's speech in a subsequent issue (Drašković, 1989).

The gathering at Lelić in March 1989 is also significant because it was there that the pro-Velimirović Serbian clergy revealed their aspirations to transport Velimirović's remains back to Serbia and lay them to rest in the bishop's native village ("Osvećena kapela Sv. Nikolaja Srpskog," 1989, p. 16). Three months later, at the regular meeting of the Assembly of Bishops of the Serbian Orthodox Church, Bishop of Western Europe Lavrentije (who at this meeting succeeded Velimirović's recently deceased nephew as bishop of Šabac and Valjevo) urged the Assembly to set up a committee which would initiate the return of Velimirović's remains to Serbia. The Assembly assigned the matter of Velimirović's exhumation and transportation to Bishop Lavrentije personally. A year later he reported back to the Assembly, stating that "secular authorities gave a green light" for Velimirović's return, on the condition that the event passed "without larger public ceremonies or mass gatherings of citizens." Bishop Lavrentije proposed that the transportation be placed under the jurisdiction of two Serbian bishops in the United States and the bishop of Žiča, Stefan Boca (cited in Janković, 2003, p. 493). It took over a year for the relevant paperwork to be completed. On April 25, 1991, Velimirović was exhumed and his remains were transported from Libertyville to Chicago, where they were cleaned and placed in a sealed coffin. On May 2, the coffin was boarded onto a regular Yugoslav Airlines evening flight to Belgrade. It arrived in Serbia the next morning. Velimirović's remains were greeted at the airport by Patriarch Pavle and a number of bishops of the Serbian Orthodox Church. Much to the disappointment of the Church leaders, only about five hundred faithful turned up at the airport, most of them from the diocese of Šabac and Valjevo. The remains were taken to the Church of St Sava in Belgrade (located next to the construction site of the much larger Cathedral of St Sava), where they were greeted by several thousand faithful. On Saturday, May 4, a Holy Liturgy in Velimirović's honor was held at the church, followed by a suitable "spiritual academy" devoted to his religious work. On Sunday, May 6, the body was taken to the diocese of Žiča, where Velimirović was bishop during 1919–1920 and 1936–1956. On May 12, the remains were brought to his native village of Lelić. The burial in Lelić was the largest Velimirović-related commemorative ceremony of the period: a mass gathering attended by a crowd of between fifteen and thirty thousand faithful. Representatives of the ruling political establishment, including the Serbian Prime Minister Dragutin Zelenović, Minister of Faiths Dragan Dragojlović, Minister of Culture Radomir Šaranović, and Defence Minister Admiral Miodrag Jokić were present, as were representatives of opposition parties, including two current war crimes indictees, Radovan Karadžić and Vojislav Šešelj. The event in Lelić attracted considerable publicity in the religious press. *Pravoslavlje* devoted a whole issue to the occasion, as did *Glas Crkve*. Both publications filled their pages with detailed reports from the burial, interspersed with extracts from Velimirović's writing and affirmative texts about his life and work. The presence of government representatives also ensured coverage in the mainstream press such as *Politika* and *Politika Ekspres*, as well as on national television. Apart from reporting the event on the daily news bulletin, the Serbian state television broadcasted a special program devoted to Velimirović, in which actor Milan Dimitrijević read extracts from Velimirović's *Prayers by the Lake*, while author Slaven Radosavljević offered a positive evaluation of his philosophical writing.

This marked change in the attitude of the mainstream media and the ruling establishment towards the Church and specifically towards the persona of Nikolaj Velimirović was a by-product of a more general transformation in relations between secular and ecclesiastical authorities in Serbia at the time. Both the arrival of Slobodan Milošević on the political scene and the rise of Serbian nationalism attracted significant support from the Serbian Church. In 1989, Archimandrite Atanasije Jevtić praised Milošević's policy in Kosovo for "looking the Kosovo truth in the eye" and for responding to the "tragedy of the Serbian population in the region" (cited in Tomanić, 2001, p. 20). The editors of *Glas Crkve* similarly recognized the "contribution of the Serbian leadership in the solution of the Serbian question. The new leadership has demonstrated the ability to use the considerable democratic energy and spiritual potential of the Serbian people which once again is thinking with its own head and is deciding its own future" ("Predlog Srpskog crkvenonacionalnog programa," 1989, p. 5). In June 1990, members of the Holy Synod of the Serbian Orthodox Church visited Slobodan Milošević, and after the meeting issued a statement declaring that the encounter symbolized the fact that "at least as far as Serbia is concerned, the difficult and ugly period in the life of the SOC has finally come to an end" (cited in Tomanić, 2001, p. 25). However, the period of cooperation between church and state was relatively short-lived. The Serbian Orthodox Church quickly became disillusioned with Milošević and regarded him as unable to fulfill the promise of a spiritual revival among Serbs (see Radić, 2002b and Tomanić, 2001 for a more detailed examination of church–state relations in Serbia at the time). For this reason, between 1991 and 2000, commemorative events in the diocese of Šabac and Valjevo and other pro-Velimirović activities, such as the fortieth anniversary of Velimirovic's death in 1996 passed relatively unnoticed, although they were not inhibited by secular authorities either.

Apart from the numerous commemorative ceremonies and publishing projects which were awash with favorable interpretations of Velimirović's legacy, memorial activity of his supporters in the late 1980s and the early 1990s included deliberate attempts at suppressing the controversies surrounding his work through censorship. There is evidence that in some editions of Velimirović's writings published in the past two decades, compromising sections, such as the praise of Hitler, or the reference to Serbs as members of the "Aryan race" were furtively omitted by publishers (see Čolović, 2002; Tomanić, 2003). Similarly, the most controversial sermons from *Words to the Serbian People Through the Dungeon Window* do not appear in several editions of the book which are currently on sale in Serbia's bookshops. These examples undoubtedly offer clearest illustration of intentionality and the want on behalf of the memory makers within the Serbian Orthodox Church to regulate the content of collective memory so as to present Nikolaj Velimirović in an unambiguously complimentary way.

Significantly, however, explanations that display an over-reliance on intentionality seldom tell a complete story with regard to transformations in collective memory. The focus on the power and intent of individuals and institutions involved in memory work translates into a rather unflattering picture of modern society. The reliance on the "simplistic, tacit assumption that collective memory work can be reduced to human agency" (Kansteiner, 2002, p. 195) implies that the public readily accepts communication from relevant power-structures—without challenging, doubting, or disputing ideological claims. In other words, such approaches imply that "facts of representation coincide with facts of reception" (ibid.). What we are left with, then, is the image of an unthinking society, one that is easily hoodwinked by propaganda and spin. In contrast, recent poststructuralist theories of culture and communication suggest that people are not passive recipients of ideology, but agents engaged in a "free play of signification," able to create their own readings of dominant ideas, as well as to challenge, dispute, and undermine ruling ideologies (Billig, 1997b; Thompson, 1984). As Iwona Irwin-Zarecka (1994) recognizes, "individuals are perfectly capable of ignoring even the best told stories, of injecting their own, subversive meaning into even the most rhetorically accomplished text" (p. 4). This suggests that the process of social remembering involves a strong argumentative component which was outlined in the introduction. To remember is not just to represent, but also to conduct an implicit argument against competing representations that coexist in the public domain. Thus, when examining why and how, in a specific context, one version of the past is "remembered" and another is "forgotten," it is important not just to explore the machinations of the human and social agency behind it, but also to look at the relevant "textual dynamics": the rhetorical and argumentative skills by means of which "remembering" and "forgetting" are accomplished in practice.

The discursive dynamic of social forgetting: Repression as replacement

As has already been noted, Iwona Irwin-Zarecka (1994) proposes that, in collective memory, aspects of the past are forgotten by not being invoked, spoken about, and remembered in public. They become "repressed" by being ostracized from commemorative ceremonies, museums, and books. Significantly, in narratives of the past, because of their chronological order and organization, it is impossible merely to omit an embarrassing episode or period of history. Silences have to be "dressed up in words" (p. 120). That which is "wilfully forgotten" must be replaced by a suitable substitute: "when we speak of forgetting, we are speaking of displacement (or replacement) of one version of the past by another. To use different imagery, when we set out to listen to historical silences, we are forced to listen to a great deal of noise" (ibid.). In that sense, social forgetting involves the creation of alternative memories, which suppress the material which is to be forgotten by replacing it with more innocuous and harmless content.

More recently, rhetorical psychologist Michael Billig has also argued that the replacement of troubling memories underpins the process of willed forgetting (see Billig, 1997a, 1999a, 1999b). "Repression demands replacement, as a dangerous topic is replaced by another… If one successfully represses an experience the result should not be amnesia—or a gap in the remembered stream of consciousness. A replacement history needs to be found, so one possible memory story is supplanted by another, which suppresses the former" (Billig, 1999a, pp. 168–169). Billig maintains that replacement plays a key role in repression both on individual and collective levels. He suggests that contrary to the assumption of traditional psychology and psychoanalysis, individual repression need not be conceived as some "mysterious inner event" which takes place in the human brain and whose working is observable only indirectly, through psychoanalytic practice. Instead, repression constitutes a discursive and ultimately a social activity. We repress both as individuals and as collectives, by developing, or acquiring through communication, a set of discursive and rhetorical strategies for avoiding having to talk, or think about uncomfortable topics. The skills of repression are essentially the rhetorical skills of effective topic change, through which attention is diverted away from the material that needs to be repressed.

Billig (1999a, 1999b) also argues that one of the key features of repression, as a subtle and "unconscious" form of willful forgetting, is that it occurs outside conscious awareness. This unconscious, or unmindful nature of repression lies in the fact that the skills involved become weaved into the routine of talk and everyday social interaction: "Sets of routines, because of their habitual and unmindful nature, draw attention away from other possible thoughts and thus can maintain [a] sort of social amnesia" (Billig, 1999b, p. 321). One example of the way in which routine facilitates forgetting is through the standardization of specific memories. When standardized memories are constructed, that is, once specific ways of talking about an event become habitual, then what was originally omitted becomes "even more forgotten" (Billig, 1999a, p. 169). Psychological research has demonstrated that the entrenchment of particular memories ensures that alternative stories are less likely to be produced (Roediger et al. 1997; Schacter, 1995). As Billig (1999a) puts it, "a well remembered anecdote functions to obviate the need for further memory work. It offers its own proof that past has been remembered" (p. 169).

This principle functions on the social level, where "cultures and groups celebrate their pasts by creating histories which simultaneously involve remembering and forgetting" (Billig, 1999a, p. 170). Billig quotes Ernest Renan's dictum:

> forgetting [...] is a crucial factor in the creation of a nation. [Forgetting is accomplished] not by general amnesia, but by the formulation of historic myths which only recount a gloriously unshadowed past [...] The more we claim to remember the past—or the more the group claims to know its history—the more that the self-serving account is preserved. The end result is that personal or collective forgetting is accomplished by means of remembering, which becomes solidified into a rehearsed story. (ibid.)

Recent literature on collective memory offers numerous examples of such solidified replacement myths in representations of the national past. Martyrological interpretations of Austria's World War II history, which proliferated in the post-war years, played an important role in repressing the alternative and more uncomfortable versions of the country's Nazi past. Similarly Polish society's resistance to accepting its share of the moral responsibility for the Holocaust was made possible by the presence of the replacement myth that Poland was in fact "a victim of history," specifically of Nazism and communism (Irwin-Zarecka, 1994, p. 120). In France too, the emphasis on the activity of the resistance movement in representations of World War II helped repress the legacy of the Vichy and keep the memory of collaboration away from public consciousness (Rousso, 1991).

The presence of a suitable replacement myth, which facilitates the repression of controversy surrounding his life, was instrumental in the rehabilitation of Nikolaj Velimirović in the late 1980s and early 1990s, and continues to play an important role in the management of his reputation in Serbia today. The myth in question is the portrayal of Velimirović as a "martyr" and a victim of Nazi persecution during the occupation of Serbia between 1941 and 1944.

Velimirović in Dachau: "Martyrdom" as a replacement myth

Throughout the initial stage of Velimirović's rehabilitation—at commemorative ceremonies organized in the diocese of Šabac and Valjevo, in sermons and speeches by religious leaders, intellectuals and men of letters, as well as in articles published in the religious press—words such as "martyrdom" and "suffering" routinely accompanied the evocation of the bishop's name. Velimirović was referred to as "the great Serbian martyr, sufferer, preacher, and cleric" (Zeljajić, 1988, p. 25), "great cleric, sufferer, and martyr for the physical and spiritual salvation of his people" ("Osvećena kapela Sv Nikolaja Srpskog," 1989, p. 16), "the Martyr of Dachau, the Hermit of Ohrid, the Archshepherd of Žiča, the holy Peasant of Lelić" (Jevtić, 1991, p. 29), "Holy Martyr Bishop Nikolaj of Žiča" (Terzić, 1991, p. 52), and "holy Martyr and hero" (Komnenić, 1991, p. 48).

On the occasion of the reburial of Velimirović's remains in his native Lelić in May 1991, the promotional poster displayed in churches across Serbia mentioned nothing about the bishop's life and work other than that he "was arrested by the Gestapo in 1941" and that he was "incarcerated in Ljubostinja Monastery, in Rakovica and Vojlovica, as well as in the camp Dachau, together with Patriarch Gavrilo." In the official sermon at the ceremony, the first thing that Bishop Amfilohije Radović said about Velimirović was that he was an "exile from his country, prisoner in Ljubostinja and Vojlovica, an intern at Dachau" (A. Radović, 1991, p. 39).

Velimirović's alleged martyrdom during World War II was also emphasized in religious art of this period. A fresco in the Church of St Constantine and St Jelena in Voždovac, Belgrade—painted in 1989 by the controversial artist Milić Stanković—portrays Nikolaj Velimirović in the company of two canonized Serbian Martyrs, Archimandrite Pajsije and Deacon Avakum, both of whom were impaled on a stake by the Turkish authorities in the 19th century. The painting shows Velimirović, Pajsije, and Avakum among dozens of emaciated and nameless Serbian victims of Ustasha concentration camps in Croatia (Fig. 13). Another fresco, found in the Serbian Monastery Nova Gračanica near Chicago, Illinois, entitled "The new martyrs of Jasenovac and Glina, and Bishop Nikolaj at Dachau," shows Velimirović as a prisoner at the camp, surrounded by a column of Serbian victims of Ustasha war crimes, represented as peasants with halos above their heads. Also pictured on this fresco are Draža Mihailović leading a column of Chetnik fighters, Patrijarch Gavrilo Dožić, and Bishop of Hvostno Varnava Nastić, who is believed to have been poisoned by Yugoslav secret service in 1964 and who was canonized on that account as a new martyr in 2005 (Fig. 14). In both frescos Velimirović is presented as an inherent part of history of Serbian martyrdom.

Similarly, in the poem "The Return of Bishop Nikolaj," published in 1993, Dušan Vasiljević describes the return of Velimirović's remains to Serbia as follows:

> Archdeacon Stefan
> and Deacon Avakum,
> walked backwards,
> with the serenity of martyrs;
> from the thurible of Saints
> they poured fire
> along every step
> of the Episcope's way'
>
> *(Vasiljević, 1993)*

Again, the choice of Velimirović's helpers in this allegorical poem is not haphazard. "Archdeacon Stefan" is St Steven, disciple of Jesus and the first Christian martyr. By this association with two canonized martyrs, the image of Nikolaj as one of their number is once again signified. Also, in the poem "Cries Against the Bishop" by Komnen Bećirević, published in *Pravoslavlje* in September 1991, Nikolaj is described as "Serbian martyr / outcast and prisoner / righteous man in constant prayer" (Bećirević, 1991).

The portrayals of Velimirović as a victim of Nazism were often accompanied by a photograph from the period of his internment in Ljubostinja, which shows the bishop in the company of a German soldier. In a speech delivered on the occasion of Velimirović's interment in Lelić, the nationalist poet Milan Komnenić was referring to this photo when he exclaimed that "there is a photo from the war days which symbolizes the suffering of Serbian clergy. In that photo there is a broken Nikolaj, incarcerated in Žiča, and beside him a German guard, as menacing as a Teutonic monster" (Komnenić, 1988, p. 32). The photo in question, which is reproduced here (fig. 15) does little to justify such interpretation. The German soldier, compared in the description to a "Teutonic monster" is no taller than Velimirović, who, according to an identity card issued in the United States in 1949, was hundred and seventy centimeters tall. Also there is nothing on the faces of the bishop and the guard to suggest either that Velimirović was "broken" or that the soldier was in any way "menacing." Moreover, one can even discern in Velimirović's posture a significant element of posing for the camera. And yet, Komnenić's interpretation illustrates the way in which Velimirović's supporters, in interpreting the photo, have assimilated the relevant visual material within the available interpretative framework dominated by the theme of suffering. This photo has become an emblem of Velimirović's alleged suffering, a striking image that assists the retention and transmission of memory (Bartlett, 1932; Yates, 1966).

The tendency to represent Velimirović as a victim of Nazi persecution persists to the present day. A recently published book on Nikolaj Velimirović bears the title *The Holy Martyr Bishop Nikolaj of Žiča* (Saramandić, 2004). The petition for Velimirović's canonization submitted to the Assembly of Bishops of the Serbian Orthodox Church by a number of high-ranking Serbian clerics in December 2002 emphasized that Velimirović's cult among the Serbian people had been reinforced by his "suffering for Christ in German prisons and concentration camps" (cited in Jevtić, 2003, p. 306). A similar theme runs through the *kondak,* a short hymn dedicated to Velimirović, which was approved by the Assembly of Bishops on the occasion of his canonization in May 2003:

> On the throne of St Sava in Žiča you held court,
> You enlightened God's people and taught them the gospel;
> You helped them repent and feel the love of Christ;
> For Christ you endured suffering at Dachau,
> For this we celebrate you, Saint Nikolaj, our new Man of God.

In spite of the frequent references to his alleged "martyrdom" at the hands of the Nazis, the status of Nikolaj Velimirović as a "martyr" is highly contestable. Although a comparison of photos of Velimirović taken in 1941 and 1945 reveals significant signs of aging during that period, there is no evidence to suggest that he endured any torture or suffering during the war. The treatment that he received during the internment in the Serbian monasteries of Ljubostinja and Vojlovica, where he spent most of the war, had been reasonably good. Recollections of eyewitnesses suggest that while in Ljubostinja, Nikolaj had considerable freedom of movement and received regular visits from locals. According to one testimony he also frequently distributed sweets and figs to local children, a privilege enjoyed by very few German prisoners during the war (letter from Bosiljka Đuričin, published in *Glas Crkve* in 1987). Also, according to his followers in the Church, during his stay in Ljubostinja, Nikolaj managed to found an orphanage for refugee children in the nearby town of Trstenik (A. Radović, 1987, p. 32) and rescue a Jewish family from capture by the Nazis (see below, Chapter 5). In Vojlovica, although under German guard, Dožić and Velimirović had two rooms each at their disposal. They were allowed to hold religious services at the monastery and had sufficient food provided both by the authorities and by local residents (Borković, 1979, p. 270). In his memoirs Bishop Vasilije Kostić (1907–1978), who was in Vojlovica at the time, recalls that food parcels from other Serbian monasteries were a frequent and welcome occurrence (Kostić, 2003). At the same time, Nikolaj is said to have been frustrated by the restriction of movement and by the lack of communication with his diocese. An SS official, Lieutenant Meier, whose duty was to visit Velimirović and Dožić at the monastery, noted in one of his reports that he often found Velimirović in a state of "mental breakdown and drunkenness" (Radić, 2002a, p. 80).

Also, there is little evidence to suggest that in the two and half months which they spent at Dachau as "honorary prisoners" Velimirović and Patriarch Gavrilo Dožić endured suffering or torture comparable to that to which other, ordinary interns at Dachau were routinely subjected. "Honorary prisoners" at Dachau lived in privileged quarters, the *Ehrenbunker*, and ate the same food as German officers. As was the case with other honorary prisoners, Velimirović's and Dožić's cells were kept unlocked, and they had free and unlimited access to a separate camp courtyard (Berben, 1975; Marcuse, 2001). Also, as men of the cloth, they were allowed to wear their priest's attire and did not have their heads shaved. A testimony by Branko Đorđević, a fellow prisoner at the camp, which was published by the Serbian Orthodox Church in the summer of 1946, states that Velimirović and Dožić did not suffer physical abuse while at the camp (cited in Tomanić, 2001, p. 50; see also P. Ilić, 2006).

Further evidence in support of the claim that Velimirović's life was never in danger during the internment in Germany comes from the fact that Nazi officials took special measures to ensure Velimirović's and Dožić's survival. The two had been taken to Dachau following a medical examination the purpose of which was to ensure that both were fit to travel. Shortly before the deportation, the SS General Heinrich Müller noted that the "death of either of the two clerics during their stay in Germany would have serious and damaging repercussions and that enemy agitation in the Balkans and throughout the world would utilize any apparent murder by the Gestapo for propaganda purposes against the Reich" (cited in Radić 2002a, p. 85; also Ristović, 2000). For this reason, all decisions regarding the treatment of the two prisoners during transportation to Germany had to be approved by the head of the German security services (RSHA) in Berlin, General Ernst Kaltenbrunner.

And yet, favorable interpretations of Velimirović's life repeatedly suggest that at Dachau, Nikolaj and Patriarch Gavrilo "endured all the horrors of this hell on Earth," underwent "enormous suffering and agony" (A. Radosavljević, 1986, p. 18), were "tortured and humiliated" by their captors (Marjanović, 1990a, p. 45) and "went though the hell of the Camp Dachau" (Ranković, 1991, p. 9). Father Žarko Gavrilović writes that at Dachau Velimirović "faced death at every second, either from execution, poisoning, from disease or anything else" (Gavrilović, 1998; p. 10). Bishop Amfilohije Radović went as far as to compare Velimirović's suffering at Dachau to "crucifixion" (A. Radović, 1991, p. 44), while Ranković compared it to Christ's experience at Golgotha (Ranković, 1991, p. 7).

In spite of the emphasis on suffering, details of "torment" and "torture" are conspicuously absent from descriptions of Velimirović's "martyrdom." Although Bishop Artemije Radosavljević (1986) claims that "numerous witnesses" testified to Nikolaj's and Patriarch Gavrilo's "suffering" at Dachau, and that the two clerics themselves recounted their experiences both "in writing and privately," practically the only publicized detail regarding "hardship" at the camp, of which there are multiple versions, refers to an incident when Velimirović allegedly slipped and grazed his knees while carrying a bucket of water (or a latrine, depending on the version) across the camp courtyard (Janković, 2002b, p. 674; Marjanović, 1990a, p. 45; Stanišić, 1977, p. 58; J. Velimirović, 1991, p. 24). Accounts of this event usually include the description of a verbal interchange between Velimirović and a German prison guard, in which the bishop outwits his collocutor (see for instance Ranković, 2003). This episode is depicted on the aforementioned icon "The new martyrs of Jasenovac and Glina, and Bishop Nikolaj at Dachau," where Velimirović is portrayed in communication with a German soldier at the camp. Crucially, none of these accounts of Velimirović's existence at Dachau come anywhere close to describing "suffering" or "martyrdom." Instead, when describing this stage of the bishop's life, most writers resort to systematic vagueness. Radovan Bigović (1998), for instance, mentions in passing that "[Nikolaj and Patriarch Gavrilo] know best what they had to endure [at the camp]" and that Velimirović used to describe Dachau as the place where "the living envied the dead" (p. 43). Similarly, in a speech delivered in 1988, and published posthumously in *Glas Crkve*, Bishop Jovan Velimirović (1991) merely notes that "it is superfluous to speak about the kind of existence that the patriarch and Nikolaj lived in Dachau..." (p. 24). The elusiveness apparent in these accounts is rhetorically significant in that the obvious absence of detail is coated in the impression that the unsaid is so dreadful that it cannot be adequately captured in words. This way, specific information is obscured, without diminishing the overall claim of martyrdom.

On other occasions, allegations of suffering are substantiated with a reference to Velimirović's physical injuries, which came to light after his death in 1956. Bishop Artemije Radosavljević writes that Velimirović "complained of pain in his legs and his back, a direct consequence of the suffering and ordeal which he endured at the camp." Also mentioned are "bruises on [Velimirović's] back," obtained at the hands of the Nazis, which remained visible until his death twelve years later. These injuries were apparently witnessed and revealed by a Russian monk who prepared Velimirović's body for burial (A. Radosavljević, 2003, p. 339; see also Marjanović, 1990a, p. 45). A private letter which the Serbian priest Milivoje Marčić sent to Bishop Lavrentije Trifunović on May 14, 1988, also mentions a testimony by a Russian monk named Vasilije who saw Velimirović's body and described his legs as being "black below the knee." Marčić concludes that "he endured pain and suffering, but did not tell anyone about it" (cited in Janković, 2002a, p. 696). The claim about Velimirović's injuries was reaffirmed recently in December 2004 by the current Bishop of Australia and New Zealand, Irinej Dobrijević, who at the time was consultant to the Holy Synod for International and Inter-Church Affairs. Dobrijević told an audience of university students in Belgrade the following:

> When I started writing my thesis on Bishop Nikolaj, I interviewed a man who prepared his body for burial. This pious Russian told me that one of the main reasons why Nikolaj used a walking stick, why he limped, after leaving Dachau was that he was wounded during his incarceration. It looked, he said, as if [Velimirović's] toes were permanently contorted, as if someone cut his feet with a blade or burned them with hot iron or cigarettes. Bishop Nikolaj never spoke of his bad experience in Dachau [...] there is only one exception where he mentions a conversation with a young German soldier. (Source: author's audio record.)

The discrepancy between these accounts (pain in back and legs, darkened skin below the knee, scars and burn marks), all of which are said to have been derived directly from a first-hand source—the Russian monk who prepared Velimirović's remains for burial—inevitably casts doubt on their credibility. And yet the descriptions are revealing of the way in which the story about the marks on Velimirović's body—attributable most probably to arthritis from which he suffered and which was undoubtedly exacerbated by the unfavorable conditions in which he spent the war years—has been assimilated into the story of the martyrdom and transformed into forensic evidence of torture and suffering which he is said to have endured at Dahau. Moreover, it is the torture which Nikolaj never spoke about. He is therefore presented not only as a martyr, but also as a brave and heroic character who quietly and modestly endured his earthly suffering.

Although most references to Velimirović's martyrdom refer to the plight in captivity, some writers also emphasize the continuation of his suffering after the war. Ljubomir Ranković referred to Velimirović's final years in exile as the "Golgothic path of emigration," arguing even that "he who suffered greatly during his lifetime became an even greater sufferer after his death" when "he, who was prisoner of the most notorious fascist camp, was declared a collaborator" (Ranković, 1991, p. 8). The writer Vuk Drašković expressed a similar opinion during the interview conducted for the purposes of the present study:

> He survived the Golgotha of the concentration camp, and the fact was that in the meantime his country rejected God, became atheist, openly anti-Christian and anti-God, a dictatorship, a country of crime in which he was unable to return. He spent the rest of his life in emigration, in a foreign land, listening to lies about himself, about General Draža Mihailović, about the king, Serbian history, and St Sava, about all that made him a Christian and a Serb. Everything was under attack and rejected, while he followed that misery from abroad, and he probably died in spiritual agony. He *was* a martyr.

Also, some of Velimirović's admirers hold the view that the bishop was murdered by the Yugoslav secret services, which enhances his status as a martyr. Deacon Radoš Mladenović, who runs the Bishop Nikolaj Velimirović Orthodox Spiritual Centre based in the town of Kraljevo mentioned during the interview conducted in the summer of 2003 that Velimirović could not be formally considered a martyr "unless it is true that he was poisoned." Mladenović went on to recount a story—in which he claims to believe—according to which the bishop was poisoned by a young agent of the Yugoslav secret services who infiltrated the seminary in 1956. The young assassin allegedly prepared coffee for Velimirović on the eve of his death, and then disappeared without a trace. This version of Velimirović's death—attributed to a young Russian monk Vladimir Mayevski—resident of the Russian seminary in Pennsylvania in which Velimirović died—was never officially endorsed by the church and is not included in Bishop Nikolaj's official hagiography. Nonetheless, it continues to feature in the public domain. Mayevski's testimony appears as a supplementary text in Bishop Artemije Radosavljević's book *The New Chrysostom*, the most widely publicized and many times reprinted biography of Velimirović, as well as in the edited volume *Holy Bishop Nikolaj of Ohrid and Žiča*, the publication of which accompanied Velimirović's canonization in 2003 (Jevtić, 2003).

The martyrdom myth in context: The narrative of Velimirović's suffering and the rise of Serbian nationalism

The view of Nikolaj Velimirović as a martyr, which is apparent in representations of his life in the late 1980s and the early 1990, was not the invention of the likes of Artemije Radosavljević, Amfilohije Radović, or Ljubomir Ranković. As early as in the 1960s, Velimirović's disciple, the dissident monk Justin Popović hailed his former mentor as a martyr. In a sermon delivered in Lelić in 1966, Popović referred to Nikolaj as the "greatest Serbian martyr after St Sava" and explained the following:

> Why do I say "after St Sava"? The martyr St Sava did not give peace to the enemies of Christ's cross. He gave them no peace until they burned his remains at Vračar in Belgrade. A martyr even after his death, a martyr even today as he watches his Serbian people, and within it thousands of traitors to the testament of St Sava. The Holy Bishop [Velimirović] was a martyr of this world, too. Those who know his intimate life will know that he wept frequently. They know of his weeping in Ljubostinja during the war. The Germans, who were our enemies at the time, well knew what Bishop Nikolaj meant to them. His mouth had to be silenced. You silence that mouth; you have silenced the Serbian stock. He who, while at Ljubostinja, mourned Serbia's miserable fate during the war, mourned the fratricide among Serbian brothers, mourned all the suffering and troubles of the Serbian people, became a prisoner at the monastery Vojlovica and was later taken to Dachau to die for God, for all of us Serbs. Martyr above all martyrs—that is our Bishop Nikolaj. (J. Popović, 1998, p. 11)

Justin Popović's influence among Velimirović's supporters should not be underestimated, and there is little doubt that the interpretation of his mentor's existence as one of martyrdom provided the foundation for the martyrological narrative which resurfaced in the late 1980s. On the other hand there is a further and arguably more important reason why, in spite of the lack of historical or material evidence, the concept of martyrdom acquired such a dominant role in the representations of Velimirović's life. In the late 1980s and early 1990s, at the time when Velimirović's rehabilitation began, the general theme of suffering and victimization dominated Serbian nationalist rhetoric both in political and ecclesiastical discourse (Radić, 2002b; Tomanić, 2001).

In an attempt to whip up nationalist sentiments among Serbs throughout Yugoslavia, the Serbian nationalist elite, including representatives of the Serbian Orthodox Church, regularly emphasized the suffering of Serbs throughout history, especially under the Croatian Ustasha regime during World War II. Church publications in particular drew parallels between Serbian victimhood in the past and the present-day plight of Serbian minorities in Croatia and the province of Kosovo. As early as in 1983, the official voice of the patriarchate of the Serbian Orthodox Church, the newspaper *Pravoslavlje*, published a series of articles entitled "From Kosovo to Jadovno," written by Atanasije Jevtić. The articles which were subsequently published as a book (Jevtić, 1987a), detailed the suffering (instances of rape, murder, assault, etc.) endured by Serbs in Kosovo and drew a parallel between their fate and that of the Serbian population in Croatia under the Ustasha regime between 1941 and 1945. In 1987, the Assembly of Bishops of the Serbian Orthodox Church issued a statement in which the predicament of the Kosovo Serbs was referred to as "genocide" (cited in Radić, 2002b).

Also, as ethnic relations in Croatia and Bosnia began to deteriorate in the early 1990s, the plight of Serbs in these regions was added to that of the Kosovo Serbs. The revival of the memory of the Serbian victims of Ustasha persecution led to the drawing of parallels between the regime of Ante Pavelić and that of the contemporary Croatian leadership. In 1991 *Pravoslavlje* published regular and graphic accounts of instances of present-day Serbian suffering in Croatia. One article by the Bishop of Slavonia Lukijan Pantelić published in March that year referred to contemporary Croatia as the "Ustasha state" (cited in Tomanić, 2001, p. 40).

In June 1990, the Assembly of Bishops of the Serbian Orthodox Church demanded of "secular authorities the exhumation of bodies of World War II [Serbian] victims buried in pits in Bosnia, and their reburial in cemeteries and other appropriate locations"(ibid. p.41). Permission was granted in 1991, after which the Serbian Orthodox

Church, encouraged by Bosnian Serb nationalist elite, embarked on the project of unearthing World War II mass graves of Serbian victims. The project was widely publicized as footage of hundreds of human sculls and piles of bones laid out in large marquees was broadcast daily on Serbian television, accompanied by pathetic speeches by nationalist politicians, academics, and artists. The purpose of the whole enterprise was to graphically illustrate the extent of Serbian suffering under the Ustasha regime and mobilize Bosnian Serbs around the nationalist political program. In 1991, Bishop Atanasije Jevtić explained that the aim was "to bury Serbian victims, who were not just murdered but also disgraced, and in doing so deliver their bodies and their souls from posthumous martyrdom and humiliation. For fifty years, the Serbian people and their Church could hear the innocent blood of Abel screaming from below the earth, but Cain did not hear the voice of the Lord. [...] Episcopes of the Church and the living Church itself were not, and must never be deaf to the cries of Abel" (cited in Tomanić, 2001, p. 41). Jevtić also made Serbian martyrdom the principal theme of the speech delivered on the occasion of his consecration as bishop of Banat, in July 1991:

> Once again the Serbian people find themselves on the cross in Kosovo and Metohija, in Dalmatia, in Krajina, in Slavonia, in Banija, Lika, Kordun, Srem, Bosnia, and Herzegovina. This is a people used to carrying a cross, because carrying a cross has been our destiny. This moment, I pray to God to let us to carry that cross with dignity the way we have carried it until now [...] Every Orthodox Serb has been crucified together with the crucified people from Kosovo to Jadovno especially from Krajina to Borovo. May God turn that crucifixion into resurrection, not only our resurrection, but even of those who in the name of Christ rose against the cross with three fingers. (cited in Tomanić, 2001, p. 56)

In the late 1980s Serbia also witnessed the revival of the Kosovo Myth, which was actively encouraged by the Serbian Orthodox Church (Bieber, 2002; Judah, 2000; Radić, 2002b). In 1988, the holy remains of the Serbian saint and martyr Lazar—the medieval prince who led the Serbs into battle against the invading Ottoman army at Kosovo in 1389—were taken on a widely publicized road trip through Orthodox dioceses in Serbia and Bosnia Herzegovina. Holy Prince Lazar was flagged as the symbol of Serbian martyrdom and the ruler of "Heavenly Serbia," an empire in heaven reserved for righteous Serbs who lived and died for the Cross and their country. Inherent in the theme of "Heavenly Serbia" was of course the notion of collective suffering. In 1988, Bishop Jovan Velimirović, who is credited with reintroducing the term "Heavenly Serbia" into contemporary nationalist rhetoric, wrote that "since Prince Lazar and [the Battle of] Kosovo, the Serbs, above all, have been creating heavenly Serbia, which today must certainly have grown to become the largest state in heaven. If we only think of those innocent victims of the last war, millions and millions of Serbian men, women and children killed or tortured in the most terrible way or thrown into pits by Ustasha criminals, then we can understand that today's Serbian empire is in heaven" (cited in Judah, 2000, p. 47).

Considering the ubiquity of the theme of martyrdom in Serbian nationalist and ecclesiastical discourse in the late 1980s, it is not surprising that accounts of Bishop Nikolaj's life reflected these broader ideological themes and concerns. This is especially so given that that individuals involved in the Church's nationalist project—Jovan Velimirović, Atanasije Jevtić, Amfilohije Radović, Artemije Radosavljević, and others—were also the leading figures in the campaign for Velimirović's rehabilitation. The story of Velimirović's life and the motif of Serbian martyrdom were effectively blended into a single ideological theme. According to the editors of *Glas Crkve*, "it has become impossible to imagine the suffering of the Serbian people and the Serbian church, without reference to the suffering [of St Sava and Nikolaj Velimirović]. In all the suffering of their people, they emerge as the heart of that suffering. They are the symbol of Serbian martyrdom" ("Žurnalistika—ili ????" 1987, p. 73).

Four years later, on the occasion of Velimirović's reburial in Lelić, Bishop Amfilohije Radović drew a parallel between Velimirović's life and Serbia's tragic history in the 20th century: "Bishop Nikolaj is a whole epoch, and we can safely say that everything that has happened to the [Serbian] people since the beginning of the century reflects the path of Bishop Nikolaj's life" (A. Radović, 1991, p. 40). The celebration of Velimirović's life thus became also a commemoration of Serbian suffering in the hands of its neighbors, while at the same time the nation's fascination with collective martyrdom provided an ideological framework within which Velimirović's return into public memory could be instituted.

Remembering in order to forget: The martyrdom myth and repression

The emerging memory of Nikolaj Velimirović as a martyr, which echoed the prevailing mood and nationalist sentiment of the late 1980s, had a very significant implication. It helped to "repress" the controversy surrounding the bishop's political views. Remembering the suffering helped to sideline the contentious elements of the bishop's biography, such as his apparent admiration for Hitler, his anti-Semitism, and the association with Dimitrije Ljotić.

The "repressive" quality of the martyrdom myth can be examined by looking at the way in which each element of the replacement myth contributed to diverting public attention away from the controversy. Just like any tale, the narrative of the bishop's martyrdom, as told by his supporters, has a beginning, a middle, and an end. It starts with accounts of Velimirović's arrest by the Germans in 1941, continues with descriptions of his stay at the camp and ends with the bishop's "release" in 1945.

Accounts of Velimirović's arrest usually contain an element of drama. Authors seldom mention that the Germans arrested Velimirović in July 1941, because of suspected links with the Chetnik insurgents in central Serbia. Instead the bishop is presented as a great, if not the greatest threat to the Third Reich who was arrested in the first days of the occupation. As we have seen in the earlier quotation from the sermon which he delivered in 1966, Justin Popović alleged that from the outset the German occupiers were set on 'silencing' Bishop Nikolaj. Velimirović's nephew, Bishop Jovan, even suggested that the Germans were so threatened by Velimirović's influence that they attempted to assassinate him shortly after his arrest (J. Velimirović, 1991, p. 23). Most frequently however, texts devoted to Velimirović's whereabouts during World War II mention that the order for the arrest came directly from Adolf Hitler. For instance, in 1990, *Ilustrovana Politika* claimed that "Hitler pointed out to General von Loehr that the greatest enemy of Germany was the leadership of the Serbian Orthodox Church, and he singled out Gavrilo Dožić, Metropolitan Zimonjić, and Bishop Nikolaj" (Marjanović, 1990a, p. 46; the same claim is made also in "Hitler je lično izdao naređenje da se likvidira episkop Nikolaj Velimirović," 1987, pp. 35–36; D. Popović, 1989, p. 24; Ranković, 1991, p. 7). In a biography of Velimirović serialized in the Serbian daily *Glas Javnosti* in 2003, Zoran Saramandić writes that "after the attempt on Hitler's life, 126 prisoners out of the 129 held in Bishop Nikolaj's barrack [at Dachau] were shot," thus suggesting (inaccurately) that Velimirović was interned at the camp among, and therefore as one of, Hitler's greatest adversaries (Saramandić, 2003, p. 17).

These dramatic versions of Velimirović's arrest, which are continually reproduced in religious publications, enhances the representation of Velimirović as an enemy of Nazism. In particular, the reference to Hitler's orders not only reinforces the view of Velimirović as a threat to Germany, but gives this overall theme a personal dimension. It sets up Velimirović's subsequent "suffering" almost as Hitler's personal vendetta against him. Such a personalized construction implicitly addresses the accusation of pro-Nazism. By ingraining the contrast between Velimirović and Hitler into the narratives of the bishop's life, the memory of the praise of Hitler in the 1935 sermon is repressed. The more Velimirović is remembered as a thorn in Hitler's side, the easier it becomes to "forget" and sideline the fact that the bishop once expressed admiration for the "current German leader." In fact, Velimirović himself invoked his imprisonment in Dachau when responding to criticism regarding his appraisal of Hitler in 1935. In a letter to the Serbian Bishop Dionisije Milivojević dated February 26, 1946, Velimirović explains that had he really been an admirer of Hitler "why would the Germans keep me under arrest from the first day [of the occupation]—until the last?" (Velimirović, 1983, p. 704).

In representations of Velimirović's whereabouts during the war, the accounts of his internment are hazy. In 1991, in a speech delivered on the occasion of Velimirović's reburial, Bishop Lavrentije intimated that Velimirović spent most of World War II in Dachau when he noted that "afraid of his influence among the Serbian people, and knowing that he does not condone Nazism, the Germans declared him an enemy and incarcerated him in one of the most notorious concentration camps at Dachau" (Trifunović, 1991, p. 3). In some instances, the significance of the internment in monasteries, where Velimirović spent most of the war is undermined. Writing in the journal *Jefimija*,

Predrag Protić (1993) refers to Vojlovica, where Nikolaj spent eighteen months, as a "mere temporary stop on the way to Dachau" (p. 21). On other occasions, monasteries are equated with concentration camps. Although Dachau is the only real "prison" that Velimirović was held at, in favorable accounts we are frequently told, for instance, that "Bishop Nikolaj together with Patriarch Gavrilo spent four years in Fascist concentration camps, including Dachau" (Čakić, 1987 pp. 76–77) or that they spent the war years in "dungeons of Nazism" (Trifunović, 1998, p. 5). Thus, in the context of accounts dominated by the theme of Velimirović's suffering, no distinction is made between Serbian monasteries or the Schliersee resort in Bavaria and Nazi concentration camps.

Velimirović himself was somewhat "economical with the truth" when accounting for his whereabouts during World War II. In a statement to the *New York Times* published on January 17, 1946 Velimirović claimed that he spent "two years" rather than two months in Dachau, and that he was rescued from the camp by "American soldiers" ("Bishop, ex captive of Nazis, is here," cited in Radić, 2002a, p.86, also P. Ilić, 2006, p. 203). Several months later, Velimirović told *Chicago Herald American* that he spent "four years" in Dachau and intimated once again that he had been rescued by allied troops ("Bishop Reveals Persecution of Church under Tito Regime," 1946). Also, following an encounter with Velimirović in November 1945, the Anglican bishop of Chichester, George Bell, noted in his diary that Velimirović spent "four years in a concentration camp, part of that time in Dachau" (Heppell, 2001, p. 106). This inaccuracy is intriguing bearing in mind the level of friendship between Velimirović and Bell and the fact that the reference to "four years" in a camp was added to an aide memoir shortly after the conversation between the two clerics. Also, in 1956 Bell mentioned in a sermon that Velimirović spent fourteen months at Dachau (Heppel, 2001, p. 91). Without dismissing the possibility that both occasions were lapses on Bishop Bell's part, it is also conceivable that Velimirović was, if not dishonest, than at least deliberately vague about his existence under occupation. Other sources in the English language contain similarly misleading information about Velimirović's whereabouts during the war. The recently published *The Blackwell Dictionary of Eastern Christianity* (2001) states that Velimirović spent two years at Dachau. This error is not surprising given that the source for the entry was the book *Serbian Patericon* by Fr. Daniel M Rogich, published in 1994, which states that "in 1941, with the German occupation of Yugoslavia, Bishop Nikolai, together with Patriarch Gabriel Dozhich, was arrested and sentenced to imprisonment in the infamous Dachau Prison Camp in Germany. He spent two years in Dachau, witnessing and suffering some of the cruelest torture of human beings the world has ever known" (Rogich, 1994).

Just like the various claims of torture and the reference to Velimirović as Hitler's nemesis, the misleading information about the length of incarceration at Dachau helps to augment the bishop's image as a victim of Nazism. The inaccurate assertions manage the bishop's moral accountability on the basis of the implicit logic that the length of incarceration is a measure of a person's anti-Nazi credentials. More specifically, the emphasis on victimization helps to repress an embarrassing detail associated with Velimirović's time at the camp, namely the fact that he is said to have written his most virulently antisemitic work, *Words to the Serbian People Through the Dungeon Window*, which was first published posthumously in 1985, while interned at Dachau. Since its publication, this work, which was quoted in Chapter 2, has become the epitome of Nikolaj's prejudice and hatefulness towards Jews and Judaism. Practically every critical article or commentary about Velimirović's antisemitism published in recent years offers quotations from this book, frequently mentioning the fact that Velimirović wrote it in 1944, and therefore at a time when he had to be aware of the real face of Nazism and the true consequences of its ideology (e.g., Byford, 2006; Byford & Billig, 2001; David, 1991; M. Đorđević, 1996; Lebl, 2003).

In an attempt to sideline these criticisms, accounts of Velimirović's life promoted by the Serbian Church seldom mention the bishop's creative endeavors at the camp. When they do, the writing of the book is presented as a subversive activity. Velimirović is said to have written it on "scraps of paper" or even "toilet paper," using abbreviations when referring to Germany, in case the manuscript was discovered by the guards (Trifunović, 1998, p. 7; see also A. Radović, 1991 and J. Velimirović, 1991). Velimirović's most antisemitic and anti-European work is presented as a "moving, apocalyptic account of that era" and essentially an indictment of Nazi Germany, because "Hitler is also Europe" (A. Radović, 1991, p. 43; for more details on the representations of this book among Velimirović's supporters, see Chapters 5 and 6). Such constructions, which are embedded in the overall motif of martyrdom, help obscure and sideline the otherwise indefensible anti-semitic rage articulated in the book.

Finally, descriptions of Velimirović's release also reveal elements of repression. In biographical accounts published in the religious press, there is considerable ambiguity regarding how and when the "martyrdom" in Dachau ended. Upon arrival in the United States in 1946, Velimirović told both the *New York Times* and the *Chicago Herald American* that he was liberated by American troops in May 1945. After noting that Velimirović and Dožić were taken to Dachau in 1944, Artemije Radosavljević's book *The New Chrysostom* claims that "both were finally released only on 8th May 1945, by the 36th American division" (A. Radosavljević, 1986, p. 18). A virtually identical version of events is provided by Ljubomir Ranković who suggests (inaccurately) that "they were the only two Church leaders in Europe who were imprisoned by the Fascists. They went through Dachau and survived the hell of the concentration camp. They were released only on 8th May 1945, by the 36th Allied division" (Ranković, 1991, p. 8). At the ceremony of Velimirović's reburial in Lelić, the then bishop of Žiča, Stefan Boca, declared that Velimirović and Dožić were "taken to Dachau, the place of horrific torment and suffering, where they stayed together until the end of World War II" (Boca, 1991, p. 33). An article published in the journal *Jefimija* in 1993 argues that "Velimirović was taken from Vojlovica to Dachau. At the end of the war he left first for England and then America" (Petrović, 1993, p. 112). In 1996 an edition of Velimirović's collected works published by *Glas Crkve* introduces *Words to the Serbian People Through the Dungeon Window* as having been written in the notorious concentration camp at Dachau between September 15, 1944 and May 8, 1945. A serialized biography of Velimirović published in the Belgrade daily *Glas Javnosti* alleges that "in September 1944 Germans transferred Nikolaj and Patriarch Gavrilo to the Dachau camp, where they remained until they were released by the American troops" (Saramandić, 2003, p. 17). The book *Church and State in Yugoslavia since 1945* by the British historian Stella Alexander also mentions that "in August 1944, shortly before the liberation of Belgrade, [Velimirovic and Dožić] were transported, ill and exhausted, by goods wagon and motor-van to Dachau and then moved from one concentration camp to another until they were set free by the U.S. Army on May 8th, 1945" (Alexander 1979, p. 18).

To the uninitiated reader, this version of events seems to suggest that the two clerics remained in Dachau, or at least in some other concentration camp, until May 1945 and the arrival of the American army. Given that it is well documented that Velimirović and Dožić departed from Dachau in November 1944 (see P. Ilić, 2006 for details), this is an important example of omission. Velimirović did encounter the US troops on May 8, 1945, but not in Dachau, which was liberated by the Allies a week earlier. It was in Kitzbuhel, a small resort town on the Austro-German border. By that time Velimirović was a free man, on his way to Switzerland accompanied by a number of Serbian collaborators and German officials who were fleeing Serbia. In Kitzbuhel Velimirović resided in the company of General Milan Nedić, prime minister in the Serbian quisling government (later extradited to Yugoslavia where he committed suicide in somewhat suspicious circumstances while in police custody) and Hermann Neubacher, Hitler's special envoy to the Balkans and the first Nazi mayor of Vienna (1938–1939), who was subsequently sentenced to twenty years imprisonment by the Yugoslav authorities. Hermann Neubacher and Velimirović maintained cordial relations, and discussed German philosophy while sharing an air raid shelter during the allied bombardment of the border town (cited in Janković, 2002b, p. 645). A testimony quoted in Janković (2002b) alleges that, before they were separated, Neubacher gave Velimirović thirty-five gold coins "just in case" (p. 670; see also Slijepčević, 1991).

The failure to mention Velimirović's release in November 1944 preserves the image of the bishop as the victim of Nazism. Victims of Nazi persecution were seldom freed by their tormentors, especially not, as Velimirović and Dožić had been, as a result of negotiations between the Nazis and collaborators. Moreover, the allegation that Velimirović and Dožić remained in Germany until the end of the war omits from the biographical narrative an important and controversial period of Velimirović's life: the stay in Slovenia, during which he gave his blessing to the collaborationist forces and spoke favorably of Dimitrije Ljotić at his funeral in April 1945.

The inaccuracy surrounding the precise time of Velimirović's and Dožić's release from captivity is particularly interesting in the light of the fact that the same ambiguity appears in representations of Patriarch

Gavrilo Dožić's life, promoted in the late 1940s and 1950s, at the time when the Church endeavored to build the patriotic credentials of its newly returned leader. The issue of the religious journal *Glasnik Srpske Pravoslavne Crkve* published on the occasion of Dožić's return to Serbia in 1946 alleged that "his Holiness Patriarch Gavrilo of the Serbian Orthodox Church was freed on May 8, 1945 by the 36th [Allied] division" ("Povratak Njegove Svetosti Patrijarha Srpskog G. Gavrila u Otadžbinu," 1946, p. 211). Another issue of the same journal published four years later, on the fiftieth anniversary of Dožić's entry into monastic life, spoke of his captivity as "the ascent to Golgotha" where "each new [concentration] camp meant a new hell" and where "patriarch suffered greatly: He was hungry, his clothes were torn [...] he was sick, exhausted, humiliated to the point of martyrdom." In the end, "suffering came to an end. The storm had been weathered. Joy replaced sorrow on May 8, 1945, in Kitzbuhel in Tyrol, where Patriarch Gavrilo, who had been arrested by Hitler's hordes in 1941, was finally released" ("Pedesetogošnji jubilej njegove Svetosti Patrijarha Srpskog Gospodina Gavrila," 1950, p. 23; see also Durković-Jakšić, 1980, p. 25). The striking similarity between these accounts and more recent narratives of Velimirović's existence during the war strongly suggests that the latter were informed by the former. What is more just, like in the case of the narratives of Velimirović's life promoted thirty years later, the emphasis on "May 8, 1945" as the release date, and the insistence that Dožić had been dragged from one "concentration camp" to another until his "martyrdom" finally came to an end, both performed the repressive function: they obscured the patriarch's journey to Slovenia and the politics behind his release from Dachau. It also helped to symbolically separate Gavrilo Dožić from Nikolaj Velimirović, who was conveniently omitted from the tales of the patriarch's "suffering," and who at the time was being dismissed as "the lackey of the Germans." Thus, the same replacement myth which in the late 1940s and 1950s sought to promote Patriarch Gavrilo Dožić as a patriot and a victim of Nazi persecution and in doing so reinforce the distinction between him and the 'traitor' and 'collaborator' Nikolaj Velimirović resurfaced thirty years later and became the principal tool for the management of Velimirović's own moral accountability.

Bearing in mind the extent of concealment, forgetting, and replacement in the narratives of Velimirović's life in the late 1980s and early 1990s, it might be tempting to suggest that the martyrdom myth is merely the product of an intentional and well-calculated campaign of propaganda and deception by those who wanted to transform Velimirović's public image. In the book *The Serbian Church During the War and the Wars Within it*, Milorad Tomanić (2001) makes such a point when he refers to the narrative of martyrdom as a collection of "cover-ups, lies, and half-truths" forced upon the Serbian public by those who subsequently brought Serbia to the "edge of destruction" (p.50). On the other hand, it might be argued that a subtler and more complex process is involved. Before the mid-1980s, Velimirović was marginalized by state authorities, and even within the Serbian Orthodox Church. As a result, detailed historical records relating to his life and work were scarce. What was known about Velimirović was largely based on hearsay, anecdotal evidence, and an oral culture transmitted among his limited fan base. These accounts were subject to distortion through repetition, which is why today we often have different accounts of the same anecdotes from Velimirović's life (such as those pertaining to his wounds, or his exact whereabouts and activities during the war). Therefore, rather than being reducible to individual motivations and machinations by specific memory makers, the selective nature of remembering apparent in the prevailing narratives of Velimirović's personal history should be seen as the outcome of a subtle dynamic of "social repression" and moral accountability management which take place at the level of discourse, communication, and the shared practice of remembering and forgetting, and which are firmly embedded in the broader social, cultural, and political contexts.

The dynamic of everyday forgetting: Continuity and the "routinization" of repression

In writing about the rhetorical aspects of repression, Michael Billig argues that the practice of remembering is always situated within a specific argumentative context. Those who are doing the remembering must always position themselves in relation to alternative viewpoints and memories. As Billig (1999a) puts it, "memory work is rarely neutral, as if speakers are recalling the past for its own sake. Instead, speakers, in talking about the past, are often conducting the business of the present. Memory talk contains what some discursive psychologists have called 'rhetorical stake.' Points are being made, arguments conducted, as the past is invoked" (p. 159). The present chapter has examined the way in which the argumentative nature of remembering manifests itself in the affirmative representations of Velimirović's life. It suggested that the enforcement of the martyrdom myth in biographical narratives has helped to repress and keep away from conscious awareness the contentious aspects of the bishop's work. Importantly however, the practice of willful forgetting is more than simply concealment through replacement. This is because the alternative, critical interpretations, the "countermemories," can never be fully replaced. Instead they continue to feature in the public domain, even if only on the margins, manifested as challenges to Velimirović's credibility from the independent media, liberal intellectuals, and civil rights organizations, or as remnants of the older communist critiques. Therefore, repression of critical versions of Velimirović's life, through the enforcement of the replacement myth, is a practice that needs to be undertaken continuously. The practice of remembering, of invoking the past, has to be organized in a way that provides the rhetorical resources by which thinking or talking about controversial matters can be actively avoided and routinely kept away from conscious awareness.

One way in which this is done is through the inhibition of memory work. Billig (1999a) argues that "if we humans possess the rhetorical skills to open up matters for discussion, then so we are equipped with the abilities to close down matters discursively. For every rhetorical gambit to push the debate forward, so there must be analogous rhetorical devices which permit the discursive exploration to be curtailed. Routinely, we are able to change the subject, pushing conversations away from embarrassing or troubling topics" (p. 51). Thus, an important aspect of repression, as a continuous practice, is the "active avoidance" of memory work, which threatens to "disturb the sovereignty of the accepted account of the past" (Billig, 1999a, p. 171). This is accomplished primarily by diverting attention away from the potentially embarrassing or damaging topics, in the direction of the preferred themes, that is, the replacement myth.

The way in which such "active avoidance" is accomplished can be illustrated using a number of examples from the discourse of Velimirović's remembrance. The following extract is from a speech delivered by the writer Danko Popović in 1989, at Velimirović's grave in Libertyville. The speaker remembers Velimirović's suffering, especially that which occurred in Dachau:

> The bishop, beside whose grave we stand, was held prisoner by the Germans during the occupation of Serbia, and was taken to the notorious concentration camp at Dachau. After the war, the prisoner of Hitler's concentration camp was declared an enemy of the people. Not their enemy, the enemy of communism, which he naturally was, but an enemy of the people. There, a prisoner from Dachau—yet an enemy of the people? [...] how is it possible—Hitler, the greatest enemy of the Serbian people, declares the bishop to be his greatest enemy, the same bishop who spends the whole duration of the war as a prisoner at Dachau, in the end is declared a public enemy? (D. Popović, 1989, p. 24)

Unsurprisingly, the paragraph constructs the image of Velimirović as a victim of Nazi persecution, and the enemy of Nazism. In that sense it outlines all the basic features of the familiar martyrdom myth. On this occasion however, the author hints at the existence of an alternative interpretation of Velimirović's life, one that has been used to portray him as an "enemy of the people." Yet the counterarguments, which are alluded to, are never articulated. We are not told why Velimirović was branded a traitor. Instead, each time the invitation for further memory work is made ("how is it possible?" and "a prisoner from Dachau—yet an enemy of the people?"), the answer is simply to repeat the principal claims of the replacement myth. The very existence of the myth "obviates the need for further memory work."

Similarly, on other occasions when the reference to Velimirović's status during the communist years is hinted at, this is done in the context of the safe and comforting narrative of his suffering. Deacon Ljubomir Ranković suggests that "Velimirović was declared a traitor and an enemy of his people. He who survived all the horrors of war, who was the prisoner of the most notorious Fascist concentration camp, was declared a collaborator" (Ranković, 1991, p. 9). Serbian philosopher and literary critic Nikola Milošević also noted that "he who spent time in the notorious camp at Dachau, was declared nothing less than a war criminal!" (N. Milošević, 1991, p. 47). In June 1987, in response to the petition from the diocese of Šabac and Valjevo which called for the "ecclesiological and historical evaluation of the life and work of Bishop Nikolaj," the Assembly of Bishops of the Serbian Orthodox Church issued a statement in which it "concludes with resentment that attacks on the late Bishop Nikolaj (Velimirović) of Žiča have been going on for years. Nikolaj was Hitler's prisoner and martyr of Dachau, yet they call him a criminal and a traitor, even though the whole of the cultured world knows that he was a prisoner for the duration of World War II and that he was at Dachau at the end of the war" (cited in Janković 2003, p. 436). In neither of these cases are arguments against Velimirović laid out in full or addressed. Instead, criticisms are merely cast aside and the claim about martyrdom is offered in their place.

Even on occasions when the nature of the controversy is revealed, the alleged martyrdom is used to undermine it. In 1990, the magazine *Ilustrovana Politika* published a two-part article on Velimirović, which contained a favorable interpretation of his life. The article aimed to answer the following question: "Why was Bishop Nikolaj, who was declared by the Germans to be their worst enemy and was kept locked away in the worst prisons including the camp at Dachau, declared after the war to be an enemy of the people?" (Marjanović, 1990b, p. 45). In providing the answer, the article reflected on just two aspects of the controversy regarding Velimirovic's life: the medal from Hitler and the eulogistic speech that he delivered at Ljotić's funeral in April 1945. And yet, both were dismissed as unwarranted by being substituted with the narrative of suffering under the Nazis. In response to the controversy, Archimandrite Atanasije Jevtić is quoted as stating simply that "the bishop was an antifascist [...] that is why he suffered so much" (Marjanović, 1990a, p. 46). The topic of discussion was therefore shifted onto the suffering in the camp as the remembrance of the specific details associated with the controversy is subtly resisted. The title of the second article in the series echoes this strategy: "A traitor—yet in Dachau!"

The avoidance inherent in the martyrdom myth is evident also in the context of spoken dialogue. In May 2003, shortly after Velimirović's canonization, Deacon Ljubomir Ranković took part in *Radio Free Europe*'s regular show, "Radio Bridge." When the show's host Omer Karabeg asked Ranković about the controversies surrounding Bishop Nikolaj's work, including his antisemitic writing at Dachau, the latter replied:

> The life of every saint should be the subject of dialog and debate, and it can be examined from different aspects. With regard to the Holy Bishop Nikolaj, he and his work should also be put to the judgment of the public. But, the examination of his life must be devoid of all prejudice and bias, of emotion and superficiality. It must be an objective judgment, which any serious critique demands. Of course, Words to the Serbian People is somehow the most controversial work by the Holy Bishop Nikolaj. However, one should bear in mind that this work came about in the greatest hell in history known to man, in the concentration camp at Dachau. Bishop Nikolaj was taken to that camp after three years under German guard. There are many written testimonies. I was lucky enough to be secretary and Deacon to Bishop Jovan Velimirović, who accompanied Bishop Nikolaj during the imprisonment in Žiča, Ljubostinja, and Vojlovica. From his story I know of their suffering, and that when they arrived at Dachau, hell began, in the true sense of the word. ("Radio Most," *RFE/RL*, June 2, 2003)

Ranković's answer to the question about Velimirović's antisemitism starts with the reiteration of the martyrdom myth which switches the topic onto the positives from Velimirović's life. The frequency with which this rhetorical move occurs both in written text and in public discussions (see for instance the quote at the start of the chapter) reveals how the perpetuation of the martyrdom myth supplies the armory with which the remembering of the controversy can be resisted. The myth does not just tell a story but also equips the public with the necessary skills of repression. The routinized narrative of the bishop's suffering provides argumentative resources required for casting aside the embarrassing questions, to be used should anyone ever shed doubt on Velimirović's integrity and dare to remember his antisemitism or the links with Nazi collaborators. The rejoinder "but he was in Dachau!"—which has become an almost automatic, routine response to any challenge to the respectability of Velimirović's writing—constitutes an expedient means of shifting the conversation away from the compromising biographical details. It ensures that the issue of antisemitism does not have to be tackled in a more meaningful way that might be damaging to the ongoing adulation of the controversial bishop as the "Greatest Serb since St Sava."

In his discursive reformulation of Freudian repression, Michael Billig argues that "wilful forgetting" is not necessarily a bad thing. He suggests that "the topic of racism illustrates why repression is not necessarily something to be mocked [...] It is possible to argue that on an ideological level, psychological repression can be justified and progressive, moral and socially beneficial. It can be a means of replacing ways of talking that belong to discriminatory times" (Billig, 1999a, pp. 259–260). And yet, in the case of Velimirović's remembrance, it is hard to find evidence of repression's "progressive" potential. The suppression of controversy surrounding the life and work of Bishop Nikolaj Velimirović, which has been shown to play a crucial role in his remembrance in the late 1980s and early 1990s, did not contribute to the suppression of antisemitism. Quite the opposite. The routine forgetting of Velimirović's controversial views has created a curious discrepancy between, on the one hand, representations of his life in mainstream Orthodox Christian culture—which "forgets" and seeks to downplay his offensive political views—and on the other, the bishop's literary output, available in practically every bookshop in Serbia, where objectionable viewpoints are openly propagated. The promotion of the martyrdom myth thus created a situation where readers would approach Velimirović's work as that of a respectable theologian, whose political and moral integrity is above suspicion most of all because of his much-publicized reputation as a victim of Nazi persecution. Favorable biographical accounts, cleansed of the controversy, invite uncritical interpretation of Velimirović's ideas, and give his contentious writings and especially *Words to the Serbian People Through the Dungeon Window* an importance and credibility they do not warrant. As we are about to discover, this harmful outcome of social repression is further exacerbated by the coexistence, in memorial discourse, of the complementary process of *denial.*

CHAPTER FOUR

From Repression to Denial

Responses of the Serbian Orthodox Church to Accusations of Antisemitism

The discussion of the role of repression in Velimirović's rehabilitation focused primarily on material which dates back to the late 1980s and the early 1990s, and therefore to the early stages of the bishop's return to the mainstream. At the same time, more recent examples have shown that the image of Velimirović's supposed affliction during the Nazi occupation remains embedded in the overall discourse of remembrance. The inclusion of the theme of suffering in the short prayer (*kondak*) dedicated to Velimirović—which was formally endorsed by the Church on the occasion of his canonization—as well the reference to it by a protagonist of the documentary "Why People Whisper in Church" or by Deacon Ljubomir Ranković on *Radio Free Europe* confirmed the fact that martyrological interpretations have become an indispensable aspect of the routine of Velimirović's celebration.

Although the martyrdom myth was shown to provide the rhetorical means for fighting off actual or anticipated challenges to the bishop's integrity, in the early stages of the rehabilitation, "wilful forgetting" owed much of its success to the relative absence, in public discourse, of alternative, critical interpretations of Velimirović's personal life. In the late 1980s, state-controlled media were silently complicit in the overall nationalist project and the efforts to bring Nikolaj Velimirović back into the mainstream. Old communist critique of the bishop's life gradually began to wane, giving the sympathetic appraisals relatively free reign. Even after the relations between the Serbian government and the Church deteriorated in the second half of 1991 (see R. Radić, 2002b; Tomanić, 2001), the efforts of Velimirović's supporters were never officially challenged or undermined by the authorities. Only a few individuals, belonging to the country's liberal intelligentsia, made occasional attempts to "remind" the public of the contention surrounding Velimirović's life. In 1991, at the time of the hype surrounding Velimirović's "return" to Serbia, Serbian Jewish author Filip David wrote an article for the independent magazine *Vreme* in which he condemned the bishop's antisemitism and warned against his uncritical rehabilitation (David, 1991). The essay on Serbian populism by sociologist Nebojša Popov published in the same magazine in 1993 examined the ideology of Nikolaj Velimirović in the context of 1930s populist culture (Popov, 1993). In 1996, the magazine *Republika* published a lengthy and unsympathetic account of Velimirović's religious philosophy (M. Đorđević, 1996). In the same year, the monthly bulletin published by the Union of Jewish Communities of Serbia featured an article "'Saint' against the Jews," which criticized Velimirović's antisemitism, while in the contribution to the edited volume *Serbia's Road to War*, historian Radmila Radić reflected on the way in which the popularization of Nikolaj Velimirović in the late 1980s and early 1990s accompanied the rise of nationalism within the Serbian Church ("'Svetac' protiv Jevreja," 1996; R. Radić, 2002b). Apart from these occasional unfavorable evaluations, critical discourse surrounding Bishop Nikolaj's life and work was undeveloped and remained confined to liberal elite circles and publications that wielded comparatively little influence in Serbian society. It failed to threaten, in any significant way, the far more organized and widespread propagation and reinforcement of the sanitized version of Velimirović's life.

In the aftermath of the fall of Slobodan Milošević in October 2000, the widespread adulation of Nikolaj Velimirović became the subject of more regular criticism from Serbia's liberal intellectuals, independent media, and civil rights organizations. This is primarily because Velimirović's rising popularity in Serbia was linked to the increase in the public presence and political influence of nationalist elements within the Serbian Church. The emerging "new" or "post-Milošević" Serbian nationalism had a notable religious component, offering a new value system based on Orthodox religious dogma. A report published in 2003 by the Serbian office of the Helsinki Committee for Human Rights concluded the following:

> The downfall of Milošević marked the end of the Communist ideology. The ensuing political vacuum was filled with anti-Communism, monarchism and Orthodox religion. The Serbian Orthodox Church

> gained a prominent role on the political scene, and that development was wholeheartedly backed by [Vojislav Koštunica]. The Church gained a dominant position in society, which enabled it to launch a campaign for the re-traditionalisation of both spiritual and public life. The Church managed to have religion re-introduced in schools and other institutions, and it is likely to have its property reinstated and see the Theological Faculty return to the fold of Belgrade University. (Helsinki Committee for Human Rights in Serbia, 2003a, p. 142)

Another report by the Helsinki Committee claimed that in post-Milošević's Serbia, the Church "imposed itself as the supreme moral and ideological arbiter in matters raging from the education of children to the overall cultural and civilisational values of Serbian society" (HCHRS, 2003b, p. 7). In this new role, the church was said to be promoting "almost without exception, archaic values of extreme collectivism, anti-westernism and xenophobia" in a manner "marked by a high degree of intolerance, even aggressiveness" (p. 21). These and similar evaluations of the "new Serbian nationalism" unequivocally link the "clericalisation" and "re-traditionalisation" of Serbian society to the widespread influence and popularity of Nikolaj Velimirović among the ecclesiastical and political elites (see for instance M. Đorđević, 2002). In an open letter to the public issued in October 2002, a group of Serbian intellectuals warned that the continuing promotion of Orthodoxy, nationalism, monarchism, and anti-communism as principal social values was pushing Serbia towards the "totalitarian and undemocratic" ideology of pre-World War II Serbian fascism. The signatories concluded that post-Milošević Serbian nationalism, advanced with the blessing of the Serbian Church, signified the "triumph of the provincial philosophy of Nikolaj Velimirović."

Velimirović's popularity has also been linked to the resurfacing of antisemitism in Serbian public discourse. Since 2000, Serbia has witnessed the emergence of a number of extremist Christian right-wing political organizations, which propagate a mixture of political conservatism, clerical nationalism, and to varying degrees—antisemitism (see Byford, 2002, 2003). The appearance on the political horizon of the likes of Otačastveni Pokret Obraz (Patriotic Movement Dignity), Udruženje Studenata "Sveti Justin Filozof" (St. Justin the Philosopher Association of Students), and Srpski Sabor Dveri (Dveri Serbian Assembly) coincided with a noticeable increase in antisemitic incidents. In February 2001, antisemitic graffiti and stickers bearing Nazi symbols appeared on the walls of a synagogue in Belgrade. A month later, vandals desecrated the monument erected in the town of Zrenjanin in honor of Jewish victims of the Holocaust. Jewish cemeteries and municipality buildings in a number of provincial towns and cities suffered similar defilement, while graffiti displaying messages such as "Death to Jews," "Jews out," etc. became increasingly common throughout Serbia. Personal threats to members of the country's Jewish community also became more frequent. According to civil rights groups and other NGOs which monitor instances of ethnic hatred in Serbia, the number of threatening letters to Jewish households, attacks on Jewish-owned property, as well as physical assaults on members of the Jewish community, all increased in the Spring of 2001 (Belgrade Centre for Human Rights, 2002; Helsinki Committee for Human Rights in Serbia, 2001). Although the culpability of the Christian Right in these incidents remains unproven, the representatives of Jewish communal bodies in Serbia did not see the emergence of Christian right-wing groups and the rise in antisemitism as coincidental: they cited the former—and especially the most aggressive of the new organizations, Obraz—as a notable threat to the peaceful existence of Serbia's Jews (President of the Union of Jewish Communities of Serbia, Aca Singer, in Bjelajac, 2001). Importantly for the present discussion, the Christian Right builds its legitimacy on the back of Velimirović's popularity. The publicity material of the aforementioned organizations is inundated with quotations from the bishop's writings, and Velimirović is repeatedly cited as the main political and spiritual authority. Moreover, the antisemitism of which these organizations have been accused by and large takes the form of the regurgitation of Velimirović's own lamentable views.

The public profile of the Christian Right in Serbia is further sustained through close organizational and ideological links with the Serbian Orthodox Church. Each of the aforementioned Christian right-wing organizations operates with the blessing of at least one Orthodox bishop. Their public activities are routinely attended and endorsed by senior clergy, and in return representatives of the Right are invited to events organized by the church. This connection between the mainstream and the extreme, which is dealt with in more detail elsewhere (Byford, 2002, 2006) has contributed to the assessment that "although it declaratively opposes any extremism, the Serbian Orthodox Church glosses over the activities of its officials who generate hatred, antisemitism, and hate speech and who negatively affect the status of religious and ethnic communities [in Serbia]" (Helsinki Committee for Human Rights in Serbia, 2002, p. 142).

The mounting concerns about the impact that the uncritical hero-worship of Nikolaj Velimirović has on Serbian political culture jeopardized the effectiveness of repression as the main defense mechanism for protecting the bishop's integrity and influence. Since the year 2000, the increasingly vocal critics of Bishop Velimirović have been "reminding" the public of his controversial stance towards Jews, of his association with Dimitrije Ljotić, and the positive evaluation of Hitler which appears in his writing. What is more, dissenting voices—which now have much greater access to the media compared to the Milošević years—habitually illustrate their criticisms with direct quotes from Velimirović's compromising writings, most frequently from *Words to the Serbian People Through the Dungeon Window* and the speech "Nationalism of St Sava." As a result, in the past seven years, and especially around the time of Velimirović's canonization—when challenges to his credibility reached their peak—damaging aspects of the bishop's life and his literary endeavor have been rescued from oblivion and have become regular currency in discussions and debates about his reputation.

In the new context, and in the face of the increasingly perceptible "counter-memories," allegations and indictments against Velimirović's credibility had to be tackled by his supporters head-on, and openly refuted, negated, and dismissed. The dynamic of repression was therefore supplemented with a complementary strategy, that of denial. The rhetoric of denial is the principal topic of this chapter and Chapter 5.

Discourse, moral accountability, and the denial of prejudice

Discursive reformulation of repression outlined in the previous chapter emphasized that social remembering and forgetting are not impartial and disinterested activities, but performances through which particular claims are made about the nature of the past. Following Billig (1999a), it was argued that by remembering some aspects of the past and repressing others, speakers were "conducting the business of the present," positioning themselves within a particular argumentative context. In the case of the memory of Nikolaj Velimirović, the remembrance through the martyrdom myth was said to be motivated—even if only implicitly—by the desire to vindicate the bishop amid the controversy surrounding his alleged antisemitism and pro-fascism.

In considering the discursive aspects of repression, Billig (1999a) writes that that which is to be repressed is determined by historical and ideological conditions: "there is no guarantee that what is repressed in one historical epoch will be repressed in another... Each moment in history will produce its own restrictions" (p. 254). Thus, restrictions which Victorian morality placed on discussions concerning sexuality—and which were at the heart of so many of Freud's patients' troubles—have all but disappeared from our sexually liberated society. Sexual emancipation lifted the former restrictions on what can and cannot be openly discussed. At the same time, contemporary morality has imposed its own limitations. The openness with which Victorian Europeans expressed racial intolerance has been confined, if not to history, than at least to the margins of politics. Blatant racism and antisemitism have become objects of shame and criticism, banished from mainstream discourse and courteous conversation. The post-World War II political morality demands that expressions of intolerance be repressed. As Billig notes, "one might say that the topic of race today has slid into the seat vacated by sexuality. There are taboos, which restrict what can be uttered. Overt uninhibited antisemitism and racism are not to be spoken in polite company. Those who wish to criticise non-whites or Jews from the outside, must find complex, indirect and apologetic ways of doing so" (p. 259).

Research on the language of racism conducted since the 1980s has demonstrated the existence of this powerful social norm against public display of prejudice (Augoustinos et al. 2002; Billig, 1990; van Dijk, 1984, 1987, 1992, 1993; Wodak, 1991; etc.). Van Dijk writes the following:

> Negative talk about minority groups or immigrants may be heard as biased, prejudiced or racist, and as inconsistent with the general values of tolerance. This means that such discourse needs to be hedged, mitigated, excused, explained and otherwise managed in such a way that it will not "count" against the speaker or writer. Face-keeping,

> positive self-presentation and impression management are the usual strategies that language users have recourse to in such a situation of possible 'loss of face': they have to make sure that they are not misunderstood and that no unwanted inferences are made from what they say. (van Dijk, 1992, p. 115)

In fact, so pervasive is the norm against bigotry that "the value of not being prejudiced is even shared by the Fascist writer who is at pains to deny his own prejudice but to pin the label upon liberal opponents" (Billig, 1990, p. 125).

In his work on the rhetoric of denial of prejudice, van Dijk (1992) noted that in the context of denial, it is not just individuals whose egalitarian self-image is attended to in talk. Often the credibility of the collective—a nation, a political movement, a community, or a religion is also negotiated through discourse. This social dimension of denial, which takes the form of statements such as "we are not a racist society" or "we are not a racist nation" is particularly apparent in the discourse of elite institutions: in the media, in political discourse, and in the language of religious institutions. The rhetoric of positive national or confessional self-presentation not only enhances the positive collective self-image of a particular social group, but also facilitates individual denial through the argument that a person is not intolerant because of their membership of the non-prejudiced collective.

In this chapter we will examine the rhetoric of social denial in the context of Serbian Orthodox culture. In responding to criticism directed at the influence of Nikolaj Velimirović in Serbian society and the allegation that his uncritical adulation has contributed to a rise in antisemitism, representatives of the Serbian Orthodox Church and the Christian Right in Serbia often invoke the self-glorifying argument that there is, and never has been, any antisemitism in Serbia, and what is more that Orthodox Christianity has always been the dominant force behind the Serbian benevolence towards Jews. As will become apparent, such generalized statements about Serbian and Orthodox tolerance help to play down the controversy surrounding the reputation of Nikolaj Velimirović and confine the problem of antisemitism in Serbia to a small number of individual extremists on the far right. Furthermore, it will be shown that by helping to generate a consensus about Serbian tolerance, social denial implicitly perpetuates the very same xenophobic and antisemitic elements of Serbian nationalist discourse that it is meant to refute. This discussion will set the scene for Chapter 5, which explores in more detail the ways in which accusations of antisemitism directed at Velimirović personally are dealt with.

In the forthcoming sections the discussion will focus primarily on two texts. The first is the public statement issued by the synod of the Serbian Orthodox Church on February 5, 2002. The release of this page-long document was triggered by the television appearance of Father Žarko Gavrilović, the maverick right-wing Serbian priest with a history of antisemitic outbursts (see Sekelj, 1997). In a program devoted to the issue of child sexual abuse, Gavrilović alleged that incest is endemic in Jewish culture, and that "it is a well-known fact that they [Jews] marry their sisters" (full transcript of Gavrilović's claims can be found in Đurđević, 2003, pp. 231–234). This assertion provoked a strong reaction from Jewish communal bodies and Serbia's liberal media, all of whom called on the Serbian Orthodox Church to distance itself not just from Žarko Gavrilović and his specific claims, but also from the increasing public profile of the Christian Right. The second text is the article "Serbs and Jews," published in the summer of 2001 in the magazine *Dveri Srpske*, the official organ of the Christian right-wing organization of the same name, which subsequently posted the text on its website (Dimitrijević, 2001). This lengthy piece (over 4000 words) constitutes thus far the most elaborate attempt by the organized Christian Right in Serbia to address accusations of antisemitism. It was subsequently published in the right-wing magazine *Pogledi* in January 2002, as well as in another "special issue" of *Dveri Srpske* in December 2004 (Dimitrijević, 2004). The author of this article, Vladimir Dimitrijević, is a right-wing journalist, commentator, and a regular contributor to magazines such as *Dveri Srpske* and *Pogledi*. He is also the editor of several books on the threat to Serbian Orthodoxy posed by religious sects and cults, which are inundated with allusions to an anti-Serbian and anti-Orthodox conspiracy, a ubiquitous topic in the discourse of the Serbian Christian Right (e.g., Dimitrijević, 1997, 2005, 2007).

The detailed examination of these two texts follows the principle that the study of ideology can benefit greatly from the scrutiny of a small number of significant texts, even from a single case study. Although such analysis is often limited with regard to the generalizability of the findings, it can nonetheless help to identify aspects of ideological discourse that might have wider significance (Billig, 1990). In this instance, the issues of how representative a text is and how generalizable the findings are have been addressed by selecting two ideologically important texts that have acquired a special status in the debate about the persistence of antisemitism in Serbian Orthodox culture. Since their publication, both texts have been referred to, within the Serbian Orthodox Church and the Christian Right, as authoritative pieces that have definitively addressed the question of antisemitism. As we have seen, Dimitrijević's text has been published three times in right-wing publications. In a contribution to the letters page of the mainstream liberal weekly magazine *Vreme* in 2004, one of the leaders of Dveri, Boško Obradović, responded to the "vicious libels" about the organization's antisemitism simply by directing the readers to the article in *Dveri Srpske*, which he depicted as an "analytical text by the writer Vladimir Dimitrijević on the exemplary relations between Serbs and Jews throughout history" (Obradović, 2004). The Synod's 2002 press release has also been cited as evidence that the Serbian Church has tackled the contentious issue of antisemitism. The book *Bishop Nikolaj and the New Testament on the Jews* by the US-based Serbian theologian Predrag Samardžić—published with the formal blessing of the Holy Synod of the Serbian Orthodox Church in 2004—dismisses the criticism of the Serbian Church by alluding to the synod's press release. Samardžić writes:

> Take the view of [Aleksandar Lebl, president of the Commission for the Monitoring of Antisemitic Incidents Affiliated to the Union of Jewish Communities of Serbia]... He writes that the book *Words to the Serbian People* by Nikolaj [Velimirović] is antisemitic, but that the Serbian Church is not inclined towards antisemitism. On the contrary, Mr. Lebl concludes that the Serbian patriarch and the Holy Synod have always condemned hooligan incidents with antisemitic undertones. (Samardžić, 2004, p. 128)

The way in which Samardžić brings the press release into play is noteworthy. It is invoked as evidence of the Church's tough stance on antisemitism, but in a way that also suggests that it has been recognized as such by the leadership of Serbia's Jews. Although rhetorically effective, this instance of "footing" (Goffman, 1979) is profoundly misleading. While welcoming the Church's move, most reactions from the Jewish community judged the statement to be inadequate in combating rising antisemitism. In an article published in the daily *Danas* in July 2002 (to which Samardžić is most probably referring in the above quote), Aleksandar Lebl acknowledged the "clear and principled stance" against antisemitism in the synod's press release, before lamenting the fact that, shortly after issuing the statement, the Church erected a monument to Nikolaj Velimirović (A. Lebl, 2002). Moreover, a year later, Lebl told a press conference that the "official stance of the Serbian Church" against antisemitism should not divert from the fact that "there are circles in the Church that are antisemitic" ("Antisemitizam ponovo u porastu," 2003).

"Serbs have never hated the Jews": Literal denial of antisemitism

Within Serbian Orthodox culture, a common reaction to insinuations regarding the presence of antisemitism within its ranks is the rhetoric of what Stanley Cohen calls "literal," "factual," or "blatant" denial (Cohen, 2001, p. 7). The customary response to criticism is simply to deny that what is alleged is true and claim outright that there is no antisemitism among Serbs, and especially not within Orthodox Christianity. Both the Serbian nation and the Orthodox Christian culture, to which authors belong and which they claim to represent, are portrayed as collectives with an untarnished liberal tradition.

This type of collective self-representation is apparent in the press release issued by the synod of the Serbian Church, as well as in the article in *Dveri Srpske.* The synod's press release begins with the following assertion:

> For centuries, the Serbian Orthodox Church taught its flock—which until recently included the whole of the Serbian people, and even other people who found themselves under her canonical jurisdiction—to love its neighbors, especially those in trouble or in anguish, who are victims of injustice and persecution. The Serbian Church remains faithful to its creed and continues to teach these values to the present day. That is why, with a clear conscience, it can be said, and

> demonstrated, that—thanks precisely to the beneficial spiritual influence of Orthodoxy as a faith and a way of life—the Serbian people are one of unfortunately very few European and Christian peoples who never harbored, and still do not harbor, any negative feelings or attitudes towards Jews. Serbs never took part in unchristian persecutions and inhumane pogroms of Jews, which remain an ineradicable stain on the history and the conscience of some other nations. On the contrary, because of their own suffering and victimhood, our people have always been able to feel the pain of their compatriots and fellow citizens of Jewish faith and nationality, and of the Jewish people as a whole; and to share their sorrow and pain and even to help lessen it wherever possible. (Information Service of the Serbian Orthodox Church, 2002)

The article "Serbs and Jews" contains an equally vigorous expression of denial. Vladimir Dimitrijević states: "It is clear, clear, clear: Serbs have never hated the Jews, Serbs have never persecuted the Jews, Serbs cannot be accused of racism and Judaeophobia." He adds: "throughout the centuries Serbs always lived in peace with their Jewish neighbors, never persecuted them for their faith, and always granted them full human and civil rights in their state" (Dimitrijević, 2004, p. 77).

Both the synod of the Serbian Orthodox Church and Vladimir Dimitrijević cite adherence to the Christian faith as itself ruling out the possibility of anti-Jewish sentiment among Serbs. In spite of the long history of anti-Judaism in the Christian theological tradition, from which Orthodoxy has not been immune, the statement by the leadership of the Serbian Church attributes the non-existence of antisemitism to the beneficial influence of the Church and its creed, which can be "demonstrated." The article "Serbs and Jews" reveals in its opening statement that "an Orthodox Christian cannot hate Jews, above all because he is Orthodox" and that "in Orthodoxy there is no basis for anti-Jewish hate" (Dimitrijević, 2004, p. 74).

The most striking feature of the claims about the absence of antisemitism in Serbia is the emphatic and categorical terms in which they are articulated. In the statement from the synod the assertion regarding the inherently tolerant nature of Serbs is expressed through the repetition of words such as *never* or *any*: Serbs are said to have "never" harbored "any" negative feelings, that there was "never" any persecution of Jews by Serbs. Dimitrijević frames the denial in absolute terms by using phrases such as "never," "no basis," "cannot be accused," "always."

Emphatic literal denial, apparent in above examples, employs a rhetorical device identified by conversation analysts as "extreme case formulations" (Edwards, 2000; Hutchby & Wooffitt, 1998; Pomerantz, 1986). This device, which refers to "descriptions or assessments that deploy extreme expressions" such as *every*, *all*, *none*, *always*, *never*, *absolutely*, etc. (Edwards, 2000, p. 347) is a common discursive resource used for legitimizing and warranting claims in an adversarial situation (Pomerantz, 1986). Terms such as "never," "always," etc. enhance the authority of a description by presenting it as factual and true, purely on the grounds of its apparent certainty, pervasiveness, and widespread acceptance. Because of their insistent tone, extreme case formulations help to forestall possible counterclaims and help mount a challenge to alternative positions (also Hutchby & Wooffitt, 1998; Pomerantz, 1986; Potter, 1996).

In the present case, extreme case formulations do not just reinforce an argument in the debate about contemporary Christian-Jewish relations in Serbia. They also provide the means by which the political controversy surrounding the issue can be dismissed—or repressed. According to Freudian psychoanalytic theory, a critical aspect of denial is its forceful and categorical expression. An emphatic "no," "never," etc. "protests too much, for it is a way of dismissing a question, rather than answering it." It is a means of "dismissing a matter out of hand and closing the issue" (Billig, 1999a, p. 200). The strength of emotion evident in the denial of antisemitism suggests that any allusion to anti-Jewish prejudice within the Serbian Orthodox Church or the Christian Right is regarded as so preposterous and outlandish that it can be instantaneously dismissed as not warranting further consideration.

A related aspect of literal denial of antisemitism is that assertions about Serbian tolerance towards Jews are accompanied by frequent allusions to "facts," "evidence," and "proof." The use of empiricist discourse reflects an important feature of denial, namely the "truth-value dilemma" (Billig, 1990; Wetherell & Potter, 1992). Because definitions of prejudice, both lay and scholarly, emphasize the lack of rational judgment as the essential characteristic of the phenomenon—for example: "thinking ill of others without sufficient warrant" (Allport 1954, p. 6; see also Jones, 1972)—, the denial of prejudice is often articulated so as to present a potentially criticizable view as rational, empirical, and factual rather than as interested, biased, and irrational. The description constitutive of denial is worked up to appear as a solid and unproblematic representation of the world as it is and therefore as separate from the speaker's potentially biased motives and intentions. The use of empiricist discourse acts as an "externalising device" (Woolgar, 1988), which draws attention away from a person's stake or interest in making a claim and their accountability for it (Edwards, 1992; Potter, 1996).

The references to the factual and empirically demonstrable nature of claims about Serbian tolerance are seldom backed with concrete evidence that might sustain such sweeping claims. Although denials frequently allude to relevant "evidence" and "proof," these are, in most instances, conspicuously absent from the argument. The statement from the Serbian Orthodox Church merely states that Serbian benevolence towards Jews can be "demonstrated." Similarly, in the interview conducted specifically for the purposes of the present study, Branimir Nešić, editor-in-chief of *Dveri Srpske* and leader of the Christian right-wing organizations which publishes it, claimed emphatically that "Serbs don't have a problem with Jews, we don't have a problem with any other nation. [...] That story about antisemitism in Serbia just won't stick, although someone might want to put it on the table. But we have so many facts and arguments to show otherwise... all this amounts merely to sticking labels." Just like the synod of the Serbian Church, Nešić never elaborated on the relevant "facts and arguments" that might justify the extreme reference to the absence of problem with "any nation."

In his work on denial of prejudice, Teun van Dijk (1992) refers to instances where the factuality and veracity of a claim are assumed rather than supported as "apparent denial." He argues that the unsubstantiated nature of the invoked "facts" actually helps to enhance and validate the speaker's argument. The absence of corroboration presents a claim as "self-evident," "based on common sense," and a view that does not require verification (van Dijk, 1992, p. 105). The argument is rhetorically designed to attract support via the appeal to the power of consensus (Reeves, 1983). In the present case, apparent denial presents Serbian compassion not just as an unproblematic feature of the world, but also as a shared view, an accepted truth. In the article in *Dveri srpske*, Dimitrijević enhances the assumed commonsensical nature of his claim by suggesting that it is "both senseless and impossible" for an Orthodox Serb to hate Jews and appeals to the wider consensus through repetition: "it is clear, clear, clear: Serbs never hated the Jews..." (Dimitrijević, 2004, p. 77). Discursive construction of consensus regarding Serbian–Jewish relations turns denial of antisemitism into what is known as a "rhetorically self-sufficient" or "clinching" argument. By providing what is seen as a "basic cultural verity," such arguments are treated as beyond question (Augoustinos et al., 2002). Once they are alluded to, "no more needs to be said, no further warrant need be given" (Wetherell & Potter, 1992, p. 92). In the present case, apparent denial and the construction of common sense surrounding Serbian benevolence closes down the topic of antisemitism and shifts the focus of attention onto other topics, ones that are less compromising for the writer.

On occasions however, "facts" and "proof" that are in most instances merely alluded to are elaborated and publicized, presumably for the benefit of those not entirely versed in the nationalist common sense. Exposition of "evidence" typically reveals the propensity amongst writers to interpret history selectively and consistently with their ideological commitments. Dimitrijević (2004) for instance backs the claim about the Serbian tradition of tolerance towards Jews with the argument that "when [the leader of the first Serbian uprising against Ottoman rule which started in 1804] Karađorđe liberated Belgrade in 1806, he issued an explicit order that Jewish houses, temples, and shops must not be touched" (p. 75). Similarly, he reveals to his readers, with great pride, that Jews acquired full citizenship in Serbia following the Berlin Congress in 1878. Although presented with an air of confidence, Dimitrijević's "evidence" of Serbian munificence consists of a sanitized version of the country's history that conceals some important details. The author of the article in *Dveri srpske* does not mention for instance that during the two-year-long struggle for national independence, which preceded the "liberation of Belgrade," Serbian rebels drove Jewish communities out of provincial towns and cities. Presumably it was this conduct that necessitated Karađorđe's order in the first place. Also, Dimitrijević fails to note in the text that once they had taken control over Belgrade, Karađorđe's fighters largely ignored their leader's prohibition. As a result, numerous Jewish homes, businesses, and synagogues were destroyed, a proportion of the local Jews were forcefully converted to Christianity, some were killed, while most fled across the Danube to the Austrian-controlled town of Zemun (Freidenreich, 1979; Ž. Lebl, 2001). Dimitrijević's reference to the granting of citizen's rights to Jews in 1878 as a great achievement of the Serbian state is similarly misleading. From 1846 onwards Serbia's Jewish community was prohibited from living outside Belgrade, and after 1861 Jews were confined, by law, to a small number of ghettos scattered around the city. Although Jews were formally granted full civil rights in 1878, this was done under considerable diplomatic pressure from Western powers, especially Britain. The Berlin Treaty, which granted Serbia its independence and statehood, required of the newly established kingdom to facilitate the emancipation of religious minorities (Freidenreich, 1979; Ž. Lebl, 2001). Moreover, resistance to this section of the treaty within Serbia was considerable, so aspects of anti-Jewish legislation remained in force until 1889, when the new constitution brought Serbia in line with its treaty obligations.

"Parrots," "idiots," and "the mummies of reason": Denial and offensive rhetoric

Denial of prejudice is more than a form of defense against actual or potential accusations. It is also an attack against opposing constructions of reality (van Dijk, 1992). Every description of a state of affairs implicitly or explicitly acts to undermine a range of alternative positions (Billig, 1987, 1990; Dillon, 1991), which are seen as "symbolic competitors in the realm of moral influence" (see van Dijk, 1992, p. 108). Thus, denial does not just involve "defensive" rhetoric—the construction of one's own position as "factual," "true," or unprejudiced, but also "offensive" rhetoric, namely the undermining of alternative views as products of strategy or interest. Potter (1996) uses the term "ironisation" to refer to the means by which alternative descriptions are portrayed as "talk which is motivated, distorted or erroneous in some way" and dismissible as the product of lies, delusions, misrepresentations, malevolence, or financial gain (p. 107).

In the case of denial of antisemitism, literal denial is routinely accompanied by the questioning of the morality of the critics and the veracity of their claims. The topic of debate is regularly re-directed towards the accusers, whose position is constructed, in very elaborate ways, as mistaken, intolerant, biased, and malicious. For instance, in the statement from the synod, claims about the benevolence of Orthodox Serbs—which are constructed as demonstrable—are contrasted with the critical opinion, attributed to ulterior motives and the deviant character of "superficial, or even spiteful circles, who readily attribute antisemitism of certain groups and individuals to the influence of Orthodoxy and the teaching of St Sava, and who cite, as the ultimate culprit for antisemitism, the Orthodox Church which leads and enlightens the Serbian people" (Information Service of the Serbian Orthodox Church, 2002). Criticism that provoked the press release—which is described as "misrepresentation"—is therefore described as the outcome of "spite" and misjudgment (superficiality). It is attributed to certain "circles," indicating that criticism does not come from isolated individuals but from interested groups. Similarly, Nešić's (2004) reference to accusations of antisemitism as nothing but "sticking of labels" intimates the unjustified and unwarranted nature of such insinuations.

The disqualification of criticisms through the use of idioms like "certain circles" or "sticking of labels" can be contrasted with far more vivid and colorful language occasionally used by representatives of the Serbian Orthodox Church, when describing their political opponents. In a speech reported on Belgrade's *Radio B92* on May 25, 2003, Bishop Amfilohije Radović dismissed the critics of the clericalist tendencies within the church as "parrots, idiots, the mummies and flies of reason, ignoramuses." References to the inferior intellectual ability of political opponents are outnumbered only by claims regarding their political motivations. In a recent article, Bishop Atanasije Jevtić referred to the critics of new Serbian nationalism as the following:

> This high-calibre anti-Serbian tirade, which surpasses both Ottoman and Communist achievements in the domain of fabrication, moaning, and slandering [...] [creating] a confusion, based on malicious but carefully worded disinformation [...] [by the] new, self-appointed unilateral, and one-party agit-prop, or Central Committee from Brussels. (Jevtić, 2003b, p. 567)
>
> All kinds of groups, consisting of well paid prompters and spitters from Belgrade, the "petty Belgraders" (people already refer to

> them as Euro-slobberers [*evroslinavci*]), who are small in number but very noisy—united by their malice and the shared totalitarian and intolerant love for Europe—which is sentimental to the point of sniveling. They persistently hate Serbs and the Church. They are Mirko Đorđević, N. Popov, V. Arsenijević and co., M. Tomanić, I. Čolović, Kandić, Biserko, Vučo, Srljanović, Pavićević, and others from the "council of the Wicked" (Ps. 1:1) or the "company of evildoers" (Ps. 26:5). (ibid., p. 568)
>
> "Let them be!" we who are the people say, let them do their well-paid job. "Children, you just do your job." Every person's deeds or misdeeds will eventually come to light. (ibid., p. 568)

Critics are dismissed as communist ("Central Committee," "one-party agit-prop"), puppets of the West (reference to "Brussels," "Euro-slobberers") but most of all as mercenaries ("well-paid job," "well-paid prompters," etc.). Apparent in the disqualification is also the populist distinction between the urban and the rural, in that the Serbian capital Belgrade is used as a term of abuse ("spitters from Belgrade," 'petty Belgraders," etc.) and is contrasted with the "people" ("people already refer to them as...," "we who are the people").

Most importantly, the Manichean distinction between the Church and liberal public is articulated in religious terms. The critics are described as the "council of the Wicked" or the "company of evildoers," with specific references to the Bible. Religious dimension is also apparent in the sentence "Children, you just do your job," used by Jevtić. This is a paraphrase of a well-known statement attributed to the elder Vukašin from the village of Klepci, one of the New Serbian Martyrs, canonized by the Serbian Orthodox Church in 2000. Vukašin was murdered at the Jasenovac concentration camp in 1943 by his Ustasha captors. According to the official hagiographic account of his life and death, Vukašin refused to praise the Ustasha leader Ante Pavelić in return for his life, and instead said to his executor "Child, you just do your job." The Ustasha soldier mutilated Vukašin's body, but the Serbian Martyr responded with the same words of defiance (Anon., 2000; Mileusnić, 2003). In alluding to Vukašin's words, Jevtić effectively draws a parallel between the Church and the martyr, while at the same time comparing his own political opponents to the murdered man's ruthless tormentors. The analogy presents the Church as engaged in a heroic struggle in which it has God's justice on its side. The same message underpinned Patriarch Pavle's assessment of civil rights groups as "sinful minds" (Patriarch's Christmas encyclical issued in January 2002, reported in "Protiv greha u nama samima," 2002).

References to political motives and interests of the critics in the context of denial are not limited to the representatives of the Serbian Church. In 2002, Bogoljub Šijaković, then Minister of religious affairs in the federal government of Serbia and Montenegro, referred to human rights groups as "political chameleons" and remnants of the communist era who now "persecute people" in the name of "human rights and European integration" ("Evropski standardi na balkanski način," 2002). A year earlier, in a statement to the daily *Glas Javnosti*, nationalist historian Radoš Ljušić, who later served a term as member of Serbian Parliament for the ruling Democratic Party of Serbia (2003–2007) responded to concerns about the rise of antisemitism in Serbia by invoking the theme of an international anti-Serbian conspiracy:

> The Helsinki Committee and other mondialists, who took over the witch-hunt from the communists, are clearly bothered by anything that is Serbian, especially if it is national and Orthodox. I think that behind these accusations directed against the Serbian people hides a political motive. To those who have been defeated in war, you can attribute what you like. The final battle with the Serbian people is not over; the powerful believe that we have not been punished enough. They start with antisemitism, then they incite the ethnic minorities to revolt; territories are then torn... Maybe these accusations are meant to justify the new consignment of Serbian arrestees for The Hague. (Kordić, 2001)

This strategy of "reversal" (Billig, 1990; van Dijk, 1992) or the "condemnation of the condemners" (Cohen, 2001) inherent in offensive rhetoric conveniently deflects attention away from any consideration of the wrongfulness of own behavior or ideological position. Also, it illustrates the inherently argumentative nature of literal denial. The construction of Serbian benevolence as obvious and commonsensical implicitly locates alternative positions and their exponents as being outside the consensus and the community of normal, fair, and ordinary people (see van Dijk, 1992, p. 104). As the denial of prejudice is reified and objectified as "self-evident truth," alternatives are dismissed as "unnatural," biased, and interested (p. 106). The denial thus becomes a weapon of counterattack, which is waved at liberal public opinion in an attempt to undermine its social relevance and impact on public opinion.

Offensive rhetoric employed in the denial of antisemitism reveals a further use of extreme case formulations. "Extrematisation" (Potter, 1996) is apparent in a way in which those who deny antisemitism represent critical opinion in the context of their counter-argumentation. Specific criticisms of Serbian clerics or the condemnation of particular ideological trends within the church, most of which are linked to the influence of Nikolaj Velimirović, are routinely interpreted as attacks on the entirety of the Serbian Church, or even more broadly on Orthodox Christianity. The statement from the synod claims, for instance, that allegations of antisemitism are directed at "Orthodoxy," "the teachings of St Sava" and "the Orthodox Church." In the above quotation, Radoš Ljušić argues that concerns about rising antisemitism in Serbia were "accusations directed against the whole of the Serbian people." Bishop Atanasije Jevtić refers to liberal critics as "the accusers of Serbs" (Jevtić, 2003b, p. 570). More recently, at a public meeting in Ćelije Monastery in April 2004, Jevtić noted that "they are attacking us, brothers and sisters—the Communists and after them the neo-communists and the anti-communists, they are all the same—accusing us of being nationalists, because they are all against the Serbian nation" (cited in "Justin je fino mirisao," 2004).

This aspect of denial reflects a more general interpretative framework apparent in Serbian religious and nationalist discourses where events in the world tend to be viewed through the prism of the national collective, and where the critique of the particular is routinely interpreted as a condemnation of a whole category or a group. For instance, the prosecution of individual Serbian war crimes suspects in The Hague is routinely constructed and opposed as an indictment of the whole of the Serbian nation. In 2004, in an attempt to arrest the former leader of Bosnian Serbs and fugitive from international justice, Radovan Karadžić, NATO troops in Bosnia raided a house in Pale near Sarajevo during which an Orthodox priest and his son were seriously hurt. (The two were, it later turned out, wrongly suspected of harboring the fugitive Bosnian Serb leader.) The fate of the two individuals was instantly condemned by the Church as an attack on "the soul of the [Serbian] people" and an attempt to "humiliate a whole Christian nation" (Information Service of the Serbian Orthodox Church, 2004a). In a similar vein, in an interview to the sensationalist weekly *Nedeljni Telegraf*, the Serbian bishop of Vranje, Pahomije Gačić, dismissed the charges of child sexual abuse brought against him by a number of youths in his diocese as an attack on the "Church as a whole" ("Linčuju i mene i crkvu," 2003).

Such radical re-formulations of critical opinion assist the overall dynamic of reversal. As Edwards (2000) notes, by "upgrading and taking to extremes" an opponent's view, extreme case formulations set up that view "for irony and disagreement" (p. 359). In the case of allegations of antisemitism, the reinterpretation of critical opinion as invoking the notion of collective responsibility presents the liberal view as violating the pervasive social norm against a moral indictment of a whole nation or a religion. The amplified or "extremicized" representation of criticism constructs the liberal opinion as malevolent, spiteful, and prejudiced against Serbs and Orthodox Christians, thereby facilitating its dismissal and rejection. The Right thus effectively appropriates the language of liberalism and equality, mobilizing it for the purposes of reversal and for the perpetuation and reification of its own ideological position. Moreover, it is precisely the "extrematization" of criticism that legitimizes the use of social denial. The generalized claims about Serbs or the Church not being racist are necessitated by the way in which criticism is interpreted in the first place.

More importantly however, the general way in which social denial is articulated fails to acknowledge that most of the charges of antisemitism are specifically directed at the influence of Nikolaj Velimirović. By treating criticisms in a general manner, debate about what Velimirović said or did during his lifetime or about how he should be remembered—which is at the heart of the controversy and the main object of criticism—is conveniently omitted, and concealed under the barrage of emphatic denial.

Comparing Serbs and Croats and the rhetoric of "competitive martyrdom": Comparative denial of antisemitism

Literal denial of antisemitism is typically accompanied by denial that is expressed in relational rather than in absolute terms. It is often argued that Serbs are not only an inherently tolerant nation with a long and unblemished history of hospitable attitudes towards Jews, but also that this is a national trait that sets Serbs apart from other nations. The statement from the synod of the Serbian Orthodox Church states that Serbs are one of "unfortunately very few European and Christian people who never harbored, and still do not harbor, any negative feelings or attitudes towards Jews." Also it reveals that antisemitism "remains an inerasable stain on the history and the conscience of some other nations," but not of Serbs (Information Service of the Serbian Orthodox Church, 2002).

A further example of comparative denial is to be found in the aforementioned article "Jews defend Serbs from accusations of anti-Semitism," published in *Glas Javnosti* in 2001. This article, which contained the statement from Radoš Ljušić about the "anti-Serbian" motivations of those concerned with the rise in antisemitism, reported also the view of Aleksandar Mošić, vice-president of the Serbian–Jewish Friendship Society. Mošić told the author of the article, Marija Kordić, that "[a]ntisemitism among Slavic people in the Balkans, namely among Serbs, Macedonians, Bulgarians, is infinitely milder than in other countries like in Romania, Austria, or Hungary. As far as Serbs are concerned, one of the reasons why antisemitism never took root in Serbia is because Serbs are ethnically particularly tolerant and liberal people. Antisemitism in Serbia has always been 'imported goods'" (Kordić, 2001).

Not only does Mošić include Serbs among a selected group of Balkan nations who are "infinitely milder" in their antisemitism compared to others, but he attributes the tolerance to an "ethnic characteristic" of the Serbs. By attributing tolerance to national character, the alleged open-mindedness is given a stable and constant dimension. This reinforces the denial of prejudice, in that references to Serbian antisemitism can be dismissed on the grounds that antisemitism is incongruous with Serbian "nature." Moreover, through the objectification of Serbian tolerance, the discussion of antisemitism is redirected towards the consideration of the "other" (whose "nature" is less tolerant).

In the same article Mošić pursues the comparative argument further. He attributes the tolerance of Serbs to the authority of the Orthodox Church, by means of a contrast with Roman Catholicism:

> In Catholic countries, antisemitic prejudice is far more common than in Orthodox countries. Politically, Catholicism is far more aggressive. The Orthodox Church never endorsed the missionary propaganda comparable to that of the Catholic Church. The Orthodox Church never emphasized those Christian dogmas that awaken antisemitism. The Serbian Orthodox Church has always been more concerned with the maintenance of national identity and with Christian ethics. (ibid.)

A similar point was raised by the leader of Dveri, Branimir Nešić, during the interview:

> The Roman Catholic Church, one must mention this, did some bad things during the World War II, they supported Hitler. So, the Catholic Church asked Jews for forgiveness... Now the problem is that Jews who have every right to feel grievance towards the Catholic Church, have extended the same argument to us. They do not understand that Orthodox peoples and the Serbian people do not have this problem with Jews... we don't have this problem in Serbia.

Besides repeating the familiar argument about tolerance being the legacy of Orthodox influence, Mošić and Nešić both present Catholicism as the main hub of [Christian] antisemitism. The comparison perpetuates a broader theme of Serbian nationalism, namely the contrast between Orthodoxy and Catholicism and, on a more basic level, between Orthodox Serbs—who are seen as "ethnically tolerant"—and the Catholic Croats whose open-mindedness is constantly challenged. In the article "Serbs and Jews," published in *Dveri Srpske*, Croats are clearly identified as the target for comparison. Throughout the text, Dimitrijević's quasi-historical elucidation of Serbian–Jewish relations, which attempts to demonstrate total absence of antisemitism in Serbia, is interpolated with contrasts with Croatia. Dimitrijević notes that unlike in Serbia, "Jews were banned from residing on Croatian territories until the 18th century, and antisemitic incidents were very frequent after that" or that "in 1941 Ante Pavelić [leader of the NDH] sent all Croatian Jews to the concentration camps," while "Serbia, even under occupation, refused to pass laws against Jews." The repeated comparison with Croatia reflects the prevailing cultural stereotype within the discourse of the Serbian Right, where Croats are traditionally seen as proselytizing, intolerant, even "genocidal" (see Milosavljević, 2002).

Comparative denial of antisemitism also manifests itself as a more favorable comparison between Serbs and Jews, especially with regards to the common martyrdom of the two peoples throughout history. The comparison between Serbian and Jewish history is closely linked to the martyrdom myth characteristic of Serbian nationalist discourse, and as such was a notable component of Serbian nationalism in the late 1980s and the early 1990s. In 1985, in his "Letter to the writers of Israel," Vuk Drašković lamented over Serbia's troubled history though an analogy with the suffering of the Jews. He wrote that "every square foot of Kosovo is Serbia's Jerusalem: there is no difference between the suffering of Serbs and Jews. Serbs are the thirteenth, lost tribe of Israel" (Drašković, 1987, p. 74). The best-known exponents of the comparison between Serbs and Jews was the controversial, government-sponsored Serbian–Jewish Friendship Society founded in 1990 by a group of Serbian nationalist intellectuals and some of the country's Jewish public figures. The society promoted the bond between Serbian and Jewish people on the grounds that both suffered persecution in the hands of Croatian fascists and German Nazis (see Gordiejew, 1999). Importantly, behind the seemingly philosemitic sentiments propounded by the Serbian–Jewish Friendship Society lay a more sinister "functionalization" of Jews, and the usurpation of Jewish symbols and history in the pursuit of Serbian nationalist agenda (see Gordiejew, 1999; Sekelj, 1997; Živković, 2000).

While the public attention which the Serbian–Jewish Friendship Society attracted in the early 1990s diminished over the past decade, the overall interpretative framework within which it functioned and the ideas which it promoted persist above and beyond the limited membership of this organization. The parallel between Serbian and Jewish suffering continues to be invoked in public discourse whenever the theme of antisemitism or of Serbian–Jewish relations is raised. In the statement from the Holy Synod of the Serbian Orthodox Church, the ability of Serbs to "feel the pain" of Jews and to share "their sorrow and pain and even to help lessen it wherever possible" was attributed to the common victimization and suffering of the two people. Similarly, in the message which Patriarch of the Serbian Orthodox Church Pavle sent to the Government of Israel in September 2003, on the occasion of the fiftieth anniversary of the Yad Vashem Remembrance Authority in Jerusalem, the head of the Serbian Orthodox Church noted that "Serbs sympathize with the profound suffering of the [Jewish] people with whom they became united like brothers through coexistence and common martyrdom" (Information Service of the Serbian Orthodox Church, 2003a). The message also reflected on the fact that that "Nazis murdered Serbs as often as they murdered Jews," and that today "we both live together, in the words of a Serbian poet [Matija Bećković] 'as the remnants of a slaughtered people'." The patriarch concluded the telegram with the hope that the "common suffering of [Serbs and Jews] will find a place in the new historical exhibition at Yad Vashem, in spite of the fact that many tried to use the recent Balkan tragedy to conceal and minimize the crime against the Serbian people during the Second World War which lies at the core of the recent conflict" (ibid.; for a more detailed account of comparative martyrdom in relation to the Holocaust, see Byford, 2007).

The theme of common suffering is sometimes invoked in more controversial ways. Following the upsurge in the ethnic conflict in Kosovo in March 2004, which resulted in the death of thirteen and the displacement of four thousand Serbian inhabitants of the province, the Serbian Orthodox Church posted in a prominent place on its website a press release from the Serbian–Jewish Friendship Society which stated that "the orchestrated crime throughout the Kosovo territory closely resembles the Nazi 'Kristallnacht' which took place in the night between the 9th and 10th of November 1938 " (Information Service of the Serbian Orthodox Church, 2004b). The press release went as far as to argue that "in terms of the number of victims" and in terms of the "evil" which motivated it, the event in Kosovo surpassed *Kristallnacht*. The unsustainable example of "competitive martyrdom" (Shafir, 2002) and the comparison with the 1938 event, when hundreds of Jews were murdered and 30,000 were sent to Nazi concentration camps, captured the imagination of the Information Service of the Serbian Orthodox Church, whose webpage continued to display a banner stating "Kristallnacht in Kosovo continues" even after the hostilities ended.

The two aspects of comparative denial, namely the contrast with Croats and other nations and the comparison with Jews, are often blended into the same argument. In the interview with Branimir Nešić, the Catholic Church's "support for the Nazis" was contrasted with the record of the Serbian Church, which "never did anything of the kind. Serbian Orthodox people and the Russian Orthodox people perished in the war together with Jews." Also, the message which the Patriarch of the Serbian Church sent to the Israeli government in 2003 contains a subtle critique of Croatia. Although those who were the cause of the common suffering of Serbs and Jews are referred to in the text simply as "the Nazis" (who "murdered Serbs as often as they murdered Jews"), a closer reading of the text reveals that the target of the patriarch's condemnation were not so much Nazi Germans, but the pro-Nazi Independent State of Croatia (NDH). In the concluding passage of the telegram the patriarch refers to "crimes against the Serbian people during World War II" which "lie at the core of the recent conflict," clearly referring to the historical background to the wars in Croatia and Bosnia. Also, the "Serbian poet's" dictum about Serbs being the "remnant of a slaughtered people," mentioned by the patriarch, was originally uttered in reference to Serbian victimization in the NDH between 1941 and 1945.

National self-glorification in a historical context

The themes of positive national self-presentation, which are constitutive of a literal and comparative denial of antisemitism, are not the invention of the contemporary Serbian ecclesiastical establishment or the emerging Christian Right. The power of these denials lies precisely in the fact that they contain themes that have a long history in Serbian public discourse. As Stanley Cohen (2001) writes, accounts that are employed in the context of denial are "learned by ordinary cultural transmission, and are drawn from a well-established, collectively available pool. An account is adopted because of its public acceptability [...] Denials we see are those offered in the expectation that they will be accepted" (Cohen, 2001, p. 59).

Many of the arguments inherent in contemporary social denial of antisemitism date at least to the early decades of the 20th century. Writing on the history of the Jewish community in Serbia, Freidenreich (1979) notes that even in the late 1920s and 30s, at a time of a notable rise in antisemitism in what was then the Kingdom of Yugoslavia, the dominant stance of government officials was that Yugoslavia "does not suffer from the poison of antisemitism" (Minister of External Affairs in 1929, Vojislav Marinković, cited in Freidenreich, 1979, p. 181). In 1938, only two years before he introduced two antisemitic measures throughout Yugoslavia (a *numerus clausus* in schools and universities and a ban on Jewish participation in the distribution of food produce), Minister of the Interior Anton Korošec noted that "among us in Yugoslavia, as everyone can testify, the Jewish question does not exist. Yugoslavia is one of the few countries that is not bothered by this question. That is the best proof that Jews among us are treated as citizens with equal rights" (cited in Freidenreich, 1979, p. 182). In the same year, in the book *Yugoslavia and the "Jewish Problem"*, Edo Gajić notes the absence of antisemitism in Yugoslavia, arguing that anti-Jewish prejudice "is alien to the Yugoslav and above all Serbian mentality" (Gajić, 1938). Nine years earlier, Yugoslav Minister of External Affairs Marinković substantiated his claim about the absence of antisemitism in Yugoslavia by invoking another theme found in more contemporary forms of denial:

> [T]he historical development of our nation was in many respects similar to the development of the Jewish nation. We had to undergo so much suffering and misfortune and so many bloody battles in which we bore so many sacrifices for freedom that we have and have always had full understanding for the Jews, whose history knows so much hardship and suffering, just because Jews too faithfully preserved their faith and community. In this regard, the same endurance, stamina and perseverance tie us together, so that it is natural that Serbs and Jews should understand each other. (cited in Freidenreich, 1979, p. 181)

Therefore, the themes and tropes constitutive of the contemporary forms of denial have been plucked from an ideological armory that has a long history in Serbian self-representation. A further reason behind the familiarity of these themes is that they contain a kernel of truth.

Most historical accounts of Serbian–Jewish relations emphasize that compared to many other European societies, and notwithstanding some less laudable periods in history, the relationship between Serbs and Jews over the centuries had been amiable (see Freidenreich, 1979; Ž. Lebl, 2001; Sekelj, 1995; etc.). This fact is also emphasized by representatives of the Jewish community and by the liberal public opinion. In fact, one of the reasons why the recent manifestations of antisemitism attracted so much interest and criticism is precisely because there is no established or long-standing legacy of antisemitism in Serbian culture. It is important to emphasize therefore that the aim of the present discussion is not to challenge national self-representation on the grounds of historical accuracy, or to challenge the prevailing affirmative view of the relations between Serbs and Jews. Rather, the objective is to explore the ideological implications of the propagation of the non-prejudiced self-image in the context of the denial of antisemitism. After all, it is not by accident that positive self-presentation is mainly invoked in the context of moral accountability management by those who find themselves under criticism. As will become apparent, national self-presentation can be and is mobilized in a way that helps to justify, legitimize, and normalize anti-Jewish prejudice in a social context in which antisemitism invites moral censorship.

Denial of antisemitism and the distancing from "extremism"

As the earlier sections have shown, literal and comparative denial helps to turn the focus of public attention away from manifestations of antisemitism in Serbian culture. Reversal constructs the denial as common sense and the only moral and credible option, shifting the debate towards a passionate "condemnation of the condemners." Comparative denial projects antisemitism onto relevant others (Croats, Catholics, etc.), thus enhancing the sentiment of national self-glorification. The emphasis on the martyrdom of Serbs and Jews brings into play the familiar martyrdom myth. The presence of antisemitism in Serbia is set aside on the grounds that Serbs, like Jews, are perennial victims of injustice, rendering any consideration of prejudice and discrimination on their part redundant.

And yet the appeal to the consensus about the inherently tolerant nature of Serbian society and its people, which runs through the three components of denial, is coupled with incidental admissions of more blatant "exceptions" to the rule. In the statement by the Holy Synod, for instance, the overall denial of antisemitism in Serbia precedes the denouncement of "certain [antisemitic] groups and individuals" who publish "anti-Jewish texts" under the banner of "defenders of Orthodox Christianity," "saviors of Orthodoxy" or "enemies of the Jewish world conspiracy" (Information Service of the Serbian Orthodox Church, 2002). As was already noted, the Church specifically condemned the television appearance of Žarko Gavrilović. Similarly, in the article "Serbs and Jews," after denying the presence of antisemitism in Serbia, Dimitrijević dismisses the publishing activity of Ratibor Đurđević, Serbia's most prolific writer of antisemitic material, whose catalog of publications includes the book *Famous People on the Jews* (a kind of antisemitic dictionary of quotations) by the well-known exponent of Holocaust denial, William Grimstad (Grimstad, 2000). Dimitrijević notes that "[a]ny lack of objectivity [among the liberal public that criticizes the manifestations of antisemitism] can be damaging, as damaging as the short-sightedness of those Serbs who publish books with quotes by 'great people about Jews' (where great people include among others Hitler)" (Dimitrijević, 2004, pp. 74–75).

Distancing from extremism apparent in these examples has important rhetorical implications in the context of denial. Denials generally appear more persuasive when at least some form of deviation from the ideal is admitted to (van Dijk, 1992). The condemnation of the lunatic fringe tones down the extreme case formulations used in the construction of Serbian benevolence, making the denial seem more plausible. At the same time, prejudice that is admitted to is treated as incidental, and an exception that proves the general rule. The statement from the synod states explicitly that only the "spiteful circles" see any connection between the exponents of antisemitism and the traditionally tolerant Serbian Orthodox culture.

The synod's condemnation of extremism contains, however, an ideologically significant omission. The only person explicitly named in the statement by the synod is father Žarko Gavrilović—a nonconformist rebel cleric who had been dismissed by the Church for his antisemitism on numerous previous occasions. Although the identity of "groups and individuals" who promote antisemitism in Serbia is well-known, and they involve the likes of Dveri and Obraz, these organizations are not named and shamed by inclusion in the category that warrants dismissal. Also, although "publishers" of antisemitic texts were mentioned, the synod missed the opportunity to condemn explicitly the activities of Ratibor Đurđević and his notorious publishing company, Ihtus Press. The purposely vague reference to "groups" and "publishers," which displays ignorance of or lack of interest in their true identity—thereby creating the impression that they are so marginal that they do not warrant specific mention—subtly excludes the organized Christian Right from the problem and leaves its credibility untouched by the statement. By setting the very narrow boundaries of the category "extremist," the synod effectively vindicates a significant source of antisemitism in Serbia from criticism and condemnation.

What is more, the formal distancing by the ecclesiastical establishment even from the narrowly defined extremists is only partial. In spite of the public condemnation of Žarko Gavrilović in 2002, this discredited priest continues to work as editor-in-chief of the magazine *Hrišćanska Misao*, one of the leading religious magazines in Serbia, and as one of editors of the publishing house of the same name on whose editorial board sit the Bishop of Montenegro, Amfilohije Radović (who was one of the signatories of the press release), and the current Serbian prime minister, Vojislav Koštunica. Also, Gavrilović is the author of numerous books on Orthodox education, which are sold and promoted in Church-owned shops. The same applies to Ratibor Đurđević, whose publications are also featured in Church stores, including that located in the building of the patriarchy, regardless of the fact that the Church formally distanced itself from him in 1995 (see Sekelj, 1997).

The dismissal of Ratibor Đurđević in Dimitrijević's article in *Dveri Srpske* is similarly equivocal. It occurs in the context of a more general condemnation of liberal public opinion. The critique of extremism is expressed in a manner that equates the antisemitic author with the liberal public: both are dismissed as equally "lacking in objectivity" and "damaging," thereby reinforcing the status of Dimitrijević's own position as that of the moral majority of level-headed individuals. In the rest of the article, however, Dimitrijević treats Đurđević and the liberal critics very differently. When referring to the latter, Dimitrijević uses strong language. Civil rights groups are branded "hysterical" (Dimitrijević, 2004, p. 74). In contrast, Ratibor Đurđević is said to be simply "short-sighted" and "misguided." Likewise, nothing like the strong and emotive terms habitually used to denounce the liberal left have ever been used by Church leaders to denounce Đurđević, Gavrilović, or other propagators of antisemitism.

"We are not antisemites, but...": Denial and the rhetoric of disclaimers

In the language of the Serbian Christian Right, nationalist self-glorification and self-presentation as tolerant, liberal, and welcoming is seldom an end in itself. Literal denial of antisemitism often occurs as part of a more complex argument. It tends to precede a potentially criticisable claim, usually containing a critique of Jews. As van Dijk notes, the "humanitarian values of tolerance and hospitality" reinforced through denial of prejudice are often followed by a controversial claim which is typically constructed though the prism of "realism," "truth," or "common sense" (van Dijk 1992, p. 111). The speakers employ the "disclaimers" (Hewitt and Stokes, 1975) to build a category entitlement of someone who belongs to a tolerant nation or subscribes to an open-minded religious belief, thereby inoculating themselves against accusations of prejudice and bigotry. Van Dijk (1993) maintains that "grand claims of virtue and superiority are the classical introductions of disclaimers such as 'we are very tolerant towards minorities, but...' stereotypically followed by a negative statement about such minorities, or a defense of actions and policies that have negative consequences for minorities [...] Such disclaimers are often a symptom of underlying prejudices or antagonistic attitudes, if not a sure sign of subtle or not so subtle racism" (p.77)

This is the case in many of the examples looked at in this chapter. A disclaimer lies at the core of the previously mentioned article "Jews defend Serbs from accusations of antisemitism," published in *Glas Javnosti* in 2001. The emphasis on Serbian tolerance (articulated through the statements from Aleksandar Mošić cited earlier) precedes the defense of the antisemitic organization Obraz. Having established that there is no antisemitism in Serbia, the author of the article, Marija Kordić, notes that Obraz had been unfairly accused of antisemitism merely because the organization's literature "identified as enemies of the Serbian people Richard Holbrooke, Madeleine Albright, Kouchner, Soros, Westendorp, Jacques Klein, Clark, Gelbard, and many other" public figures "whose role in the Yugoslav war is well known" (Kordić, 2001). Kordić accentuates the culpability of listed individuals by framing it as "well-known," thereby invoking consensus on this matter. However, while Kordić does not specify that the named persons are of Jewish extraction, other sections of the article openly blame Jews for the Yugoslav crisis. Aleksandar Mošić, who attributed tolerance to the essence of Serbian "ethnic" being, reveals that the prevalence of Jewish names among Serbian enemies is not accidental. Continuing the theme of ethnic characterology, Mošić asserts that "American Jews, whose ancestors came from Russia, carry within them a deep-seated hatred towards the Russians. For them Serbs are just little Russians, so it is no wonder that they immediately adopted anti-Yugoslav propaganda. This includes James Rubin, the former spokesman for the State Department, Sandy Berger, advisor to Bill Clinton, Abramovich, and others from the top of American power" (Kordić, 2001).

The reference to "anti-Yugoslavism" being "no wonder" constructs the view as self-evident. More importantly, within the context of Mošić's contribution to the article, the contrast between the tolerant Serbs and the hateful American Jews is clearly established. What makes this statement especially perplexing is that Mošić is Jewish and the vice president of an institution that calls itself the Serbian–Jewish *Friendship* Society.

In the article "Serbs and Jews," the presence of a disclaimer is even more apparent. The exposition of denial, which ends with the statement that it is "ludicrous and impossible" for Serbs to hate Jews, is followed by the following counterargument:

> On the other hand, not every exploration of the role of the Jews (or the representatives of any other people of a different national or state ideology [*sic*]) in the destruction of traditional Orthodox states is a priori—"racism." In such explorations a whole people is not accused of being responsible for the suffering of another people, but facts are being laid out which might help elucidate what really happened. Hysterical accusations of antisemitism against anyone who, for instance, notes the curious fact that today among American Jews there have been numerous Serbophobes, although Serbs, at least when Jews are concerned, never deserved this, does not do anyone any good, least of all those who initiate such campaigns. (Dimitrijević, 2004, p. 74)

This time it is the criticism of Jews that is presented as "facts" or a "curious fact" that reveals what "really happened," while any counter-arguments are dismissed and presented as "hysterical." The role of the Jews in the "destruction of traditional Orthodox states" is introduced, in a rather matter of fact way, as a "national or state ideology," and therefore as a legitimate, non-controversial, topic of "exploration." Consistently with the overall aims of denial, Dimitrijević displays eagerness to modify his criticism of Jews by arguing that his "elucidation of what really happened" is not and indictment of "a whole people," but criticism of selected individuals, the "numerous Serbophobes" among "American Jews." This, however, is just another disclaimer. The contention that Serbs "never deserved" the "hysterical accusations [...] at least when *Jews* are concerned" (emphasis added)—indicates that the particular "American Jews"—who are cited as "representatives" of a "national or state ideology" and who are thought to be "numerous"—are invoked *as* Jews.

Another ongoing theme of the article is the portrayal of Jews as a people whose prejudice and "Serbophobia" stand in stark contrast with traditional Serbian and Orthodox Christian tolerance. After stating that "Serbs never hated Jews, never persecuted Jews," he argues that "it is a fact that, since the early 1990s, the Serbian people have been satanized in the world media and that an active role in this was played by some influential Jews—above all in Europe and America (Richard Holbrooke, Madeleine Albright, Bernard-Henri Lévy, Steven Spielberg, Wesley Kanne Clark...)" (p. 77). The suggestion that "after the resurrection of Christ Judaism developed in a resoundingly anti-Christian way" precedes the following contrast between Serbs and Jews:

> It is a fact that there had been (and still are), among followers of Talmudic Judaism, those who hate Christians [...] But, Apostle Paul says: "Call down blessings on your persecutors—blessings, not curses" (Romans 12:14). Isn't the Serbian Church a prime example of religious tolerance—from ancient times to the present? The patriarch condemns every instance of hate towards other nations including Jews. Even if some hate us, it is never an excuse to retaliate with hatred. (p. 74)

In this instance, "Serbophobia" is no longer interpreted as a "national ideology," but as a manifestation of the ancient hatred of Christians by Jews. The political stance of certain "American Jews," such as Madeleine Albright, Richard Holbrooke, or Wesley K. Clark, whom Dimitrijević singles out as especially "Serbophobic," is characterized as a feature of longstanding inter-religious conflict. What is more, of the five individuals, only Holbrooke, Spielberg, and Lévy are Jews. Albright is a Catholic of Jewish descent and Clark, whose father was Jewish, was raised as a Christian. The fact that Dimitrijević cites them as Jews indicates the he is well-versed in Serbian conspiracy theory. During the NATO bombing of Serbia in the spring of 1999, Albright's and Clark's Jewish ancestry was widely publicized in the Serbian media and, in some cases, even woven into causal explanations of the war (see Byford, 2006; Byford & Billig, 2001). By implying a decisive role of Jews in the Balkan conflict and by interpreting it as a manifestation of a long standing inter-religious conflict, Dimitrijević comes close to embracing the kind of outlook disseminated by Ratibor Đurđević, the antisemitic conspiracy theorist from whom he attempts to distance himself earlier in the article.

Significantly however, not all instances of literal denial and national self-glorification examined in this chapter have been articulated in the context of a disclaimer. The statement from the synod of the Serbian Orthodox Church, issued in February 2002, does not include a critique of Jews. The signatories used the theme of positive national and religious self-presentation to dismiss the accusations as unfounded, without mentioning the Jewish community, whether in Serbia or the West. The "other" in the press release was not the Jews, but the "spiteful circles" among the liberal public opinion, the independent media, or the various pro-western NGOs. This important difference is indicative of the boundary that still exists between the mainstream and the extreme in Serbian Orthodox culture, at least when it comes to public criticism of Jews.

On the other hand, the noticeable similarities in the rhetoric of denial employed both in mainstream ecclesiastical discourse and in the language of the Christian Right reveal that divisions between the mainstream and the fringe are not airtight. The equivocal condemnation of extremism in the synod's press release and the offensive rhetoric apparent in the Church's polemic with the critics suggest that in the Manichean world of Serbian religious politics, the Christian Right is still seen as less of a danger to the interests of the Serbian Orthodox Church than the country's liberal public opinion. This is evident in the fact that in the autumn of 2004 the synod of the Serbian Church instated Branimir Nešić, editor of *Dveri Srpske*, at the helm of Serbia main religious publication, *Pravoslavlje*. Since then, numerous articles written by associates of Dveri, including those which are critical of the liberal public opinion and human rights organizations, have been published in this mainstream publication.

More importantly, the Church's role in the perpetuation of the themes and tropes of literal denial indirectly contributes to the persistence of antisemitism in Serbian society. The Serbian Orthodox Church is one of the most influential institutions in Serbian society, which commands unparalleled respect among the country's Orthodox population. In recent years, by enforcing its links with the state, the Church has also acquired considerable power over the media (in that its activities are treated as newsworthy), as well as through the introduction of religious education in schools. Because of its access to the public, the Serbian Orthodox Church, as an elite institution, is able to produce and enforce "self-definitions, evaluations of the situation, selection of problems, and agendas that may have significant public impact" (van Dijk, 1993, p. 45).

In speaking out about relations between Serbs and Jews, as it has done in the aforementioned press release, the Church helps to shape the interpretative and argumentative framework underlying everyday experiences and interactions relevant to ethnic affairs. It provides views on what it means to be antisemitic or what constitutes extremism. Moreover, the Church does not just enforce particular agendas or representations, but also provides the public with argumentative resources by means of which a particular ideological *status quo* can be maintained and reproduced. For instance, by perpetuating the consensus about Serbian tolerance, without at the same time unequivocally denouncing anti-Jewish prejudice in all its forms, the Church reinforces the self-glorifying appraisal of inter-ethnic relations in a way that makes the controversial disclaimers found in the literature of the Christian Right appear more plausible and publicly acceptable. As we have seen, the perceived legitimacy of the argument explicated in the article in *Dveri Srpske* relies on the existence of consensus regarding Serbia as the "tolerant community," which the Orthodox mainstream helps to perpetuate. Also, the statement by the synod helps to disseminate the Church's own image as the paragon of virtue, tolerance, and charity, while at the same time enabling it to maintain its traditionalist and conservative religious dogma.

Finally, by propagating the belief that antisemitism does not exist in Serbia—other than on the distant margins of society, far removed from the church or the mainstream—the ecclesiastical establishment helps to keep the topic of antisemitism off the public agenda. As van Dijk (1992) notes, if tolerance is promoted as a national myth, then "it is much more difficult for minority groups to challenge remaining inequalities [...] They may be seen as oversensitive, exaggerating or over-demanding" (p. 96). Furthermore, "successful resistance [to prejudice] requires public attention, media coverage and at least partial recognition of grievances. If leading politicians and the media refuse to acknowledge that there is a serous problem, there will be no debate, no change of public opinion, and hence no change in the system of power relations" (ibid.).

Once it becomes accepted that there is no antisemitism in Serbia or within the Church, then there is little else left to discuss with regards to this matter. All those who challenge the nationalist common sense are simply dismissed as "Serbophobes" or "Euro-slobberers," members of the "spiteful circle" of "petty Belgraders," unwilling to accept the "truth" about the unblemished history of Serbian benevolence towards Jews.

CHAPTER FIVE

"He was merely quoting the Bible!"

Denial of Velimirović's Antisemitism

The previous chapter highlighted the frequency with which the narrative of national self-glorification and the rhetoric of literal and comparative denial appear in ecclesiastical and nationalist discourse, whenever the topic of antisemitism is raised. Bearing in mind the prevalence of this broader strategy of denial, it is not surprising to find that generalized claims about the absence of antisemitism among Serbs are also invoked when accusations of anti-Jewish bigotry are directed specifically at Nikolaj Velimirović.

In the article "Serbs and Jews" quoted extensively in the earlier chapter, the exposition of denial of antisemitism concludes with an explicit defense of Bishop Nikolaj Velimirović. The author, Vladimir Dimitrijević, refutes the criticisms of the bishop by claiming that "[i]n our quasi-democratic press it is frequently mentioned that Bishop Nikolaj was an 'antisemite.' This accusation is senseless as was the accusation made by the communists—that Nikolaj was a follower of Hitler. Every honorable man knows that the holy Serbian teacher and educator of the Serbian people could not have been a racist, because this is not in the tradition of the people to which he belongs" (Dimitrijević, 2004, p. 78). Similarly, in response to a criticism of Velimirović in the daily *Danas* in April 2003, a reader from Belgrade, Nada Bunjak, substantiated her defense of the bishop with the assertion that "in Serbia before the war Jews were well-respected and valued; my family had the best business relations with Jews and in the former Serbia [*sic.*] no one thought ill of Jews, let alone speak ill of them" (Bunjak, 2003).

During the interview conducted for the purposes of this study in the summer of 2003, the writer and politician Vuk Drašković also invoked the tradition of Serbian hospitality and benevolence when he noted that he does not "believe that Nikolaj was an antisemite":

> This antisemitism, and this is the most interesting thing, has no foundation in the Serbian Church and the Serbian people. When, during the time of the Inquisition, they were murdering Jews in Spain and other countries of Western Europe whenever they caught them drinking wine, saying: "you drink the blood of Christ"—here in Serbia, which was under Turkey, under Islamic occupation, Jews were greeted without any negative feelings. In fact many sang in choirs in Orthodox churches. I regret that from time to time in the Orthodox Church one may notice some individual expressions of antisemitism. That is against God and our tradition.

Finally, Slobodan Mileusnić, curator of the museum of the Serbian Orthodox Church and a leading experts on Serbian saints, attempted, during our conversation, to exonerate the bishop by constructing him as part of the broader category of "Orthodox Serbs" among whom antisemitism is an unknown phenomenon:

> Bishop Nikolaj, just like the whole of the Serbian Orthodox Church and the whole of the Serbian people—for the Church is not merely the clergy—has an extremely correct stance towards Jews, and it is well-known that some of the suffering [endured by the Serbs and the Jews] in the past is also similar. This was especially the case during World War II. One could say that [the suffering of Serbs and Jews] went hand in hand. The two people fell to a common enemy—we do not have the exact number of victims but we know that it was horrific, that it was genocidal, that it was unprecedented and a martyrdom. Today, the relations between the two people are good. The Serbian Orthodox Church always denounced antisemitism and all the writings and other things that went in that direction…

The above quotations contain several themes examined in the previous chapter. Mileusnić invokes literal denial of antisemitism among Serbs, while the justification of this generalized claim is based on the familiar notion of common suffering between the Serbs and the Jews. Likewise, Dimitrijević mentioned the "tradition" of munificence and added to his argument a dose of "condemnation of the condemners" when he attributed criticism of Velimirović to the "quasi-democratic press," which follows the dishonorable tradition of the "communists."

Vuk Drašković not only argued that antisemitism is against "our tradition," but also used this argument to distance himself from "individual expressions" of prejudice, which in this instance did not include Nikolaj Velimirović.

The extract from the conversation with Slobodan Mileusnić is noteworthy also because this was the only occasion, during the hour-long interview, that Mileusnić commented on the widespread criticism of Velimirović. He otherwise showed considerable reluctance to give his view on specific aspects of the bishop's contentious writing. Mileusnić evaded the issue of the *Words to the Serbian People Through the Dungeon Window* by arguing that he "never studied the bishop's writing of that historical period" and recommended that the interviewer should talk to "individuals more competent to speak on this matter." The roots of the visible caginess expressed during the interview might be sought in the embarrassment which Mileusnić endured in 1992, when he was dismissed from the post of editor-in-chief of *Pravoslavlje* following the publication of the article "Jews once again crucify Christ," which alleged that Christians are being persecuted in Israel ("Jevreji ponovo raspinju hrista," 1992). Although there is no evidence that Mileusnić shared the hateful views expressed in the article, or was directly responsible for its publication, it appears that in the aftermath of this experience, antisemitism became a subject which he feels is best avoided.

On the other hand, Mileusnić's refusal to comment on Velimirović's views on Jews—which, he suggested, requires specialized knowledge of the bishop's work and is therefore beyond the realm of everyday casual conversation—was not accompanied by silence on the issue. Rather than saying nothing about the bishop's stance towards Jews, Mileusnić filled the conversational space with themes inherent in the common sense of national self-presentation, the culturally available narrative which can be summoned when accusations of antisemitism need to be dealt with.

Rising above the criticisms: *Refusal to engage in controversy as a form of denial*

The avoidance of questions about Velimirović's position on Jews, apparent in the interview with Slobodan Mileusnić, is a common strategy among Velimirović's supporters. Some of them cite the refusal to engage in the debate as the preferred approach, although the justification for doing so differs considerably from that offered by the late curator of the Museum of the Serbian Orthodox Church. In May 2003, in a speech reported on *Radio B92*, Bishop Amfilohije Radović refused to be drawn into the argument regarding Velimirović's antisemitism, not because he regarded himself insufficiently competent, but because "attacks on Bishop Nikolaj" are "shameful and unworthy of consideration." Others appear to draw inspiration from what is believed to have been Velimirović's own approach to criticism. As early as in 1986, in the postscript to the book *The New Chrysostom* by Artemije Radosavljević, Atanasije Jevtić noted that Bishop Nikolaj never responded to accusations that he is a "heretic," "bigot," "freemason," "English," or "German agent," "collaborator," "enemy of the people," "clerical nationalist," etc. and therefore that neither should his followers. Instead, Jevtić argues, they should follow Bishop Nikolaj's example: "through inner peace, and through Christian forgiveness, [Velimirović] demonstrated to his slanderers what he referred to many times as 'the love for Christ, the love for fellow man and love for the people'" (Jevtić, 1986e, p. 51). Several years later, on the occasion of the reburial of Velimirović's remains in 1991, historian Milutin Veković cited a similar reason for refusing to enter into confrontation with the "the spiritually blind, simple souls, retards, political poltroons, and Satan's apprentices." He quoted a passage from Velimirović's book *Prayers by the Lake*: "Lord, bless my enemies. I too send them my blessings and will not curse them. The enemies are the ones who push me further into your arms... Just as the hounded animal finds cover quicker than one that is not hounded, so I, hounded by enemies, found the safest cover, under Your tent where neither enemies nor friends could make me lose my soul" (Veković, 1991, p. 54).

The contention, apparent in the quoted statements, that Velimirović's spiritual superiority and adherence to the principles of Christian forgiveness and tolerance somehow prevented him from responding to criticism, overlooks the fact that the bishop eagerly polemicized with Rabbi Isak Alkalaj in 1928, just as in a letter written in 1946, he confronted his critics over the meaning of the 1935 sermon in which he praised Hitler (see Chapter 3). In fact, Atanasije Jevtić invokes Velimirović's letter containing the defense of the controversial sermon, only a few paragraphs after stating that the bishop never responded to criticism. Clearly, what is presented as a tactic of non-confrontation and "righteous silence" is in fact an argumentative device, deeply embedded within the very same polemical context which its users are supposedly eager to avoid being drawn into. Similarly, the proclaimed adherence to "inner peace" did not prevent Atanasije Jevtić from writing a number lengthy texts of polemic with Velimirović's critics (e.g., Jevtić, 1986e, 2003b), in the same way that Veković's high-minded refusal to "curse" his enemies did not prevent him from labeling them "spiritually blind Satan's apprentices." The refusal to engage in the dispute is therefore a form of "offensive rhetoric." The focus on the moral dichotomy between on the one hand the calm and honorable followers of Christ seeking refuge under God's "tent" and on the other hand the aggressive and bellicose "slanderers" and "enemies" who "hound" the righteous, diverts attention from the actual subject of controversy—namely Velimirović's antisemitism, while at the same time exonerating his reputation by maligning the critics.

In July 2003, in a regular column in the magazine *Pravoslavlje*—in which he purports to be answering readers "questions on matters of faith and religious life"—the then editor-in-chief, Protopresbyter Ljubivoje Stojanović, elaborated on the benefits of non-confrontation. He was responding to a letter from a reader who was "puzzled by the existence of certain objections [to the canonization of Nikolaj Velimirović] and by 'accusations' directed at him." The reader sought advice on how to "respond to the allegations regarding all manner of things" (Lj. Stojanović, 2003, p. 26). In the response, Stojanović recommends to the readers to ignore accusations: "it is unnecessary to wear ourselves out with empty discussions, in order to defend the Holy Bishop from 'attacks'... The lack of understanding among the indecisive, which sometimes manifests itself as malice, must not provoke hate within us towards them. We must also be careful, in 'defending" the bishop, not to identify ourselves with those who, in attacking him try to conceal their weakness of faith" (p. 26). He goes on to suggest that "we will not defend ourselves from the attacks, we will not respond to the insults, but we will always demonstrate the secret of our strong faith which lies in the purity of our conscience" (ibid.). Just like in earlier examples, the debate is deemed to be pointless because of the "other side's" "indecisiveness" and "malice." Stojanović writes that critics "either will not or cannot understand or genuinely accept" the bishop's sanctity (p. 26). Those who are unsympathetic towards Velimirović are said to be "rash," "malicious," or to have taken things "out of context." Although the identity of the critics is not revealed, Stojanović hints at the intended target when he notes that "the living Church is above all unions, forums, and committees" (p. 26). This is an allusion to the Helsinki Committee for Human Rights, Forum for the Monitoring of Antisemitism, affiliated to the Union of Jewish Communities of Serbia, and to the group of intellectuals who, in the autumn of 2002, issued a press release citing Velimirović in a negative context.

The contrast—in terms of integrity, strength of faith, and sincerity—between Velimirović's critics and his followers, is also accentuated through the advice to the readers of *Pravoslavlje* to adopt a moral high ground on this matter. Because criticism of the bishop is attributed to weakness of faith and character, the columnist advocates rising above "rashness" and "malice," refraining from "insults" and "disputes," and calls for patience with those who are "insecure in their faith," as they are not "our enemies." Stojanović also advises the readership that—when faced with criticism—they ought to abide by the Evangelical principle of "come and see for yourself," rather than adopt the approach of "shut up and listen." He proceeds to argue that "we are least likely to persuade them by imposing our view and by treating theirs with disdain, because in doing so we would be reflecting their weakness of faith" (p. 26). While these comments might be seen as a subtle criticism of those within the Serbian Church who, in Stojanović's eyes, defend the bishop a bit too eagerly, in the end it is critics—the human rights organizations, the intellectuals, and the liberal media—who are portrayed as zealots, impatient to impose their beliefs on others. Admirers of Velimirović, in contrast, are presented—at least in a normative sense—as tolerant, calm, and armed with the kind of self-assurance characteristic of those who have God on their side.

In substantiating the claim that disputes should be avoided, Stojanović also "externalizes" his position on Velimirović. He says, "We are reminded of this by our Holy Fathers and teachers who say, 'every word can be contrasted with another, but no word can be compared to life itself'" (p. 27). Criticisms are thus associated with empty "words" of interested and ideologically-minded critics, while the belief in Velimirović's sanctity and the assumed purity of his character are regarded as reflecting the reality of "life" itself. It is this distinction between "life" and "words" that gives Stojanović the grounds for optimism. When interviewed for the purposes of this study, Stojanović concluded: "I am an optimist. People will eventually realize the significance of Nikolaj Velimirović."

"Tiny mosquitoes" and the mighty "eagle": Who has the right to remember Nikolaj Velimirović?

The self-righteous stance adopted by Velimirović's supporters in relation to the evil and morally and intellectually inferior critics is underpinned by the fundamental and unwavering belief in the bishop's unsurpassed greatness and importance. The following extract from Artemije Radosavljević's *The New Chrysostom* offers an illustration of the level of hero-worship among Velimirović's admirers:

> There is no doubt that no Serb has ever written as many brilliant books as Bishop Nikolaj, books on which the Serbian Church and the Serbian people will live spiritually for many centuries to come. On the world stage, both in terms of the quantity and the quality of books written, Nikolaj stands shoulder to shoulder with Origen, St John Chrysostom, and the Blessed Augustine. In terms of the breadth of topics which he covered and the ease with which he had done so, he has hardly any rivals in the world. (A. Radosavljević, 1986, p. 22)

The assumption regarding Velimirović's unprecedented greatness is often viewed as imposing limits on the capacity of ordinary mortals to understand and evaluate his work. Shortly after Velimirović's death, his disciple Dimitrije Najdanović wrote that "Bishop Nikolaj was not just a colossal writer, a giant whose size cannot be evaluated or depicted. He was of almost unsurpassable greatness in terms of his life, his everyday existence, every inner or outer move or action; He was a giant in terms of the whole of his being and his existence" (Najdanović, 2001, p. 85). A similar argument can also be found in the writing of another of the bishop's disciples, father Justin Popović. In 1966, on the tenth anniversary of Velimirović's death, Popović compared ordinary people, the Serbs, to "tiny mosquitoes," and contrasted them with the mighty "eagle," Nikolaj Velimirović. Popović spoke about ordinary mortals as "tiny little candles," insignificant compared to "the

Sun [that] floats over the Serbian sky, the other sun, that is Bishop Nikolaj. We are ticks, Serbs of today, nothing but ticks who cannot see the sun" (J. Popović, 1998, p. 9). He prefaced another sermon full of praises for the bishop by saying, "Oh Lord, what have I, a small and insignificant worm, done to deserve this opportunity to speak about this magnificent light..." (cited in Stanišić, 1976, p. 15). The implication of these words of humility, which were followed by uncritical reverence of Nikolaj Velimirović, is that ordinary mortals can never fully appreciate the greatness of the "New Chrysostom."

More recently, the bishop of Šabac and Valjevo, Lavrentije Trifunović, alluded to the incomprehensibility of Velimirović's work when he mentioned "the English journalist and writer Stella Alexander"—author of *Church and State in Yugoslavia since 1945*, published in 1979—who "tried seventeen years ago to comprehend, collect, and review the Holy Bishop Nikolaj's rich literary and spiritual work." According to Bishop Lavrentije, Stella Alexander "gave up after a while admitting that 'Nikolaj is an ocean that I can neither comprehend nor describe'" (Trifunović, 2003, p. v).

The stipulated limits to the ability to understand and assess Nikolaj Velimirović are sometimes confined only to those who are critical of the bishop. It is not just suggested that *no one* can fully appreciate Velimirović, but that those who disapprove of him are particularly inept at evaluating and appraising the merits of his religious philosophy. In *From All-Man to the Man of God*, Radovan Bigović suggests that Velimirović "is a very multifaceted, complex at moments, even a controversial person, who so far has been respected, underestimated but never adequately appraised. It will take a long time before this can be achieved. Because of his magical personality and complexity many have stumbled over him. Some out of ignorance, some out of malice. Few people have had so many slanderers and enemies who wanted to destroy and undermine them..." (Bigović, 1998, p. 47). Although Bigović defines the inability to "adequately appraise" the bishop in general terms (in that presumably Velimirović had not yet been "adequately appraised" by anyone), the only ones who are specifically cited as having "stumbled" over his "magical personality" are "the ignorant," the "malicious" "slanderers," and the "enemies." Similarly, in 1987, Bishop Amfilohije Radović quoted Justin Popović's sermon cited earlier and noted that we must take Popović's dictum on Velimirović for granted because "our eyes cannot see what the eyes of the holy people see. That which the holy Elder of Ćelije saw, many Serbian eyes, blinded by prejudice and passion, still cannot see. That is why the words of the holy Elder of Ćelije are a great truth about a great man" (A. Radović, 1987, p. 29). Once again, the inability to see what "the eyes of the holy people see" is initially attributed to everyone ("our eyes"), only to be confined later in the same sentence to "many Serbian eyes" that are "blinded by prejudice and passion." More recently Amfilohije Radović proposed that Velimirović's merit cannot be discussed or questioned because "we are not worthy of that," before once again imposing the division between supporters and critics by suggesting that, precisely because no debate on this issue is possible one can only be "with [Velimirović] or against him" (cited in Tomanić, 2003).

Finally, Protopresbyter Milan Janković, the secretary of the synod of the Serbian Orthodox Church and editor of a three-volume collection of documents relating to the life and work of Nikolaj Velimirović—who declined to be interviewed for this study but provided a written response to five questions posed by the author—suggested in his answer the following: "Let's be clear about one thing: for the last hundred years, those who hate Bishop Nikolaj, those who envy him, who are incapable of understanding all that He, Holy and Great, speaks and writes about, only they speak about the controversy surrounding his writing. When hearing about the antisemitism being imputed to him, a normal person does not know whether to laugh or to cry. Whether to cry over the hatred or laugh at the ignorance." Accusation of antisemitism is imputed to those who "are incapable of understanding" the "Holy and Great Bishop." Moreover, critics are contrasted with the "normal person" who is driven to tears and laughter. This construction not only portrays the favorable stance towards Velimirović as the only normal and rational one, but also presents the alternative position as one that is so removed from reality that any form of dialogue or attempt at persuasion is futile. The "normal person" can only laugh or cry.

Implicit in the above arguments is that only practicing Orthodox Christians, those who can "see," and who are not "blinded" by passion and prejudice have the ability and the right to accurately judge Velimirović's genius. Bishop Amfilohije Radović's suggestion that, when trying to assess Velimirović's importance, we must accept the verdict of Justin Popović, implies that the latter's status as one of the "holy people" with superior faith gives him a privileged vantage point over this matter. The aforementioned claim by Ljubivoje Stojanović that "weakness of faith" prevents the critics from "realizing [Velimirović's] greatness" insinuates that having faith is a necessary prerequisite for assessing and understanding the bishop. In the same vein, during our conversation in the summer of 2003, Deacon Radoš Mladenović defended his refusal to comment on Velimirović's antisemitism by stating the following:

> Don't be angry, but my answer will be very clear and very short. I don't think that these attacks warrant a response. Instead Nikolaj should be presented the way he was... I will not respond to [critics of Velimirović], they are educated ignoramuses who don't understand a thing; they never came here to experience the immanent spirit of Orthodoxy, the immanent spirit of Žiča Monastery and its monastic life, to experience Bishop Nikolaj from the period when he was at Žiča. Instead they are putting him on trial, condemning him from a distance.

For Mladenović, the only way of seeing Nikolaj "the way he was" is by experiencing the "spirit" of Orthodoxy at the monastery in which Velimirović once officiated. Mladenović reiterated this point on several occasions during the interview, by inviting the author of this book to spend a few days in Žiča before reaching a conclusion on Nikolaj Velimirović. Presumably, this was because, as the example of "educated ignoramuses" demonstrates, the bishop cannot be adequately understood "from a distance" but only from "within."

This division between "insiders" and "outsiders," those who are "with" or "against" the bishop, is crucial to the pro-Velimirović discourse because it elevates the Serbian Church to the position of the only relevant and legitimate arbiter of Velimirović's integrity. The bishop of Raška and Prizren, Artemije Radosavljević, made this point explicitly, when he wrote in the journal *Jefimija* in 1993:

> To speak of Bishop Nikolaj from any aspect is not easy. Not because there would be nothing to say, but because it would be hard to capture him with words. What we say about Nikolaj might be good, but it would not be Nikolaj. Plenty will remain outside our words, for-

> mulae and definitions. This is why Velimirović can only be somewhat captured and understood if viewed and appraised by the Church and within the Church, given that he grew out of the Orthodox Church and became embedded in it. And God's Orthodox Church alone has the perfect criteria and standards with which people and their deeds can be measured. Those criteria and standards are the eternal and, in the Church, omnipresent godlike personality of Lord Jesus Christ. Only he is the only true and unerring measure of all people and all things" (A. Radosavljević, 1993, p. 9)

During the conversation held in the summer of 2003, Branimir Nešić from Dveri went as far as to argue that any remembrance of Nikolaj Velimirović that strays from the official line should be prohibited. Angry at the accusations of antisemitism directed at the bishop, he said that "I think that there should be a people's court that would suppress and punish the stupidities that some people come up with, so that people would realize that they cannot talk nonsense." While it is unlikely that Nešić advocated the creation of an actual Serbian Orthodox equivalent to the Spanish Inquisition that would deal with what he views as blasphemous and heretical comments about Nikolaj Velimirović, his reaction illustrates the extent to which the dispute over Velimirović's posthumous reputation involves a battle not just over the content of memory, but also over the right to remember.

The letter from "a Jewish woman": Bishop Nikolaj as the savior of Jews

Another strategy used to defend Velimirović from accusations of antisemitism include the building of his credibility as someone who not only did not hold any prejudice against Jews, but in fact did everything he could to rescue them from their tragic fate at the hands of the Nazis. The claim regarding Velimirović's humanitarian effort during the war is of relatively recent origin. In October 2001, Ela Trifunović née Najhaus, a resident of Belgrade, wrote a brief letter to the synod of the Serbian Orthodox Church in which she requested from the ecclesiastical authorities written confirmation that she had spent eighteen months during World War II in hiding at Ljubostinja Monastery. The confirmation was needed, the letter explained, so that Trifunović could apply "for a pension which the German government pays to Holocaust survivors." The letter revealed that the author's father, "Aleksandar Najhaus, a dentist who before the war had lived in the town of Trstenik," was "a great friend and adopted brother [*pobratim*] of the bishop, doctor Nikolaj Velimirović." Shortly after the beginning of the occupation, Bishop Nikolaj is said to have "advised her father to flee," before "risking his own life" to save Dr. Najhaus's wife and daughter. Velimirović is said to have hidden the child—the author of the letter—in a sack, dressed her mother in a nun's attire and taken them both in a carriage through a number of German checkpoints before hiding them in Ljubostinja. The fugitives remained there for a year and a half, until Velimirović obtained false personal documents enabling them to leave the monastery and survive the war.

Since the first appearance of this letter—the authenticity of which has been confirmed by the representatives of the Jewish community (see A. Lebl, 2002)—Velimirović's supporters have endeavored to popularize its content. The book *Holy Bishop Nikolaj of Ohrid and Žiča*, published on the occasion of Velimirović's canonization, includes a transcript of Najhaus's letter under the title "Bishop Nikolaj saved Jews—a letter from a Jewish woman" (Jevtić, 2003a, p. 179). The letter appears in the book among numerous other testimonies to Velimirović's good character and moral greatness. The publishers even reproduced Ela Najhaus's original signature on the page, as well as her full address, presumably to enhance the credibility of the reported testimony and prove that the letter is genuine. The letter was also published in the February 2003 issue of the religious journal *Žički Blagovesnik* under the same title, "Bishop Nikolaj saved Jews—a letter from a Jewish woman." In the issue of another journal (*Hrišćanska Misao*)—published once again around the time of Velimirović's canonization and under identical title—the letter was printed in a textbox embedded within a favorable article on Velimirović. Although the longer article did not reflect on the controversy surrounding Velimirović's writing, the editors nonetheless printed the letter, as a reminder of the bishop's good nature. The second edition of the book *Bishop Nikolaj and the New Testament on the Jews* by Predrag Samardžić also includes a transcript of Ela Najhaus's letter (Samardžić, 2004, pp. 89–90).

The reason behind the frequent inclusion of this letter in various Orthodox Christian publications can be sought not just in the general desire to popularize Velimirović's kindness, but also as a response to the controversy surrounding the bishop's claims about Jews. The event described in the letter functions in a similar way to the martyrdom myth examined in Chapter 3. By continuously reminding the public of the charitable act towards the Najhaus family the Church is effectively appealing for the bishop to be judged on this particular commendable action, not on his *Words to the Serbian People Through the Dungeon Window*. The image of the "Jewish woman," Ela Najhaus concealed as a child in a potato sack, is meant to obliterate from memory the image of another Jewish woman, "Rebeka Natan," the epitome of evil described in Velimirović's book *Indian Letters*, which, incidentally, he wrote shortly after rescuing the young Ela and her mother from certain death. Moreover, the promotion of the story of Velimirović's valor turns the representation of Nikolaj as the savior of Jews into a rhetorical resource that can be invoked when the critics voice charges of antisemitism. At a public panel discussion devoted to Velimirović's stance on Jews which Dveri organized in December 2004, the host Boško Obradović read Ela Trifunović's letter as part of his introductory address. He described it as a "response" to accusations against Velimirović and one of the "basic arguments" in his defense. Similarly, shortly after Velimirović's canonization, Deacon Ljubomir Ranković wrote in *Večernje Novosti*:

> Accusations of antisemitism are unfounded. In his orphanage in Bitolj, the bishop accepted children of all nationalities, Muslims, Gypsies, Albanians, Turks, and Jews. Between the two wars, rich Jewish traders helped the bishop with the publication of his books and the renovation of monasteries. Ela Trifunović-Najhaus, a Jew from Belgrade, following the accusations of antisemitism, sent a letter to the Holy Synod in 2001, in which she testifies how Bishop Nikolaj dressed her and her mother in monastic attire and hid them in a convent in his diocese, risking his own life. (Ranković, 2003b)

Ranković made the identical claim in an article published a week later in the weekly magazine *Vreme* (Ranković, 2003c), as did Bishop Atanasije Jevtić in a statement to the daily *Politika* around that time (Kuburović, 2003). During the interview conducted for this study Ljubomir Ranković also invoked the letter in this way. Moreover, he endeavored to substantiate the veracity of the claim about Velimirović's act of compassion by suggesting that he has a copy of the letter. He kept saying "I have it," "I will show it to you." And yet, in spite of these claims of in-depth knowledge of the letter's content, in the article in *Novosti* Ranković writes, inaccurately, that Ela Trifunović sent the letter "following the accusations of antisemitism," implying that the writing of the letter and the accusations are causally related. The misinterpretation of the motive for the letter (which was linked to a claim for a pension) reveals that the correspondence from "a Jewish woman" is not just a valuable asset in the overall discourse of apologetics but also something that in the mind of Velimirović's supporters has become an inextricable part the polemic surrounding his reputation.

The letter was also alluded to by other interviewees:

> Antisemitism of Bishop Nikolaj? You will find in that text by Ela Najhaus that she says that Bishop Nikolaj smuggled her in a sack, risking his own life and sucking up to the Germans. (Deacon Radoš Mladenović)

> Here's one of the controversies: They say that Bishop Nikolaj was an antisemite, that he wrote some bad things about Jews. In the most recently published book—I read it in the original—is a letter from a Jewish woman, I can't remember her name. In that letter, written by a Jewish woman, she says and admits that Holy Bishop Nikolaj hid her in a sack and placed it among other sacks on a horse-drawn carriage, dressed her mother in a nun's dress, and took them both out of Nazi-occupied Belgrade, risking his own life. They remained in Ljubostinja until the end of the war, [Nikolaj] ordering the nuns to look after them. He also saved her father, according to the woman's testimony. In any case he was in Dachau. This letter and the fact that he was in a German concentration camp says enough, it clearly suggests that Bishop Nikolaj did not hate any people, and of course he did not hate the Jewish people. (Branimir Nešić)

Branimir Nešić's response reveals the way in which the martyrdom myth and the image of Velimirović as the savior of Jews are used concurrently to address accusations of antisemitism and repress controversy. Bishop Nikolaj could not have been an antisemite for two reasons: he was in Dachau, and he saved Jews. Discussion closed.

Important moral objections can be raised with regards to the way in which the events related to the fate of Ela Najhaus and her mother are used in the context of denial of antisemitism. As Aleksandar Lebl notes, routine repetition of the rescue whenever Velimirović's credibility is challenged is profoundly misleading. The fact that the bishop saved concrete individuals, more importantly the family of a personal friend, does not and should not in any way undermine the valid criticism of antisemitic views which appear in some of his writing. Lebl points out that "there is proof that the greatest antisemites, including Hitler and his accomplices in the Holocaust as well as Ante Pavelić and other Ustasha leaders, out of whatever motive, saved a certain number of Jews, while at the same time being responsible for the death of others, sometimes millions of them" (A. Lebl, 2002, p. iv). Lebl does not allege that Velimirović was in any way responsible for the death of Jews, but highlights an important broader issue. A single act should not be used to divert attention from Velimirović's broader perspective, which was demonstrably antisemitic. Noting a similar tendency in representations of the stance of the Catholic Church towards Nazi Germany, Daniel Goldhagen (2002) refers to this strategy as the "prettifying procedure," where the audience is "mislead with concrete stories and memorable images" of relatively rare instances of commendable conduct which are used to conceal the far more common instances of contempt for the Jews (p. 59). In Velimirović's case the episode described in the letter by Ela Najhaus, qualifies Bishop Nikolaj for the status of what Hilberg (1993) calls a "selective helper": someone who assists specific individuals (often friends or former business associates) as an extension of the bonds which existed before the war (p. 213). And yet in popular representation, this event is often treated as representative of Velimirović's overall stance towards Jews. In the above quotations Nešić interpreted the letter as proof that Nikolaj "did not hate any people, and of course he did not hate the Jewish people," while Ranković uses it to support the claim that "objectively" there is no antisemitism in Velimirović's work. In the book *Bishop Nikolaj and the New Testament on the Jews*, Predrag Samardžić is referring to Najhaus's letter when he notes that "it is a fact, and there are living witnesses to support this: the Bishop only did good for everyone, and this includes Jews" (2004, p. 12). In an article published in *Danas* in July 2002, Branislav Skrobonja, editor of the publication *Glasnik Kosova i Metohije*, went as far as to claim that one of the reasons why in 1942 German authorities moved Velimirović from Ljubostinja to Vojlovica, "where the conditions were a lot worse," was that they discovered that he was "protecting a Jewish family" (Skrobonja, 2002). This claim is not based on any historical evidence but its aim is clear: to link the myth of martyrdom to the story of the rescue, and present Nikolaj as someone who suffered because he helped Jews.

The most serious manipulation with the fate of the Najhaus family can be found in the aforementioned book by Predrag Samardžić, where he makes the following claim:

> We have received information that Nikolaj was about to be included among the Righteous Among the Nations by the Jewish state, for his role in the rescue of Jews during World War II, for which there is incontrovertible evidence according to the strictest criteria. However, his inclusion among the Righteous gentiles was slowed down by this anti-Serbian and anti-Orthodox campaign, concealed behind Nikolaj's alleged antisemitism, to which you, "comrade" professor, made a significant contribution. (Samardžić, 2004, p. 141)

This paragraph (in which Samardžić is addressing the author of this book) is profoundly misleading. It mentions Nikolaj Velimirović's inclusion among the "Righteous Among the Nations," the highest accolade awarded to those who helped Jews during the Nazi era, not as something that Samardžić considers to be desirable or deserved, but as something that seemed inevitable until it was delayed by the ongoing "anti-Serbian and anti-Orthodox campaign." And yet according to information obtained from the Yad Vashem Remembrance Authority in Jerusalem in March 2005—and therefore three months after Samardžić's book was published—Velimirović was not only never considered for this honor, but was never even recommended for it by anyone. Although the origin of Samardžić's claim remains a mystery, its intention is more transparent. Like other similar efforts, it reinforces the view of Nikolaj as a hero and a savior of Jews and places the events in Trstenik, along with the martyrdom at Dachau, at the centre of his war-time efforts. In the same vein, the somewhat vague headline "Bishop Nikolaj saved Jews"—which habitually precedes the transcript of the letter—might be interpreted by readers as suggesting that this was Velimirović's principal preoccupation during the war.

The reference to Velimirović's status as a benefactor and savior of Jews, as well as the argument that his writing cannot be satisfactorily appraised, especially by those "outsiders" with inadequate strength of faith, can both be said to have significant repressive qualities. Both are a form of "topic change," a way of minimizing the relevance of controversy as an object of memory. And yet, in recent years, the attempts to keep Velimirović's antisemitism off the conversational agenda have co-existed with a greater willingness by the bishop's supporters to openly and often spontaneously discuss the controversy in the media, in public appearances, and in newspaper articles. This became acutely visible in the interviews, conducted for the purposes of this study, with a number of Velimirović's supporters. Interviewees were told that the researcher, who is resident in the UK, is conducting a study on "the role of Orthodoxy in contemporary Serbian society" and that part of the project involves the examination of the "role of Nikolaj Velimirović in present-day Serbian culture." The project was deliberately described in a way that did not explicitly mention, as the main focus of research, the controversy surrounding Bishop Velimirović's personal history. This minor deception was motivated by the desire to allow the respondents to choose whether or not they would engage in the debate about the controversies surrounding Velimirović's work.

Rather than sidestepping the issue, most of the interviewees engaged in very elaborate expositions of denial. The willingness of the respondents to speak about contentious matters confirmed van Dijk's observation that denials "can be pre-emptive," "focusing on possible inferences of the interlocutor" not ones that are explicitly made (van Dijk, 1992, p. 91). On the other hand, the willingness to openly deal with criticism of Nikolaj Velimirović, in an interview situation that was in no way adversarial, can be said to be illustrative of an important aspect of moral accountability management. Denial of prejudice is not merely a discourse of justification, but also self-justification. The need to evade blame and disapproval associated with accusations of prejudice is not just a feature of the way individuals argue with those who do not share their views, but of the very way in which they think and remember. In other words, in the broader social context marked by the proliferation in critical discourse, controversy has become so deeply embedded in the discourse surrounding Velimirović's life that denials are now an intrinsic part of the memory of Bishop Nikolaj.

Some attempts to directly address the controversy surrounding Velimirović's antisemitism, in particular that found in the book *Words to the Serbian People Through the Dungeon Window*, have been apparent since the late 1980. From the very early days, supporters occasionally trivialized the book's significance, claiming that Bishop Nikolaj never wanted his sermons to be published. At the time of the publication of the first edition of the book in 1985, Bishop Lavrentije Trifunović explained the delayed publication of the controversial sermons by revealing that Velimirović attached to the manuscript a note, stating "not for publication" (Trifunović, 1998). On several occasions since then—when called upon to reflect on the books antisemitic message—Atanasije Jevtić invoked Bishop Nikolaj's alleged moratorium as a means of undermining the significance of the book. He noted for instance that *Words to the Serbian People Through the Dungeon Window* was not "actually uttered as a message to the Serbian people," but was "merely" a "collection of casual notes, written on toilet paper, notes which Nikolaj never intended for publication" (Jevtić, 1986a, p. 12). Yet the distancing from the book's message is only partial. Only a few sentences after referring to the work as a collection of "casual notes" for private consumption, Atanasije Jevtić described it also as a work whose "theological, philosophical, historiographic, and literary value should not be undermined by politically motivated misinterpretations" (ibid.).

Another form of distancing involves the argument that controversial passages from the book, which are regularly quoted in critical literature, had been "taken out of context." In 1987, nationalist historian Borivoje Karapandžić argued that Velimirović's critics, the "atheistic journalists in Yugoslavia, out of the 172-page book, quote just one sheet of paper, two pages, which the communist press satanically picked out in order to denigrate the bishop as an antisemite and an enemy of Judaism" (speech delivered in Cleveland, Ohio, in 1987; cited in Janković, 2002b, p. 203). Ljubomir Ranković said in the interview that "you cannot throw away 12,000 pages on account of this one page from Words to the Serbian people." In *Bishop Nikolaj and the New Testament on the Jews*, Predrag Samardžić speaks of the "incriminating words" are "in proportion to Bishop Nikolaj's overall opus just a speck of dust" (Samardžić, 2004, p. 116; see also Jevtić, 1986a; Krstić, 2002). Protopresbyter Milan Janković stated in his written response to my questions that "certain gentlemen (let us call them that) base their hatred on what appears on two pages, in only a couple of sentences of the seventy-seventh sermon [in *Words to the Serbian People Through the Dungeon Window*] and they spit their hatred like a snake in all directions."

This distancing appears to suggest that Velimirović's supporters implicitly acknowledge that, in isolation, the controversial passages in the book appear prejudicial. However, by claiming that the infamous quotations present de-contextualised exceptions whose meaning has been deliberately "taken out of context" and subverted so as to portray the author in a negative light, supporters play down Velimirović's stance on Jews as a marginal aspect of his life's work. Crucially, by limiting the distancing to "just one sheet of paper, two pages" out of *Words to the Serbian People Through the Dungeon Window*, the rest of Velimirovic's work where antisemitic claims are also to be found is conveniently absolved from criticism. This is similar to the strategy employed by Slobodan Mileusnić who refused to comment on Velimirović's antisemitism on the grounds that he "never studied the bishop's writing of *that historical period*" (see earlier quotation; emphasis added). In all of these instances, Velimirović's controversial views are presented as isolated incidents and as such are treated as being of little interest and, therefore, as "forgettable."

The widespread tendency to argue that critical perspectives on Velimirović stance on Jews are the result of the misinterpretation is often followed by attempts to provide the "correct" and appropriately "contextualized" reading. As we will see, the favorable interpretation on which supporters insist involves the renegotiation of the boundaries of the term "antisemitism" and the management of a semantic distinction between the seemingly unobjectionable creed of Christian anti-Judaism on the one hand, and the anti-normative ideology of secular, Nazi antisemitism on the other.

The two kinds of antisemitism: The rhetoric of interpretative denial

Research on the rhetorical and argumentative aspects of language and communication frequently points out that terms used to label and categorize social phenomena should not be regarded as predetermined, natural phenomena, with decidable and demonstrable referents in empirical reality, but as contestable, fluid, and locally contingent entities which are constituted in social interaction (Billig, 1987; Billig et al., 1988; Edwards, 1997; Wetherell and Potter, 1992). The socially constructed nature of categories reflects their inherently argumentative quality. Categories are invoked, negotiated, and disputed in the context of discursive acts, the aim of which is to accomplish rhetorical goals such as to legitimize or to contest a particular version or description of reality.

The argumentative nature of categorization has been shown to have important implications for the study of prejudice. Because prejudice depends on the existence of categories, allegations and denials of prejudice inevitably involve a debate about the meaning of relevant social objects such as "gender," "race," "ethnicity," etc. (Billig et al., 1988). Moreover, terms such as "racism," "tolerance," "discrimination," and "equality," around which the language of intergroup relations revolves, are themselves topicalized in discourse. Their meaning is constructed and their relevance negotiated in the context of manufacturing accusations, refuting criticism, apportioning blame, or positioning a view in relation to prevailing ethical norms (Billig, 1987; Edwards, 1997).

The term "antisemitism" is a good example of a disputed and negotiated social category. In recent years, scholars, journalists, commentators, politicians, and intellectuals in the West have debated the meaning of the term in the context of the controversy surrounding the distinction between the "old" antisemitism of the Right and the "new" antisemitism of the liberal Left (see Chesler, 2003; Foxman, 2003; Iganski and Kosmin, 2003). At the heart of this often-heated dispute has been another contested categorization, that which distinguishes the critique of Jews from the critique of Israel (see contributions on the topic in Iganski and Kosmin, 2003; and Rosenbaum, 2004). Public attention has recently focused also on some older distinctions related to the problem of antisemitism. The release in 2003 of Mel Gibson's film *The Passion of the Christ* revived the debate about the persistence of Christian antisemitism and its status in the moral universe *vis-à-vis* twentieth and twenty-first century variants of antisemitism (Lawler, 2004; Pawlikowski, 2004; United States Conference of Catholic Bishops, 2004; etc.).

An impassioned debate about the nature and the meaning of the term "antisemitism" dominates the argumentative context surrounding Velimirović's remembrance in contemporary Serbia. In affirmative accounts of Velimirović's position on Jews—articulated in public discourse around the time of the canonization—denials and justifications of his contested stance centered around the discussion of what antisemitism "really" is and how Velimirović's viewpoint fits into the negotiated definition of the term.

Shortly after the canonization of Nikolaj Velimirović was announced by the Assembly of Bishops of the Serbian Orthodox Church, Deacon Ljubomir Ranković discussed the new saint's contentious views in a debate on *Radio Free Europe*. He argued the following: "The antisemitism, let's accept that term, of Bishop Nikolaj was on a theological, or rather biblical level. That kind of antisemitism is present in the Bible itself, from the beginning, namely the Book of Moses, all the way through until the arrival of Lord Jesus Christ in the New Testament" (*RFE/RL*, June 2, 2003). A week earlier Ranković similarly noted that "the mention of Jews in *Words to the Serbian People Through the Dungeon Window* is a purely theological question" (Ranković, 2003d). Matija Bećković, one of Serbia's best-known nationalist poets and a regular participant in commemorative activities devoted to Nikolaj Velimirović, remarked in the interview conducted for the purposes of this study that the controversial writings on Jews are "purely biblical discussions, and the 'antisemitic' phrases [in his writing] are actually far more common in the writings of Jews themselves, in the Old Testament... you could call them [antisemitic] only in the context of a malicious interpretation."

Apparent in these quotations, which are representative of the material examined in the study, is first of all the attempt at distancing from the term "antisemitism." The qualification is accepted reluctantly ("let's accept the term") or placed in inverted commas (whether literally, in writing, or by intonation in interviews and audio records). On other occasions, the word antisemitism is prefaced with the word "so-called." The opening sentence of Predrag Samardžić's book *Bishop Nikolaj and the New Testament on the Jews* defines its subject matter as the "so-called 'antisemitism' of Bishop Nikolaj" (Samardžić, 2004, p. 5). The use of inverted commas and the word "so-called" suggests that the validity and the appropriateness of the term "antisemitism," as the descriptor of Velimirović's position on Jews, are treated as problematic. The insinuation that the bishop was antisemitic is attributed, in the words of Matija Bećković, to disingenuous, "malicious interpretation." At the same time, accusations are not rejected outright. It is not denied that Velimirović was critical about Jews, but the nature of the alleged offence is "re-categorised as something less negative or more excusable" (Wetherell and Potter, 1992, p. 212). Speakers employ the tactic of particularization (Billig, 1987) or what Stanley Cohen (2001) calls "interpretative denial": Velimirović's stance towards Jews is offered as a special case, a specific type of antisemitism ("biblical" or "theological"), which is understood to be different, in terms of both substance and consequence, to that against which there exists an implicitly acknowledged social norm.

The emphasis on the "theological" or "biblical" nature of Velimirović's antisemitism implies that a contrast can be drawn between this legitimate form of criticism of Jews and some kind of "real" antisemitism that warrants moral censure. Velimirović's stance is repeatedly referred to as "purely theological" or "purely biblical." The notion of "purity" in this case suggests that Velimirović's views are confined to the acceptable category of criticism of Jews, and therefore unpolluted by elements of other discredited antisemitic traditions. During our conversation in August 2003, Deacon Ljubomir Ranković revealed that the "other" kind of antisemitism is that propagated by the Nazis:

> [Velimirović 's] antisemitism is, in the real sense of the word, of the only kind that it can be, namely biblical. [...] The Old Testament criticizes the Jewish people for rejecting God, while the "antisemitism" of the New Testament is when Jews are criticized for crucifying the Lord Jesus Christ. [...] All of this—shall I say animosity—that may exist among Christians towards Jews is there because they are enemies of Christ. That and such [antisemitism] exist in the writing of Bishop Nikolaj. We might say that that is anti-Judaism, a critique of Judaism, but in no way is it antisemitism. When one says antisemitism, the allusion is to Hitler, crematoria, etc. This is not the case at all in Velimirović 's writing.'

Similarly, in the article "Serbs and Jews" examined in the previous chapter, Vladimir Dimitrijević contested the view that Bishop Nikolaj was antisemitic on the grounds that he had nothing to do "with Nazi theories of race," or with the "crazy, pagan racism of Hitler's followers" (Dimitrijević, 2004, p. 78). Predrag Samardžić (2004) also discusses the definition of antisemitism. He notes that "the term antisemitism is of recent, neopagan origin." Antisemitism existed as a social problem "in the era before the New Testament, in Egypt, around Alexandria, where a significant Jewish community lived at the time of the Roman empire" (2004, p. 31). Having skipped almost two thousand years of history, Samardžić then suggests that antisemitism returned only in "neopagan times," when Wilhelm Marr, who coined the term "antisemitism," began to argue for the social exclusion of Jews in Germany. Christian antisemitism is conveniently disqualified from this historical account, presumably because the phenomenon is not seen as fitting the category "antisemitism." Samardžić acknowledges that in the intervening period "persecution of Jews was carried out most frequently in the name of some Christ and some Christianity," but the qualifier "some"—which precedes the reference to Christ and Christianity—absolves the Christian Church and its teaching as a whole from any responsibility. This is because "authentic Christians must not, or rather cannot hate or persecute anyone, least of all the Jews. This is, if for no other reason, because they are of Christ's 'kinfolk by natural descent' (Rim. 9:3–5). And because 'it is from the Jews that salvation comes' (John 4:22)" (p. 32).

The differentiation between antisemitism and anti-Judaism, implicit in the distinction between "biblical" or "Christian" antisemitism and that of the Nazis, is common across Christendom. Carroll (2002) writes that the demarcation between "antisemitism and anti-Judaism, with the clear meaning that the latter [is] an appropriate part of the defense of faith" (p. 40) had been a common feature of Catholic education prior to the Second Vatican Council. Most post-Holocaust Catholic scholars distinguish between "normal anti-Judaism" which relates to the core theological disagreement between Christianity and Judaism, and abnormal antisemitism, which, in the words of Robert Chazan, consists of "embellishments that are extremely harsh, that lack grounding in fundamental Christian texts and teachings and that never gained the respectability of widespread ecclesiastical approbation" (cited in Carroll, 2002, p. 274). The declaration *We Remember: Reflection on the Shoah* issued by the Vatican in March 1998 also distinguished between traditional Christian anti-Judaism and the "late 18th and early 19th century racist theories which provided the foundations of National Socialism," although on this occasion the Vatican expressed regret over the "longstanding sentiment of distrust and hostility" towards Jews implicit in "anti- Judaism" (cited in Carroll, 2002, pp. 381–382).

This exercise in the redrawing of boundaries of antisemitism can play an important role in the denial of prejudice. Billig et al. (1988) have demonstrated how, in the discourse of the Right, a controversial political position on matters of race and ethnic relations can be effectively justified by means of a favorable comparison with a more radical view that is unambiguously extremist (see also Billig, 1990). For Velimirović 's supporters, contrasting "theological antisemitism" with a more extreme and widely discredited position, namely "Nazi antisemitism," constitutes an easily accessible and convincing means of constructing the bishop's stance towards Jews as acceptable. Wodak (1991) documents a similar phenomenon in contemporary Austria, where equating antisemitism with Nazi racist theories is used to divert attention away from other antisemitic traditions, including that rooted in Christianity.

It is also noteworthy that in Christian rhetoric, both in Serbia and elsewhere, the veracity of the distinction between anti-Judaism and antisemitism tends to be assumed rather than supported with suitable empirical or historical evidence. As Goldhagen (2002) notes, "Those asserting [the difference between antisemitism and anti-Judaism] do not do the minimum necessary to show it, such as seriously discussing the nature of antisemitism and its varieties, and compare the two kinds antisemitism in depth according to clear evaluative criteria, in order to ascertain what their relationship is. They do not discuss the actual historical relationship of the Church's antisemitism and modern European antisemitism" (p. 78).

This feature of the argument is of rhetorical significance as it points once again to the strategy of "apparent denial" (van Dijk, 1992, 1993) examined earlier. The absence of corroboration is used to present a version of reality as self-evident and based on common sense. In the present case, the distinction between "anti-Judaism" and "antisemitism" is articulated in a way that presents the differentiation between acceptable and unacceptable critique of Jews as consensual. In the discourse of Velimirović's remembrance, the claim that the ideas of Christian anti-Judaism have nothing in common with Nazi antisemitism is invoked and presented as so normal and obvious, that it does not require elaboration or validation.

Repeating the word of God: Authority of the Gospels and the reification of antisemitic discourse

The distinction between anti-Judaism and antisemitism, which is constitutive of denial of prejudice, rests on the assumption that the former is an acceptable ideological position. This assumed legitimacy and acceptability needs to be worked up discursively. In the case of the management of Velimirović's moral accountability, by far the most common strategy of legitimization involves the argument that anti-Jewish proclamations apparent in the bishop's writing originate directly from the Holy Scriptures.

Mladen Obradović, leader of Obraz, argued in the interview conducted for this study that, in writing about Jews, Velimirović "merely states some historical truths":

> I will remind you for instance that in the Old Testament you have their own, Jewish Old Testament prophets, therefore members of that same people, who said many [similar] things about their own people who rejected God… Also, you have the very words of the Lord Jesus Christ when he says to the Pharisees that they are a "brood of vipers" or that their father is the Devil; Bishop Nikolaj merely quotes the Gospels.

Deacon Ljubomir Ranković wrote the following in the daily *Glas Javnosti*:

> When he says of Jews that "their father is the Devil," the bishop quotes and interprets the words of the Lord Jesus Christ—a Jew in body—words which were noted down by a Jew, the apostle and evangelist John: "Your [Jews'] father is the devil, and you choose to carry out your father's desires. He was a murderer from the beginning, and is not rooted in the truth; there is no truth in him. When he tells a lie he is speaking his own language, for he is a liar and a father of lies" (John 8:44). (Ranković, 2003d)

Ranković made the same claim on *Radio Free Europe* when he said that "when Bishop Nikolaj speaks of Jews that their father is the devil, he is practically quoting the words of Christ the Lord" (*RFE/RL*, June 2, 2003).

A similar argument was invoked by Protopresbyter Milan Janković, secretary of the synod of the Serbian Orthodox Church. In response to the invitation to comment on the controversy surrounding Velimirović 's writing on Jews, he noted that references to Jews in *Words to the Serbian People through the Dungeon Window*

> were not invented by Bishop Nikolaj, but were uttered by Lord Jesus Christ, so the bishop merely cites them [Jews] as a bad example which the Serbian people should not follow. Those who do not believe this should read the words of the Holy Evangelists, especially John the Evangelist (John 18:12–19:24), who concludes: "It was there from the beginning; we have heard it; we have seen it with our own eyes, we looked upon it, and felt it with our own hands [...] we have seen it and bear our testimony; we declare to you the eternal life which was with the Father and which was made visible to us" (John 1:1–2).

The cited extracts maintain that Velimirović's controversial claims are a paraphrase of the Bible. In making this claim speakers resort to what Daniel Goldhagen (2002) refers to as the "widespread convention" within contemporary Christian rhetoric, whereby it is denied that "[a] member of the Church was antisemitic even if he believed and may also have spread the anti-Jewish libels of the Christian bible... [on the grounds that] their antisemitism was 'only' of the sort that was deeply embedded in Christianity itself" (p. 22).

Claims about the biblical origins of Velimirović's antisemitism are accompanied by words such as "practically" or "merely": Velimirović "is practically quoting" Christ's words and "simply quotes the Gospels." The use of these terms is not haphazard. "Just," "merely," or "only" marks a response as a defense, by means of which the speaker rejects, in this case Velimirović's culpability for making a potentially criticisable claim (Billig, 1999a; Shweder and Much, 1987). By suggesting that Velimirović was "merely" quoting the Gospels, his supporters shift the responsibility for his controversial stance to the most reliable of sources, Christ's apostles.

In the above examples, speakers often quote the New Testament and refer to the authors of the Gospels as eyewitnesses who directly experienced the described events. Deacon Ljubomir Ranković emphasizes that Christ's words—which he quotes from the Gospels—were "noted down" by an observer, "the apostle and evangelist John." In Janković's case, the effectiveness of corroboration is enhanced with the passage from the First Letter of John, which stresses the three modalities by which the "truth" of the New Testament had been experienced by the apostles: "we have *heard* it, we have *seen* it with our own eyes, we looked upon it, and *felt* it with our own hands" (emphasis added). Nikolaj Velimirović himself resorted to a similar defensive strategy when fending off attacks on his reputation. In 1928, shortly after the Belgrade Rabbi Isak Alkalaj accused him of promoting antisemitism, Velimirović depicted Rabbi Alkalaj as belonging to the unreasonable minority of Jews by stating that "I know from conversations with many conscientious and cultured Jews, that they have distanced themselves from the unfair judges of Christ and have condemned their narrow-mindedness and blindness in the attempt to detach the Jewish people from those who led and misled them astray" (Velimirović, 1928c, p. 42). He defended his controversial sermon by citing, as the greatest authority, "a very small book, called the New Testament, and the unparalleled drama described in it":

> That book was written by four Jews, followers of Christ. Why four and not just one or two? For courts in this world, two witnesses are enough. Through God's providence, four witnesses wrote this book: twice the number required by any court of this world—so that people would believe in the truth of the testimony. All four witnesses described the trial of Jesus Christ in Jerusalem... Each stage of the trial of Jesus Christ is described in detail in the Gospels. (p. 43)

By emphasizing that there were four witnesses, Velimirović not only attended to the requirement for corroboration, which is essential for establishing factuality of potentially disputable claims (see Potter, 1996; Wooffitt, 1992), but also incorporated within it the rhetoric of quantification (Reeves, 1983). Four witnesses is twice the number required by ordinary courts, suggesting therefore that even the greatest of skeptics ought to be convinced. Also, Velimirović makes the reference to "conscientious and cultured Jews," who have sided with him. The orientation to these contemporary Jews as "conscientious" is significant. Although the crucifixion is blamed on the "unfair judges of Christ," allusion to Jewish "conscience" implies that even contemporary Jews *qua* Jews have something to feel guilty about, which is the very assumption that provoked Rabbi Alkalaj's protest. Furthermore, Velimirović hints at the possibility that the culpability for crucifixion might not be limited to the "unfair judges" given that those judges "led and misled" the whole of the Jewish people astray.

The effort to build up the credibility and reliability of the New Testament as a historically accurate story of Jesus' life and death acts as an "externalising device" (Woolgar, 1988) which turns the attention away from Velimirović as a morally accountable agent and exonerates him from culpability for the claims which he makes. A "mere" citation from the Bible is presented as separate from the bishop's potentially biased motives and intentions and therefore as unproblematic. For the same reason, around the time of the controversy surrounding his film *The Passion of the Christ*, Mel Gibson defended his contentious portrayal of Jews by noting that he merely conveyed the story as it was told by "reliable sources," "eyewitnesses," "guys [the apostles] who were there" (Boyer, 2004, p. 324). Gibson also called for the inclusion in the film of the controversial passage from Matthew 27:25 ("His blood be upon us and upon our Children") by suggesting that "it happened, it was said" (Boyer, 2004, p. 316). Defenders of *The Passion of the Christ* frequently cite the verdict about the film "it is as it was" attributed (inaccurately, according to official sources) to Pope John Paul II as absolving the film from criticism. Just as in Velimirović's case, these arguments against accusations of antisemitism rest on the conjecture that something that is "true" cannot be prejudicial, and consequently that everything found in the Gospels is *a priori* above suspicion.

The premise regarding the factuality of the Gospels is, however, highly problematic. Orientation to the Bible as the definitive source of truth neglects the historicity of the Gospels and the fact that they were not written by eyewitnesses, but by people who lived in the period after the destruction of the Temple in 70 AD, and in a manner that reflected the conflicts and debates of first-century religious politics (Carroll, 2002; Hellig, 2002; Kosidowski, 1998; Ruether, 1974; Wistrich, 1991). The Gospels were created at a time of vicious competition over spiritual influence between Judaism and the emerging Christian religion. The story of the life and death of Jesus was written with the aim of disparaging Jews and Judaism in the context of bitter religious rivalry, and persuade the population tempted by the promises of Judaism that, by failing to accept Jesus as the Messiah, Jews renounced their status as the chosen people and became the "reprobate people" who did not "hear the word of God" and therefore "did not belong to God." In other words, early Christianity effectively theorized its existence "as an ongoing opposition to the Jews" (Bauman, 1991, p. 38) and conceived its teaching as a polemic against Judaism. The status of Judaism as "Christianity's negative other" (Carroll, 2002, p. 564) was exacerbated by the deicide accusation epitomized in the sentence in Matthew 27:25: "His Blood be upon us and upon our Children!" This indictment against Jews, which presented the death of Jesus as the responsibility of the Jewish people *en mass* and forever, cast the Jews—the "children of the devil"—as "cosmic villains in the Christian doctrine of atonement" (Hellig, 2002, p. 168).

Tabak (2000) argues that the belief in the inherent truth of the Gospels—a constant theme in the rhetoric of Velimirović's supporters—is possibly even stronger in the Orthodox world than in other Christian denominations. For the Orthodox, the Holy Tradition, which includes the Bible, Service and Prayer books, decrees of Ecumenical Councils, writings of the Holy Fathers of the Church, and the "whole historical experience of the church" set down before the end of the 8th century is deemed as being "from God." The "sacred character" of the Holy Tradition makes its religious and cultural value unquestionable. For this reason in Russia and elsewhere in the Orthodox world, "the most extreme Orthodox antisemites can logically claim that their monstrous anti-Jewish invective is based upon 'Church teaching'" (Tabak, 2000).

The status of the traditional Christian contempt for Jews in Orthodox Christian cultures is enhanced by the high esteem in which Orthodoxy holds the Holy Fathers of the Church, the likes of St John Chrysostom, Origen, St Augustine, and others. The entire work of the founding fathers, including the notorious Adversus Judaeos tradition—which laid the foundation for medieval Jewish demonology (Trachtenberg, 1983)—is considered part of the Holy Tradition, and is therefore viewed as sacred and incontestable. As is the case with the

Gospels, the unquestioned veneration of the Church Fathers overlooks the historical contingency of their work. The so-called "Patristic period," spanning from the 2nd to the 4th century was a time of continued competition between Christians and Jews over the hearts and minds of converts in the Hellenistic world (Carroll, 2002; Ruether, 1974; Wistrich, 1991). As a result, the writing of the founding fathers contains numerous propagandist anti-Jewish declarations, such as St John Chrysostom's verdict that that the synagogue is "the temple of Demons" or that Jews are "dogs, stiff-necked, gluttonous drunkards [...] beasts unfit for work [...] fit for killing, for slaughter." Within the formal religious dogma of the Orthodox Church even these statements are regarded as valid interpretation of God's word, although they are seldom articulated or reiterated.

The "holy" status, within Orthodox culture, of the anti-Jewish tirades of the founding fathers has important implications with regard to the denial of Velimirović's antisemitism. As was noted earlier, following the trend started by Father Justin Popović in the 1950s, Velimirović is customarily referred to, in religious literature, as the "New Chrysostom," the "Second Chrysostom," or the "Serbian Chrysostom." Bishop Nikolaj is occasionally compared to other theologians of the patristic period. In the quotation cited earlier in this chapter, Bishop Artemije Radosavljević said that Nikolaj "stands shoulder to shoulder with Origen, St John Chrysostom, and the Blessed Augustine," all of whom are known for their antisemitic diatribes (see Ruether, 1974). Importantly however, Velimirović's supporters seldom invoke the authority of the fathers of the Church with the purpose of justifying Bishop Nikolaj's antisemitic views. The reason for likening Velimirović to St John Chrysostom lies not in their shared perspective on Jews, but in what is deemed to be comparable significance as theologians, preachers and evangelists. Nonetheless, Velimirović's controversial writings derive authority from the parallel. The comparison with Chrysostom enhances the view of Velimirović's work as being of immense merit and importance. Two individuals, whose work is separated by sixteen centuries of history, are presented—through continuous association—as identical, at least in terms of relevance and moral authority. In July 2002, in an interview to the daily *Danas*, Mirko Đorđević—sociologist of religion and a vocal critic of Nikolaj Velimirović—commented on the tendency among the bishop's fans to refer to their hero as the "New Chrysostom." He suggested that the only thing that the two theologians have in common is their antisemitism (M. Đorđević, 2002, p. v). A month later, in a lengthy rejoinder published in *Danas*, Deacon Radoš Mladenović and Vladimir Dimitrijević dismissed Đorđević's claims by invoking the difference between anti-Judaism and antisemitism:

> The sermons [by St John Chrysostom] are not against Jews but against Talmudic Judaism as a religion, which declared Christ, the Son of God a "false prophet" and "son of a loose woman." The tradition of criticism of Talmudic and Rabbinical Judaism dates back to the time of the Holy Apostles Paul and John (who were themselves Jews, and therefore cannot be branded "antisemites"), through St Justin the Philosopher to St John Chrysostom. That, broadly speaking is apologetics, because the Holy Fathers were not only arguing against this type of Judaism, but also against paganism and Gnosticism. French Cardinal Lustiger, a baptized Jew, refers to the tendency to attribute Hitler's antisemitism to the Holy Fathers as the "reading of Chrysostom in the light of Mein Kampf" and regards it as morally unacceptable and theologically illiterate. (Mladenović & Dimitrijević, 2002, p. 8)

In proposing the distinction between anti-Judaism and antisemitism, Mladenović and Dimitrijević were defending not just St John Chrysostom's views, but also those of Velimirović. Whatever counts for one seemed also to count for the other, hinting at the possibility that the representation and perceived significance of the two theologians is superimposed in the historical imagination of Velimirović's supporters. In his article "Serbs and Jews," published a year earlier, Dimitrijević already indicated that he regards Chrysostom's and Velimirović's "anti-Judaism" to be comparable when he wrote that "Holy Bishop Nikolaj criticized Christians who departed from Christ and adopted the view of those Jews who believe Christ to be a 'false prophet.' St John Chrysostom criticized those Christians who renounced their church and went to pray in the Synagogue. That has nothing to do with the crazy, pagan racism of Hitler's followers" (Dimitrijević, 2004, p. 78).

The equivalence between Chrysostom and Velimirović apparent in these examples is particularly important because it removes the latter's outlook from the ideological context of the political culture of the 1930s, and elevates it onto the same plain as the already de-contextualized and de-historicized writing of the fourth century founding fathers of the Church. Velimirović's stance towards Jews is made to appear not as an objectionable, obsolete, and historically contingent political position, but as something that, along with St John the Chrysostom's work belongs to the "eternal Truth" proclaimed in the Holy Tradition. Mladenović's and Dimitrijević's insinuation that it is "theologically illiterate" and "morally unacceptable" to read Chrysostom's antisemitic harangues "in the light of Mein Kampf" is also applied to Velimirović's writing, thus conveniently overlooking the fact that Velimirović's and Hitler's works, in spite of the important differences, do in fact belong to the same historical period.

In invoking the "Biblical" nature of Velimirović's antisemitism, the bishop's supporters seldom forget to note that the authors of the New Testament were themselves Jews. Ranković for instance mentioned that Christ was a "Jew in body," while Velimirović, in the 1928 polemic with Rabbi Alkalaj alluded twice to the fact that the Gospels had been written by "four Jews." This feature of the account presents the controversial stance not as indexical of the bishop's prejudices and ideological commitments but as a common view, shared even by representatives of the people against whom he is alleged to be biased (see Edwards, 2004). This point is sometimes made explicit. In the aforementioned letter published in *Danas* in August 2002, Mladenović and Dimitrijević defended Velimirović's antisemitic passages on the grounds that they are comparable to the writings of apostles Paul and John, "who were themselves Jews, and therefore cannot be branded 'antisemites'" (Mladenović and Dimitrijević, 2002, p. 8). Velimirović's views are compared to the Old Testament tradition for the same reason. Matija Bećković was cited earlier as stating that the bishop's position on Jews is to be found "in the writing of Jews themselves, in the Old Testament." Mladen Obradović also noted during our conversation that "in the Old Testament you have their own, Jewish Old Testament prophets, therefore members of that same people, who said many [similar] things about their own people who rejected God [...] These are the words of prophet Jeremiah: Jews abandoned God and became the sons of Satan." The rhetorical value of the comparison with the Old Testament prophets relies not just on the fact that they were Jews, but also on the exceptional attributes traditionally ascribed to biblical prophets. Jews, as well as Christians, believe them to have possessed superior knowledge about the nature of the world, which originates directly from God.

An extension of the comparison between Velimirović's writings on Jews and the biblical texts is the portrayal of the bishop's "theological antisemitism" as motivated by divine love for the Jews and a righteous concern for their spiritual wellbeing. In the article in the daily *Glas Javnosti* published shortly after Velimirović's canonization, Deacon Ljubomir Ranković wrote that "those who today defend the Jews from the bishop are causing the greatest damage to Jews themselves" (Ranković, 2003d). Implicit in this argument is the claim that the only hope of redemption for Jews lies in their acceptance of Jesus and conversion to Christianity. Critics of Nikolaj Velimirović are seen as obstructing this desired outcome. In a commemorative speech in May 2003, reported by *Radio B92*, Bishop of Montenegro Amfilohije Radović—one of the most influential and highly regarded religious dignitaries in Serbia—likened Velimirović's views to the lamentations of "Isaiah, Jeremiah, Ezekiel, and Daniel" and interpreted them as motivated not "by hate, but by the most profound love, pain, suffering, and concern" for the Jews. On another occasion, Radović noted that "the bitter and crude things" that Nikolaj said about "the people of Israel" were an attempt to "sober up those he addressed and return them to the path of Christ" (A. Radović, 2003, p. 510). The same claim was made by Dejan Apostolović, a contributor to the letters page in the daily newspaper *Danas* where he regularly defends the integrity and reputation of Nikolaj Velimirović:

> So, does the Holy Bishop Nikolaj hate anyone, or Jews in particular? Did Jesus hate the Jews and other people when he criticized them, or hated their sins? If Jesus had had within him any hate towards others would he have willingly suffered for those same people, or have prayed for them while dying on the Cross? It is the duty of holy people to educate humankind and to scold them. Saints are not politicians who play up to public opinion. God gave them the duty to deliver the souls of their people and those of other peoples. Therefore, just as Poles, Serbs, Russians, and other people are not immune to criticism, Jews should not be either. Therefore, Bishop Nikolaj clearly warns that there must

> not be any hatred towards man. From this I conclude that if I do not try to rid myself of the plague [sin] and I do not help my brother to do the same, then I nurture both plagues [sins], and in doing so I nurture evil. No people, including the Jews, should defend themselves (if attacked) with anything other than with facts. Just like in a court of law. All the talk about religious hate, antisemitism, minority rights, and so on, are nothing but the simple masking of the truth and deception of the public. Maybe it would be better, instead of defending oneself, to take a look in the mirror, and recognize which criticisms are really well-founded. The road to salvation does not lead through the courts but through genuine repentance. (Apostolović, 2003)

Here too, Nikolaj's words about Jews are compared to those of Jesus, and presented as the words of divine love. Criticism of Jews is presented as part of Velimirović's God-given, saintly duty to tell harsh truths rather than pander to public opinion. Crucially, it is above all the Jews who are constructed as being in need of enlightenment. Bishop Nikolaj is presented as someone who attempted to help rid his Jewish "brothers" from sin, and prevent them from their continuing nurturing of "plague" and "evil." Apostolović also argues that "people," in this case the Jews, ought to defend themselves from Christian antisemitism with "facts." Yet in the very next sentence he implies that such facts do not exist, requiring the Jews to resort to "deception" and the "masking of the truth." According to Apostolović, instead of "defending themselves," Jews ought to "look into the mirror," in other words face the reality of the Christian interpretation of Jewish history and "repent." The letter does not make it explicitly clear what it is exactly that Jews are meant to repent for, but judging from the overall context it is for the rejection of Christ and deicide. Later in the article Apostolović provides directions to the "path to salvation" when he recommends that sinners should "read Bishop Nikolaj's books and head for the Church to find out for themselves where the genuine truth lies."

Implicit in the motive of "divine love" is one of the main tenets of Christian antisemitism, namely that Jews are collectively responsible for the death of Jesus and that their only hope of redemption lies in the acceptance of Christ and conversion to Christianity (Carroll, 2002; Hellig, 2002). In Velimirović's remembrance, the ideological and prejudicial undertones of this claim are moderated and concealed by the language of love. The bishop's supporters are drawing on the representation of love that assumes that sometimes one must be "cruel to be kind." Velimirović's writings are presented as a necessary pedagogical method, because, in the words of Amfilohije Radović, Nikolaj "criticized those he loved, because he loved them" (A. Radović, 2003, p. 510). Or as Branimir Nešić stated in the interview—it was "like with parents. Parents chastise those they love."

"Then we are all antisemities!": "Anti-Judaism" and Orthodox Christian identity

The invoked parallel between Velimirović's position on Jews and that of the Jewish protagonists of the Bible not only reifies the affirmative interpretation of the bishop's views, but also ironizes critical opinion. Deacon Ranković proposes that if Velimirović is to be considered an antisemite then "the Old Testament, which is in fact a Jewish book, [is] the biggest antisemitic pamphlet ever." Branimir Nešić suggests that if Nikolaj is an antisemite then "we are all antisemites and the New Testament ought to be banned." Protopresbyter Radovan Bigović mentioned during our conversation that "they claim that he was some kind of ideologue of antisemitism. I always say: if you follow that logic, then all Old Testament prophets would be branded antisemites. Jesus Christ would be an antisemite."

In these instances condemnations of Velimirović's views are reinterpreted in an exaggerated and overstated way that makes them look biased and unreasonable. Critical appraisals of the bishop's stance on Jews are presented as attacks on the fundamentals of the Christian faith and therefore as excessive, intolerant and spiteful. At the same time, the amplified representations of criticism reinforce the analogy between Velimirović's work and Biblical writings. The bishop's controversial stance is reaffirmed as being no worse or more criticizable than the contents of the Christian Bible.

Once Velimirović's position on Jews is constituted as part of Christian common sense, it becomes promoted not only as acceptable, but also as a normative feature of Orthodox identity. Branimir Nešić was cited earlier as stating that if Velimirović is an antisemite then "we," namely Orthodox Christians, "are all antisemites." Later in the interview, Nešić explained:

> It is a clash of two religions, the Jewish faith on the one hand and Christian faith on the other [...] Jews believe that Christ was not the Son of God. We are talking simply about a clash. It is a fact that we, Christians, believe that Jews crucified Christ. This is a fact and it is obvious. Christ said: My blood on you and your children, but he never said that Jews should be murdered, and neither did Bishop Nikolaj, although he did say that the Jews had betrayed Christ. One cannot expect an Orthodox bishop to say that the Jews were right and that Christ was not the Son of God. Of course he will condemn the crucifixion. From that standpoint I think that the criticism of Jews is correct. I as a Christian believe that what they are doing confirms the story of the New Testament...

A few sentences later, Nešić once again misattributes the words "my blood on you and your children" to Jesus, before stating, in a matter-of-fact way, that "they crucified him, he was not crucified by some other people, Jews crucified him." Essential to Nešić's argument is that anti-Judaism, which stems "simply" from the clash between two religious beliefs, is embedded in Christianity and is an issue of profound theological significance. The deicide accusation is introduced as common sense and collective Jewish culpability as something that is a "fact" and "obvious." Moreover, the belief in the collective guilt of Jews is to be expected of an Orthodox bishop and is something that Nešić himself, "as a Christian" believes in.

Poet Matija Bećković made a similar claim when he argued that "I don't know whether among Christians you could find someone who could not be accused of antisemitism, if you were to examine this issue from a biblical perspective. However, it is difficult to imagine calling an antisemite someone who identified with Christ and devoted his whole life to him, unless you consider Christ himself to have been one." Earlier in the interview, Bećković insisted on the semantic distinction between anti-Judaism and antisemitism (see above). Here he reiterates this point and notes that antisemitism "from the Biblical perspective" (namely anti-Judaism) is something that is inherent in Christian belief (in the sense that it would be hard to find a Christian who could not be accused of antisemitism "from a biblical perspective"). At the same time, Bećković dismisses the accusation of antisemitism (of the non-Biblical kind) against Nikolaj Velimirović. He sets up the accusation for disparagement by likening it to an "extreme" and easily dismissible view, in this case the assumption that Christ was himself an antisemite. The same ironising effect is achieved by Ranković who in an earlier quotation equated the critique of Velimirović with the claim that "the Old Testament, which is in fact a Jewish book, [is] the biggest antisemitic pamphlet ever," by Nešić who suggests that if Nikolaj is an antisemite then "we are all antisemites and the New Testament ought to be banned," or by Bigović who said that Nikolaj was as "antisemitic" as Jesus.

During the interview, Deacon Ljubomir Ranković noted that the reference to Jews as "sons of the Devil" in *Words to the Serbian People Through the Dungeon Window* is "merely a repetition of Christ's words" and as such is "to be expected of a priest who upholds Christ and his teachings." In the end Ranković showed signs of frustration with having to account for Velimirović's views on Jews: "Let's cool down this whole 'antisemitism' story! So I am an antisemite, so what? He was an antisemite, against a people like that, of course he was and he had to be, if he was a Christian. They are totally anti-Christian and anti-Evangelical [...] He was against a concept and a doctrine of Jewish religion."

The term "antisemitism"—invoked here in a dismissive and defiant way—is constructed as a position that Velimirović, as "a Christian," had to embrace, because he was a Christian. Importantly, the utterance contains two contrasting interpretations of what it is that Christians are supposed to be against. While arguing that Velimirović was against a "concept and a [religious] doctrine," Ranković also claims that Velimirović had to be "against a people like that." Also it is the people ("they"), not the religious dogma, that is interpreted as being "anti-Christian and anti-Evangelical." The distinction between the "sinner" and the "sin" implicit in the old Christian adage "love the sinner, hate the sin" thus shows itself to be not entirely impermeable.

The defiance apparent in Ranković's tone is noteworthy also because it constructs the persistence of antagonism towards Jews in Orthodox Christian teachings—and the resulting conflict with secular political morality—as a testimony to the Orthodox Church's unquestionable devotion to traditional and genuine religious values. A comparably categorical and uncompromising stance towards the issue of religious tolerance is articulated in the article "Serbs and Jews." Its author, Vladimir Dimitrijević, notes that "in the domain of religion there can be no concessions: there is either only one Truth, revealed in God, or no truth at all" (Dimitrijević, 2004, p. 74). He then goes on to criticize the legacy of the Second Vatican Council by condemning the readiness of the Catholic Church to "wear sackcloth and ashes, and even reject Christ himself, just to prove that it is not 'antisemitic'" (ibid.). In the interview conducted for this study, Deacon Ranković interprets the Jewish-Catholic rapprochement over the past 50 years as indicative of Catholicism's unpardonable "tendency towards pragmatism," which stands in stark contrast with Orthodoxy's exemplary traditionalism. For him, "toning down the views of Apostle Paul or Jesus" turns religion into a "flea market."

Constructions of the anti-Jewish tradition as an immutable aspect of the Christian faith confirm not only that the "teaching of contempt" for Jews has come to be regarded, within the conservative circles of Serbian Orthodox culture, as constitutive of Christian identity, but also that among contemporary champions of Nikolaj Velimirovic the rejection of interfaith dialogue has itself been elevated to the status of a *sine qua non* of the Orthodox Christian religious creed. Velimirović's remembrance, and the ideological dispute that surrounds it, have brought the traditional derision of Jews out of the woodwork and transformed the justification and the rationalization of antisemitism into a viable means of "being a Christian" in sections of contemporary Serbian Orthodox culture.

Questionable boundaries between anti-Judaism and antisemitism

So far it has been argued that the justification of Velimirović's controversial stance towards Jews rests on the distinction between, on the one hand, the seemingly legitimate doctrine of Christian anti-Judaism—said to be rooted in the Holy Scriptures and motivated by the divine love for the Jews—and, on the other hand the anti-normative ideology of secular, Nazi antisemitism.

Scholarly literature on Christian–Jewish relations acknowledges the possibility and even the necessity of preserving the formal, theoretical distinction between anti-Judaism—as a theological abstraction—and the secular variants of racial and conspiratorial antisemitism

(Hellig, 2002; Ruether, 1974). At the same time, Christian anti-Judaism and modern antisemitism are said to be tied by a profound historical connectedness, which undermines the relevance and appropriateness of this differentiation in practice (Caroll, 2002; Goldhagen, 2002; Hilberg, 1985). Baum (1974) for instance argues:

> While it would be historically untruthful to blame the Christian Church for Hitler's anti-Semitism and the monstrous crimes committed by his followers, what is true, alas, is that the Church has produced an abiding contempt among Christians for Jews and all things Jewish, a contempt that aided Hitler's purposes. The church made the Jewish people a symbol of unredeemed humanity; it painted a picture of Jews as a blind, stubborn, carnal and perverse people, an image that was fundamental in Hitler's choice of Jews as a scapegoat. (p. 7)

Daniel Goldhagen (2002) refers to the Christian teachings about Jews as the "ideational seedbed from which ideas grew that animated the perpetrators of the Holocaust" (p. 71) and "the trunk that never ceased bringing nourishment to the modern European antisemitism that had branched off from it" (p. 78). James Carroll (2002) argues that the "Church-absolving wall between anti-Judaism and antisemitism teeters at its base" (p. 274), because hatred of Jews in the Gospels "achieved its climax in the Holocaust" (p. 22). Specifically,

> When Nazism defined Jews as the negative other, in opposition to which it defined itself, it was building on a structure of the European mind that was firmly in place before Hitler was born. If nothing else is clear by now, it is that that structure of mind had its foundations in Christianity and moreover that defining the Jew as the negative other had served as a self-protecting Church's modus operandi down the centuries, from the Gospel of St John, to the Sermons of Luther, from Saint Ambrose to anti-Dreyfusards. (p. 478)

Norman Cohn (1957) describes "the [conspiratorial] fantasy" which characterizes contemporary antisemitism as a secularized version of medieval Christian "demonological terrors [that became] blended with anxieties and resentments which are typically modern" (p. 27). Zygmunt Bauman (1991) takes the same view when he writes that "[t]he age of modernity inherited 'the Jew' already firmly separated from the Jewish men and women who inhabited its towns and villages. Having successfully played the role of the alter ego of the Church, it was prepared to be cast in a similar role in relation to the new, secular, agencies of social integration" (p. 38). The link between the two traditions has led Ruether (1974) to propose that in "diabologizing" the Jew as the "Son of Darkness," the "brood of vipers," and the apostate man, Christian anti-Judaism inevitably "takes social expression as antisemitism" (p. 116).

While most of the cited literature locates the seeds of modern antisemitism in the teaching of Christianity generally, the primary focus of the research has been on antisemitism within the Catholic, and to a lesser extent the Protestant churches. Hardly any space in studies written by western scholars is devoted to relations between Eastern Orthodox Churches and Jews. In a statement to *The Jerusalem Post*, published in 1998, Ephraim Zuroff of the Simon Wiesenthal Centre attributed the heavier scrutiny that the Vatican has come in for—compared to the Orthodox Churches—to the greater "moral authority of the Catholic Church" around the world (O'Dwyer, 1998, p.14). As we saw in the previous chapter, this bias towards the exploration of Vatican's stance towards Jews has led some protagonists of this study to present Christian antisemitism as a specifically Catholic rather than a pan-Christian phenomenon, thereby exonerating the Orthodox Church from accusations of antisemitism. However, as we can see, there is ample evidence to suggest that the inherently blurred nature of the boundaries between anti-Judaism and antisemitism are highly visible in the Orthodox context as well.

The association between "antisemitism" and "anti-Judaism" is not merely historical. In the decades preceding World War II, in Churches around Europe, traditional conceptualization of Jews inherent in the Christian ceremonial and religious doctrine was not propagated in a social vacuum, isolated from the more contemporary variants of antisemitism that were rapidly becoming part of everyday discourse. Christianity, even if only inadvertently, assimilated the emerging racial and conspiratorial antisemitic perspectives into its culture. Using examples from the Catholic and Protestant contexts, in his book *The Moral Reckoning* Daniel Goldhagen (2002) notes that what makes the distinction between anti-Judaism and antisemitism problematic is that the differentiation "is founded on a fiction, a sanitised account of the Church's so-called anti-Judaism. The antisemitism of the Church, certainly since the last part of the nineteenth century and throughout the Nazi period, was far more 'modern' and far closer in precept and practice, to the Nazi antisemitism than has been acknowledged" (p. 79).

The work of Nikolaj Velimirović provides an illustration of this trend within Serbian Orthodox culture. As was noted earlier, in Velimirović's *Words to the Serbian People Through the Dungeon Window* references to Jews as the reprobate people who rejected Christ are interspersed with claims about Jewish power, and the responsibility of Jews for the evils of the modern era. The latter themes belong to the more recent ideological tradition of conspiratorial antisemitism and feature in Nazi rhetoric, too. In Bishop Nikolaj's writing, the two supposedly distinguishable sets of arguments are so closely intertwined that they cannot be plausibly and convincingly separated.

The blurred nature of the boundaries between "theological" and modern secular antisemitism is apparent also in the rhetoric of those among Velimirović's supporters who insist on preserving the distinction. For instance, in the aforementioned letter in *Danas*, in which Deacon Radoš Mladenović and Vladimir Dimitrijević alluded to the "tradition of criticism of Talmudic and Rabbinical Judaism" and distinguished it from antisemitic ideas found for instance in *Mein Kampf*, the two authors also suggest the following:

> Nikolaj talks of Jews [in *Words to the Serbian People*] only to the extent that some of them took part in the secularization of Europe, and especially of Russia. (Were not Trotsky, Zinovyev, Kamenyev, Buharin, Sverdlov all Jews? Was the leader of the Union of godless militants not called Yaroslavski-Gubelyman? To be fair, Osip Mandelstam, who said that "every cultured man is a Christian" and Boris Pasternak, who wrote some of the finest Christian verses of the 20th century, were also Jews, but they were not the ones running Russia, nor did Nikolaj know about them... (Mladenović and Dimitrijević, 2002, p. 8)

In this instance, the justification of Velimirović's position is extended to aspects of the bishop's argument which concern 20th century politics. Although the quotation starts by undermining the overall importance of the portrayal of Jews in Velimirović's writing (he talks of them "to the extent that"), the antisemitic references are defended on the grounds of factuality. The rhetorical question about the ethnic background of the leaders of the Russian Revolution asserts not only that they were Jews, but also that this is common knowledge, and therefore not something that can be either prejudicial or controversial. Also, while acknowledging that not all Jews were responsible for the secularization of Europe (note the reference to "some of them," and the praise of Mandelstam and Pasternak) the allusion to Jews who were "running Russia" is a clear reiteration of one of the most notorious and inherently false (see Poliakov, 1987) conspiratorial myths of the 1920s, which features extensively both in Velimirović's worldview and in Nazi rhetoric (Cohn, 1957).

Similarly, in the interview for this study Ljubomir Ranković follows a description of Velimirović 's antisemitism as being "of the only kind that it can be, namely biblical" with the following claim:

> One ought to read Dostoyevsky's *The Jewish Question*. Did you see what he writes? He says they have no home, they have nothing, they only save money. Why do they save money—in case one day they are called upon to start a war against all people and create their own state. Imbued with hate towards everything around them [...] towards the Russian peasant [...] they are using him. I don't believe that Dostoyevsky lied. I really don't know them well at all, but through Dostoyevsky [...] also I read their—they say that it is an apocryphon—*The Protocols of the Elders of Zion*. That is monstrous. Even if just one per cent of what is in there is true, then it really is horrifying. I can admire their unity, their national consciousness, and devotion to their nation, but I will always be against their anti-Christian endeavors, call them whatever you want. If they are decent, loyal citizens of this country, and I am all for that, I wouldn't mind if one became the president of the state. As for everything else, a barrier needs to be in place. I believe that was Bishop Nikolaj's position too. What does that mean: they can do to us what they like, and if you object, you are an antisemite [...] as if ! There is no logic in that.

The truthfulness of Velimirović's verdict on Jews is, on this occasion, not substantiated through an analogy with either the Old Testament Prophets or the protagonists of the Christian Bible. Instead, Ranković cites Dostoyevsky's 1876 antisemitic pamphlet as well as the notorious *Protocols of the Elders of Zion.* Ranković displays an attempt at partial distancing from the evaluation of Jews which he produces by noting that the assessment is not derived from personal experience ("I really don't know them well at all"), but from secondary sources of which one (the *Protocols*) might be of questionable authenticity. At the same time, Dostoyevsky is cited as a reliable source ("I don't believe that Dostoyevsky lied") and the forgery claim is attributed to unknown others ("they say that it is an apocryphon"), thereby implying that it is merely an allegation, not an established fact. Also, Ranković refers to the alleged apocryphon as "their" *Protocols,* thereby implicitly attributing authorship of the pamphlet to Jews. Most importantly, the forgery claim and the notoriety of the *Protocols* are not seen as undermining the usefulness of this document in substantiating Velimirović's views. On the contrary, the notion that *Protocols* might be a fake is invoked in a way that supports the overall antisemitic message. Even if it is an "apocryphon," Ranković maintains, at least "one per cent" of it might be true and even this would be enough to indict the Jews. By stating that the view expounded in Dostoyevsky's pamphlet and in the *Protocols* was "Bishop Nikolaj's position too," Ranković effectively extends the boundaries of the "purely" Christian anti-Judaism to include claims and sources which fall within the ideological traditions and practices of modern fascistic antisemitism from which he attempted to distance himself earlier in the interview.

In contrast to above examples, some followers of Nikolaj Velimirović acknowledge that the bishop's writings contain conspiratorial themes of questionable merit which need to be examined separately from his otherwise praiseworthy theological work. Predrag Samardžić's book *Bishop Nikolaj and the New Testament on the Jews* begins with the suggestion that Velimirović's "so called 'antisemitism'" ought to be examined on "two levels." The two levels, the author explains are "[f]irst, that which finds its recognizable base in New Testament literature and second, one of a 'speculative' kind (which, if singled out, en bloc, belongs at the lowest point of the scale of the bishop's philosophical achievement) provoked by broader contemplations about world affairs and the concrete situation in which the bishop found himself at the time—imprisoned in the concentration camp at Dachau" (p. 5).

While acknowledging that "speculative" thoughts on Jews are not the pinnacle of Velimirović's creative endeavors, Samardžić does not see in these "contemplations about world affairs" anything that warrants condemnation. He explains that "Bishop Nikolaj expressed these views at the time when he was at his weakest, in the jaws of Nazi Germany together with millions of Jews, in many ways with all of them." In Samardžić's view, the status of victim "excludes the possibility of rabblerousing in [Velimirović's] thinking" (p. 8). At the same time, Velimirović's "speculative" writings are also said to contain some important historical truths: "Did some Jews actively participate and lead those movements [presumably communism, freemasonry, etc.] of which Bishop Nikolaj talks in the speculative extract from *Words to the Serbian People*? Without a doubt they did" (p. 10).

By interpreting Velimirović's views on Jews as being directed at "some Jews" rather than the whole of the Jewish people, Samardžić employs a strategy commonly used in Serbian antisemitic discourse to dispel criticism. For instance, Serbia's most prolific writer of antisemitic material, Ratibor Đurđević, routinely distinguishes in his writing between "ordinary Jews" and the evil and scheming "Judaists." However, these distinctions are unconvincing and have been shown to constitute nothing more than poor attempts at masking racist views (see Byford, 2003, 2006). Evidence for this can even be found even in Samardžić's book. On page sixteen, the author notes that some of the leading critics of Nikolaj Velimirović among the Serbian diaspora in the US in the 1950s were intelligence agents who received "instructions from their political mentor Oskar Davičo." This allegation is followed by the insinuation that Davičo, a well known poet and writer, was a Jew. Samardžić writes: "I am reluctant to see behind this some kind of Semitic anti-Serbianism and anti-Christianism, although I know of analysts who think otherwise." Although he distances himself from the claim made by others that Davičo's Jewish background constitutes a fitting explanation for the latter's critical stance towards Velimirović, Samardžić nonetheless introduces this notion—attributed to more than one "analyst"—as an account that warrants a mention. Moreover, he does not unequivocally reject this view, in which not only is a distinction not made between "some Jews" and all others, but also "anti-Serbianism" and "anti-Christianity" is cited as "Semitic" traits. Instead, Samardžić merely expressed "reluctance" to accept it, hinting that the "other analysts who think otherwise" might in fact be onto something.

Finally, more moderate voices in the Serbian church have argued that Velimirović's venerable theological and spiritual writing must be distinguished from his dubious views on Europe and Western civilization. In *From All-Man to the Man of God* Radovan Bigović (1998) separates the bishop's contribution to Orthodox theology from the "political" critique of the West within which the indictment of the Jews is to be found. Bigović recognizes that "in spite of a number of lucid observations," the bishop's verdict on Europe "looks more like an ideological critique of a specific type of culture than a sober theological evaluation," and that "panicky negation of culture, in essence, is meaningless" (Bigović, 1998, p. 371). Bigović also points out that Velimirović's "opinion of Roman Catholicism and Jews would not survive serious critique" (p. 372). However, a "serious critique" of Velimirović's political ideas is absent from Bigović's otherwise very detailed and comprehensive analysis of the bishop's religious philosophy. In fact, the author concludes the review of Velimirović's stance on Europe by noting that "although they may seem one-sided and propagandist," his position on the Catholic Church and Jews "is not completely misguided" (p. 371). Bigović explains that while Jews may not be responsible for "all the evils in Europe" as Velimirović contends, "objectively speaking, the influence of Jews, Roman Catholicism, and Protestantism on Europe's spiritual development is not insignificant." It is revealing that Bigović does not speak of "Judaism" along with "Roman Catholicism" and "Protestantism" but about "Jews." It is not the influence of a religious dogma, culture, or tradition, but of a people. Moreover, in acknowledging at least partially the legitimacy of Velimirović's views, Bigović validates the view that Jews contributed significantly to the development of the very same aspects of European culture (secularism, democracy, religious tolerance, etc.) which Bishop Nikolaj and his followers continuously denounce in their writing as essentially anti-Serbian and anti-Christian.

The equivocal nature of Bigović's distancing from Velimirović's views on Jews became even more apparent in the interview. In response to a direct question on Velimirović's antisemitism, Bigović explained:

> It is interesting that he articulated this one-sided position on Jews when he was in Dachau. Why not before then or after, that is a different question—we can only speculate. In any case the position was, to say the least, one-sided. And it cannot be defended. But there is also something else there. You should not read into his writing what many people read into it; they even turned into an ideology, that he was some kind of ideologue of antisemitism. I always say: if you follow that logic, then all Old Testament prophets would be branded antisemites. Jesus Christ would be an antisemite. Velimirović was, by that logic, also an anti-Serb. No one criticized his own people and their weaknesses as often as Nikolaj had done, many times, for over 50 years. That is evident and it is pointless to try to draw… anyway, how do you if he hated someone or not. We can only speculate. On the other hand one must say that these are one-sided arguments that cannot be defended. Whenever something is stated as a generalization it becomes questionable. I think that everyone in our church is aware that his position [on Jews] should not be defended and cannot be defended. There are also his claims about the West. Some of what he says might be true but when you draw a general conclusion based on negative examples that is methodologically very dangerous. I think that he was sometimes prone to generalization. […] On the other hand, it can hardly be seen as some kind of open antisemitism. He said it in that period and I used to ask myself whether he wrote these things in order to save his head, his life, because he was in Dachau, he wrote the book on toilet paper, we can only speculate, maybe that is how it looked to him at that time. In any case, to accuse the Jews for all evil in Europe is senseless. […] We cannot defend that…

The continuous shifting between condemnation and justification of Velimirović's lamentable stance on Jews illustrates clearly Bigović's ambivalence towards the views expressed in *Words to the Serbian People Through the Dungeon Window*. The quoted passage contains attempts at distancing (Velimirović's views "cannot be defended"), which are followed by explanations and justifications which are typical of pro-Velimirović apologist rhetoric. Also, Bigović describes Velimirović's antisemitic diatribes as presenting a "one-sided," biased view. This euphemistic characterization in itself indicates that the distancing from Velimirović's opinion is only partial: a biased, one-sided view is not inherently wrong. Bigović confirms this when he condemns Velimirović only for being "prone to generalization" and for drawing conclusions "based on negative examples." He reinforces the view expressed in his book that although Velimirović's views about Jews "cannot be defended," he may nonetheless have got some things right. Furthermore, Bigović presents the rejection of Velimirović's position on Jews as a shared opinion within the Serbian Church. This claim is unjustifiable, given that no one within that institution has ever openly distanced themselves from Velimirović's writing. Even Bigović has not done so explicitly, unequivocally and in public.

In *From All-Man to the Man of God*, in the very last comment on the issue of Velimirović's views on Europe, Bigović offers what he calls a "psycho-historical" rather than "theological" justification for Velimirović's most controversial views: "He wrote *Words to the Serbian People through the Dungeon Window* as a prisoner at the camp Dachau, knowing that the Catholic Church played a role in the genocide against the Serbian people. With these psycho-historical rather than theological factors in mind, his views can be to some extent justified and comprehended" (p. 372). These remarks, which are offered as a conclusion to the section that deals both with Velimirović's antisemitism and anti-Catholicism, purport to explain only the bishop's stance towards the Vatican. Bigović cites in his book no relevant "psycho-historical" arguments that might explain Velimirović's stance on Jews. And yet, during the interview, Bigović invokes, in his response, the possibility that Velimirović wrote the controversial book to save his life. Knowing what we know today about Velimirović's existence during the war, of which Bigović is unlikely to be ignorant, this explanation cannot be given serious consideration. Rather, just like Bigović's hesitation on this issue, apparent both in the book and in the interview, it should be seen as symptomatic of an important dilemma faced by Bigović, and probably by other liberal voices in the church. Ambivalence is a way of negotiating between a genuine admiration for Nikolaj Velimirović and profound disagreement with some of his views. In a broader ideological climate within the Church, dominated by the uncritical apotheosis of the "Holy Bishop Nikolaj," the swinging pendulum of argumentation is a way of managing the impasse created by the demand for equivocal condemnation in an ambience of widespread hero-worship.

Deicidal justification of Jewish suffering: The Holocaust as divine retribution

As was noted in Chapter 3, one interpretation of *Words to the Serbian People Through the Dungeon Window* in official accounts of Velimirović's life is that the book is an indictment not just of the secularized European civilization, but also of its most sinister creation, namely Nazism. It is claimed that Velimirović wrote the book in secret, often using coded references to Germany and Nazism in order to avoid punishment in case his captors discover the seditious manuscript, written on scraps of toilet paper. This "heroic" interpretation of the book enabled Velimirović's supporters within the church to repress, from representations of the bishop's life, the fact that many elements of the portrayal of Jews in the prison writing did not deviate that much from the views held by his captors.

As the specifics of Velimirović's writing at the camp started to penetrate the public domain in recent years, the promotion of the myth that *Words to the Serbian People Through the Dungeon Window* was the product of Velimirović's subversive anti-fascist mind could no longer be plausibly propagated, especially in situations such as in the interviews, where Velimirović's antisemitism, and the circumstances in which it emerged, constituted a prominent topic of conversation.

During our conversation in August 2003, Deacon Ljubomir Ranković attempted to rationalize Velimirović's stance on Jews by citing a letter that the former bishop of Šabac and Valjevo, Jovan Velimirović (whom Ranković served as deacon for more than a decade), received from his uncle Nikolaj after World War II:

> In a letter to [his nephew] Bishop Jovan, describing his suffering in the Dachau camp, Bishop Nikolaj wrote about how he watched while they took away bunches of children and people, prisoners, murdered them and threw them into gas chambers, and above all he watched the suffering of Jews. "I kneeled," he wrote, "and prayed to God"; and he says, "I watched before my eyes as Christ's prophecy, or rather their curse under Christ's cross, was being realized: His blood be upon on us and upon our children! I kneeled and prayed to God to forgive them that sin of deicide at Golgotha, and deliver them from the suffering and torture."

Ranković offered an almost identical account of this letter in an article published in the daily *Večernje Novosti* in June 2003 (Ranković, 2003a). The description of the events at Dachau includes a significant amount of specific and vivid details: bunches of children being taken away, interns being murdered, people being thrown into gas chambers. What makes this description intriguing is that it does not accurately depict the conditions at Dachau. Sereny (2000) writes that in spite of the symbolic significance of Dachau in the collective memory of the Holocaust, the camp was one where comparatively few Jews were interned and more importantly where there were not the mass executions of the kind that went on in Auschwitz or Treblinka: "[Dachau] was primarily a bitterly harsh, punitive camp for political prisoners, and while many died of overwork and starvation, and the bodies (just like in the extermination camps, all located in occupied Poland) were burned in the camp crematorium, no one was 'exterminated' there" (p. 157).

Dachau did have a gas chamber, disguised as a shower-room, but it was never used (Marcuse, 2001). Also, writing about executions at the camp, Berben (1975) notes that most of the killing at the camp took the form of executions by shooting, conducted mainly off-site. These facts about life at Dachau are in no way intended to minimize or trivialize the horror that went on inside it. They are noted in order to suggest that it is unlikely that Velimirović—as an honorary prisoner who lived in separate quarters away from other interns—in reality could have witnessed the events described by Ranković. What is more, in his statement to the *New York Times* in 1946, Velimirović stated that he "did not know" what went on outside the barrack he was in, and that all they could hear was a mixture of "beautiful music... Mozart and Beethoven" and "gunfire" ("Bishop, ex captive of Nazis, is here," 1946).

And yet, while it is not possible to ascertain what the letter actually said, or even if it exists, Ranković's description, as a description, is revealing. The memory of the letter, as articulated in the interview, is enriched with familiar imagery and shared representations of victimization and horror in Nazi camps. These details serve a rhetorical purpose in the context in which they are produced. In Ranković's depiction, reference to Velimirović actually watching prisoners being murdered, taken away, or thrown into gas chambers works up the martyrdom myth. It enhances the image of the bishop as survivor of Nazi terror, and someone who actually experienced and witnessed first hand the workings of the murderous Nazi machine. Given that eyewitnesses are generally seen as entitled to superior knowledge of the events they observed, the emphasis on Velimirović actually being there also enhances the validity of his interpretation of Jewish suffering as the realization of Biblical prophesy.

Going back to the implications of the alleged correspondence between Bishop Jovan and Nikolaj Velimirović as an account for the latter's antisemitic stance, it is noteworthy that Ranković equates Velimirović's antisemitic rage in *Words to the Serbian People Through the Dungeon Window* with "prayer," a term which has compassionate and benevolent connotations. Velimirović is no longer portrayed as someone who "chastises" the Jews with "bitter and crude words" in the manner of Old Testament prophets. Instead, as an authentic Christian, he "prays" for the deliverance of Jewish victims of Nazism. Branimir Nešić from Dveri also invoked the notion of the prayer when he claimed that "Nikolaj prayed for Jews to repent, in the same way that he prayed for Serbs to repent their sins." He added: "[Nikolaj] is not an antisemite because he prayed for Jews to repent and avoid sin but he prayed for all people to repent, so that this would not happen. I think that is OK, I see nothing antisemitic in that. It was a prayer of a Bishop who in Dachau witnessed the suffering of the Jewish people and among other prayers he also prayed for Jews [to repent]."

In talking about the need for repentance, Nešić speaks of it as of something that will help the Jews avoid "sin" rather than "suffering." Because of the assumed causal relationship between the two concepts, in interpreting the history of Jewish suffering Nešić treats them as practically synonymous. The implication of this is that the responsibility for the suffering, and for its alleviation, is even more unequivocally laid on the shoulders of the victims. Nešić's answer also trivializes Velimirović's antisemitism by claiming that the "prayer" for Jews was just one among many prayers. He even suggested later in the interview that Nikolaj prayed also for the German people. In doing so he "dilutes" the focus on Jews in Velimirović's work, and sidesteps the fact that Jews were the only people for whom Velimirović "prayed" as the "sons of the Devil," and whom he accused of being the source of all the evil in the world. Also, on several occasions during the interview, Nešić contrasted Velimirović's compassion and kindness towards Jews (manifested in the "prayer" for their repentance and salvation) with the selfishness of Jewish rabbis: "Show me one Jewish rabbi who prayed for Serbian victims."

Both Nešić's and Ranković's arguments revolve around the assumption that the suffering of Jews was divine retribution for the "sin of deicide at Golgotha," the fulfillment of "Christ's prophecy," and the realization of the curse: "His blood be upon us and upon our Children." Also, both explanations assume that the perpetual suffering of Jews, of which Holocaust was a manifestation, can end only with repentance by Jews for the crime of deicide. Shortly after stating that "Christ was not crucified by Jews per se, but by sinful people who failed to appreciate his greatness and significance," Nešić suggested that crucifixion is a "Jewish sin because Jews are the ones that passed verdict on him. Christ went to other people, but they did not put him on trial..." before adding: "You know the Holocaust was a tragedy, but this is not normal... Evidently, God punishes, and he merely used the Nazis to punish Jews. That is how I see it. You know, from an ontological point of view. Not in terms of earthly existence. I would stand in defense of any Jew, but I gather that that's how God punishes people, in the same way that he punished us with the Ustashas and the Turks."

Deacon Ljubomir Ranković similarly noted that "I must once again quote their book, the Bible, the verse: 'he who sows wind will reap a storm.' Therefore, that wind that they sowed while fighting against Christ, they reaped during World War II, in the storm of the Holocaust which they endured." In arguing that Hitler was effectively God's tool for the punishment of Jews (even if only "from an ontological point of view"), Ranković and Nešić were following the religious logic of Velimirović's prison writing: "So the innocent blood [of Christ] became the whip that drove them like cattle through the centuries, from land to land, like fire that burns their repository of schemes against Christ" (Velimirović, 1998, p. 194).

Deflecting the guilt for the Holocaust onto the Jews is not an invention of the Serbian Christian Right. This deicidal justification of the Holocaust (see Hellig, 2002; Shafir, 2002) is a frequent theme in the rhetoric of Fascist and neo-Nazi groups in Slovakia, Romania, and other parts of Eastern Europe (Shafir, 2002). Moreover, it is an idea that had been advanced even by some fairly respectable mainstream men of cloth. In a media interview in the 1960s, Heinrich Gruber, the German evangelical pastor, anti-Nazi activist, and former intern at Dachau, who was profoundly opposed to Hitler and his regime, interpreted Auschwitz as part of God's plan and likened Hitler to Nebuchadnezzar as the "rod of God's anger" against Jews (cited in Hellig, 2002, p. 162).

In a polemic with Gruber, Jewish theologian Richard L. Rubenstein dismissed the view of the Holocaust as divine punishment as morally repugnant and as symptomatic of a profoundly false logic of Christian theology, which, in its extreme manifestations, legitimizes the murder of Jews. The disputed aspect of Christian dogma is "the theologizing of history" (Ravitch, 1982), namely the tendency to interpret history, particularly that of the Jews as part of a predestined divine plan. In the attempt to explain the legacy of the persecution of Jews, the theologization of history essentially projects religious and ethnic prejudices of ordinary mortals, including Christians, onto the will of the Almighty. The presence of deicidal justification of the Holocaust reflects the more general symbolic role that "the Jews" occupy in the Christian *weltanschauung*. Because traditional, conservative Christian theology presents Jews as the perennial outcasts and sinners, their suffering is made to seem as not just as the expected and normal consequence of their deicidal sin, but also as necessary. For as Hellig (2001) asks "if Jews do not suffer, who would bear the guilt for the sacrifice of Jesus?" (p. 168).

Michael Shafir (2002) notes that the deicidal justification for the Holocaust is not the only strategy used to deflect the guilt and responsibility for the murder of European Jews onto the Jews themselves. He notes that among conspiracy theorists in Eastern Europe, there is also the view that Jewish power, led by "international Jewry and Zionism" and "Freemasonry" produced Hitler for their sinister purposes (in most cases so as to legitimize the creation of Israel). So far, such extraordinary claims have not penetrated Serbian conspiracist culture. In Velimirović's writing, however, although no allusion is made to a direct, collaborative link between Jews and Hitler, the emergence of Nazism is nonetheless attributed, at least in a broader symbolic sense, to Jewish influence in European culture. In *Words to the Serbian People Through the Dungeon Window*, Velimirović accredits Nazism to the secularization of Europe and portrays it as the outcome of Western civilization's fatal departure from traditional Christian values. Yet in the same book he asserts that the much-maligned secularization stems from Jewish influence and the fact that Europe "knows nothing other than what Jews serve to her" (p. 194). The implication of this argument is that Nazism was not just a new "whip" brought on by the "innocent blood" of Christ, or yet another burst of the fire that "burns [Jewish] repositories of schemes against Christ." It is also the work of the Devil and his disciple, the Jew. In the fifty-second sermon in *Words to the Serbian People Through the Dungeon Window* Velimirović explains:

> Europe plotted its malice together with the Jews and wanted to create peace with propaganda. Europe became fat and heavy, its eyesight worsened, its hearing deteriorated, and its heart became wooden. Just like in the old Israel, and just like Caiaphas's recipe prescribes…
>
> That is why we have today a horrific hatred of the Europeans towards Jews. Everyone hates their own vices in others. Europe breathes with the spirit of Jewishness, which is why it is persecuting Jews. Europe does not need Jews any more. They have finished their mission in Europe. European civilization will become a worthy replacement in the animosity towards Christ and God. (Velimirović, 1998, p. 131)

The Jews are therefore not only accountable for the Holocaust by the virtue of their rejection and murder of Christ. Velimirović also suggests that Nazism, which breathes with the "spirit of Jewishness," is an invention of a Satanic, Jewish "plot" that has now turned against its creators. Ranković also invoked this perverse connection between Nazism and Judaism when he compared the *modus operandi* of the Nazis with that of the Jews in the Bible: "There, it says here… One prophet, Isaiah I think, they sawed him in half. Didn't they chop off St John the Baptist's head? Christ described him as the greatest man ever borne by a woman. What happened to them afterwards, with Hitler and everything? The same thing… precisely the same thing. Who taught people to saw people in half? They did it to their own prophets…"

The various indefensible and deplorable interpretations of the Holocaust, which are to be found both in the writings of Nikolaj Velimirović and in the arguments of his followers, have an important common element. In "blaming the victim," they divert attention away from the responsibility of the Nazis and their collaborators for the Holocaust. Actual perpetrators of crimes against Jews are devoid of agency and consequently of responsibility. The identity of the murderers and the history of animosity towards Jews that made their crime possible are obscured by the perennial preoccupation with Jews as sinners who must "reap" the consequences of collective sin.

According to Richard L. Rubenstein (1966), such misguided readings of recent Jewish history reveal that Nazism not only inherited from Christianity the image of Jew as the perennial villain, but also that Christian logic is capable of providing a justificatory account for the crimes of the Nazis. Rubenstein went as far as to suggest that this interpretation of the Holocaust exposes Hitler's policy towards Jews as "the terminal expression of Christian antisemitism" (p. 46). This conclusion is simplistic insofar as it overlooks the complexity of the historical relationship between Christian anti-Jewish tradition and Nazism. At the same time, it accurately identifies deicidal justification of the Holocaust as an important manifestation of the ideological link that binds the seemingly legitimate biblical anti-Judaism and the modern secular racial antisemitism. The presence of this type of argument in the discourse of Velimirović's remembrance suggests that while challenging the legitimacy of the "reading of Chrysostom in the light of *Mein Kampf*," some of Velimirović's followers have been unable to resist the temptation of interpreting Hitler's views in the light of the writings of St John Chrysostom or the Gospel according to Matthew. This can be taken as further evidence of the haziness of the invoked differentiation between two categories of belief about Jews and which annihilates the much-misused distinction between anti-Judaism and antisemitism.

One of the principle aims of the present chapter has been to demonstrate the way in which attempts at refuting the accusations of antisemitism directed at Nikolaj Velimirović have turned one of the oldest premises of traditional Christian antisemitic rhetoric—the idea that Jews killed Christ and have drawn upon themselves eternal damnation that will end only when they repent and accept Christian teachings—into a seemingly acceptable, natural, and even normative aspect of Christian identity. The rhetoric of denial based on the drawing of a parallel between Velimirović's antisemitic work and the words of the Bible has been shown to depoliticize and legitimize the bishop's anti-

Jewish stance by placing it under the banner of the normal and acceptable "theological" "anti-Judaism." In the broader context of apologetics, this strategy helps to boost the authority of literal denial, examined in the previous chapter. The enforcement of the dubious distinction between antisemitism and anti-Judaism enables the Serbian church to maintain more convincingly and persuasively that there is no antisemitism within Orthodox culture. Moreover, by constructing the despicable anti-Jewish sentiments expressed by Velimirović as a theological matter that cuts to the bone of Christian belief and identity, Velimirović's supporters are able to dismiss criticism of their hero's work as malicious and spiteful attacks on Christianity as a whole. The ultimate consequence of this strategy is that Velimirović's ideological position continues to be unchallenged within the Serbian Orthodox Church. Most disturbingly, the spontaneity with which Velimirović's supporters invoke the rhetoric of interpretative denial suggests that normalization and legitimization of anti-Jewish sentiment has become entrenched in the routine of Velimirović's remembrance. Bearing in mind Velimirović's popularity in Serbia today, and the regularity with which "remembering" occurs, it is clear that the apologist rhetoric is gradually becoming part of the ideological common sense, an outcome that cannot have a positive impact on Christian–Jewish relations in the country.

CHAPTER SIX

Antisemitism as Prophecy

Social Construction of Velimirović's Sanctity

> "When he prophesized—Nikolaj roared, when he prayed—Nikolaj healed, when he wrote—Nikolaj prophesized." (Predrag Dragić-Kijuk, editor of the nationalist publication *Književne Novine*)

On 19 May 2003, the Assembly of Bishops of the Serbian Orthodox Church announced its "unanimous and undisputed decision" to "include the name of Nikolaj (Velimirović), bishop of Ohrid and Žiča, in the calendar of saints of the holy [Serbian] Orthodox Church." The announcement stated that, in canonizing Bishop Velimirović, the Assembly "solemnly confirmed the widespread belief in his sanctity, which exists not only within the Serbian Church, but throughout the Orthodox World" (Information Service of the Serbian Orthodox Church, 2003b). The magnitude of the importance attributed to St Nikolaj of Ohrid and Žiča (sometimes also referred to as St Nikolaj of Lelić or even St Nikolaj of Serbia) was reflected in the decision to allocate two days in the church calendar to his veneration: March 18, the day of Velimirović's death in exile in the United States in 1956; and May 3, the day in 1991 when his remains were brought back to Serbia, before being laid to rest in his native village of Lelić.

The formal canonization ceremony was held at the Cathedral of St Sava in central Belgrade only five days after the initial announcement. The special liturgy was officiated by Patriarch Pavle of the Serbian Orthodox Church in the presence of twenty-eight Serbian bishops and several thousand faithful. The sacred remains of the new saint were transported to Belgrade especially for this occasion and were displayed in an open casket to be worshipped by members of the public.

Although the inauguration of Nikolaj Velimirović as Serbia's seventy-seventh national saint came as a surprise to many journalists and commentators, the decision appears to have been premeditated and carefully planned. Several commemorative events were organized by the Serbian Church to coincide with the announcement. On May 14, five days before the canonization was declared, a museum exhibition devoted to Velimirović's life and work, which had toured Serbia in the preceding months, opened in Belgrade in the presence of the Serbian patriarch and numerous high-ranking bishops. The patriarch's speech at the opening ceremony hinted at the impending decision by the Assembly of Bishops in that the head of the Serbian Church—who was until then probably the only senior church official who consistently refused to refer to Velimirović as a saint—referred to him as the "Holy Bishop." Also, the announcement concerning the canonization coincided with the publication of the much-publicized book *Holy Bishop Nikolaj of Ohrid and Žiča* (Jevtić, 2003a) and a luxury limited edition of Velimirović's book *Symbols of Faith.*

This chapter examines the campaign for Velimirović's canonization which began in the 1980s and concluded in 2003. It will be suggested that while the cause for Velimirović's canonization tended to overlook his antisemitism, certain constructions of the bishop's holiness have been intrinsically tied to the controversy surrounding his earthly existence. This includes the claims that Velimirović had been graced with special mystical experiences and powers—those of epiphany, prophecy, and healing—which are regarded, within the Christian tradition, as important characteristics of saints. Building on the arguments developed in previous chapters, the analysis of Velimirović's "path to sanctity" explores the ways in which the assertions about the "mystical" dimension of the bishop's personal history endowed the antisemitic aspect of his ideology with almost divine significance and in doing so have helped to legitimize further the lamentable anti-Jewish invective found in *Words to the Serbian People Through the Dungeon Window.*

The first stage of the campaign for canonization: The making of a religious "cult"

In the Orthodox Church, unlike in the Roman Catholic tradition, there are no formal procedures associated with canonization. Proclamation of saints is not preceded by a formal diocesan inquiry, sessions by the Congregation for the Causes for Canonization, or well-defined courses of action regarding the verification of miracles. Also, no distinction is made between "beatification" and "canonization." The Orthodox churches are believed to follow the tradition of early Christendom, when canonization was the means by which ecclesiastical authorities simply formalized the veneration of a martyr or a confessor already worshipped as such by the wider community of faithful. Slobodan Mileusnić, curator of the Museum of the Serbian Orthodox Church and one of the leading experts on Serbian saints, suggests for instance that "in contrast to the [Catholic] Western Church, which declares its saints through an almost administrative process, the Serbian Orthodox Church merely sanctions a cult that already exists." According to canonical law, the cult of future saints manifests itself as "celebration and commemoration of [the Saint's] deeds on Earth, prayers to the Saint as intercessor before God, daily worship of the Saint's memory, and the building of churches in their name" (quoted in Grujić, 2000; see also Jevtić, 1987b; Lazarević, 2003; Mileusnić, 2003; J. Velimirović, 1991).

The less stringent rules for canonization in the Orthodox world are regarded by many Serbian clerics as the only authentic and apposite practice of declaring saints. In 1987, Archimandrite Atanasije Jevtić dismissed formal procedures followed by the Vatican as "papal innovation" and "frivolity before God" (Jevtić, 1987b, p. 30). A year earlier, in a statement to the magazine *Intervju,* Jevtić rejected the rumors that the Serbian Church planned to canonize Velimirović by stating that "in the Orthodox tradition there had never been a special inauguration of saints," but only the recognition of someone's widespread veneration. He defined sanctity as a matter determined by "God and the people," not by Church authorities (Z. Simić, 1986, p. 23). Similarly, in 1988, Bishop Jovan of Šabac and Valjevo explained that "our church does not declare someone a Saint so that people can celebrate them as such, but the other way round; people are the ones who pronounce someone a saint, and the church only formalizes that status" (J. Velimirović, 1991, p. 22).

Because of the enduring and widespread belief that canonization represents little more than an ecclesiastical formality by means of which the church ratifies an existing cult, in the early stages of the social construction of Velimirović's sanctity in the late 1980s Velimirović's supporters invested considerable effort into demonstrating the existence of a "living cult" devoted to the bishop. Articles published in *Glas Crkve* and speeches delivered at commemorative ceremonies organized in Velimirović's honor regularly emphasized the extensive veneration of Nikolaj among Serbs. Public gatherings, commemorations, celebrations, literary evenings, etc. that were part of the campaign for rehabilitation were routinely interpreted as evidence for the vast following that Velimirović has among the Serbian people. Although most of these events were organized by the pro-Velimirović clique within the Serbian Church, and were attended by a small proportion of the public, they were nonetheless flagged as reflecting the "will of the people," and as manifestations of the overwhelming public adulation of the bishop.

Also, in the late 1980s and early 1990s, campaigners for Velimirović's canonization seldom presented the alleged cult surrounding the bishop's name as a new development. The veneration of the bishop was construed as the continuation of a longer tradition dating back to the 1950s. In fact, as early as in 1945, and therefore eleven years before Velimirović's death, an icon bearing his image was painted on the walls of a church in the village of Rataje, near the town of Aleksandrovac (see Jevtić, 2003a). Bishop Jovan Velimirović noted that in the immediate aftermath of his uncle's death, Serbian and Russian *émigré* communities in the US, as well as nuns and monks from a number of rural Serbian monasteries—most notably from Ovčara, Vračevšnice, and Ćelije—instantly recognized Velimirović's sanctity and prayed to him as a Man of God, thereby sowing the seeds of his mass following (J. Velimirović, 1991; also Jevtić, 1987b). In a public lecture before students at the University of Belgrade in December 2004, Irinej Dobrijević (currently bishop of Australia and New Zealand) revealed that Nikolaj was regarded a saint among the Serbian diaspora in the United States as early as the 1970s. Apparently, monks at the Russian St Tikhon's Monastery in South Canaan (Pennsylvania), where Velimirović died, remembered and venerated him as "St Nikolaj of South Canaan." The veneration in the United States was evidently not limited to a single monastery: in the Serbian Orthodox Church of Holy Trinity in the town of Parma in Ohio, there is a fresco bearing the title "Synaxis of the Saints of North America" on which Nikolaj is depicted as "St Nicholas of South Canaan." However, according to information which I obtained from St Tikhon's Monastery, the title

"St Nikolaj of South Canaan" although not entirely unknown, is rarely used there. Moreover, monks at this monastery have been celebrating Nikolaj Velimirović's sanctity only for the past ten years or so, rather than since the 1970s as Dobrijević suggested.

Accounts of the origins of the cult surrounding Velimirović's name regularly cite Father Justin Popović as playing a key role in its creation. Popović is said to have mourned Bishop Nikolaj and prayed for his soul only on the first three days after his death. On the fourth day he prayed to him as a saint and intercessor before God. Popović's authority on the matter of Velimirović's saintliness is reflected in the following words of Bishop Amfilohije Radović: "If he [Justin Popović] who knew so much about sanctity through knowledge and experience felt that he was dealing with a holy man [Velimirović], then what can the rest of us, of much lesser spiritual importance and experience claim to know?" (A. Radović, 1987, p. 29).

The earliest efforts in the drive for canonization occurred in and around Velimirović's native diocese of Šabac and Valjevo, where his cult following was greatest. In 1982, clergy from this diocese celebrated Nikolaj in a ceremony traditionally reserved for saints. This was a prelude to the key event in the campaign for canonization which took place five years later. In March 1987, on the thirty-first anniversary of the bishop's death—at an event led by Bishops Jovan Velimirović and Amfilohije Radović—Nikolaj was informally canonized. March 18, the day of his death, was declared a religious holiday in the diocese. An article published shortly afterward in *Glas Crkve*—whose editors promptly adopted "Holy Bishop Nikolaj" as the journal's patron saint—applauded the informal nature of this act and relished in its spontaneous and populist character. The article emphasized the following:

> The bishop's canonization was not declared from the pulpit, it was not a spiteful reaction, a provoked reflex, but the desire of the whole of the Serbian nation. Those several hundred people, gathered in the churchyard, were the ones who canonized the bishop. They did so in the manner and in the spirit of ancient Christian tradition, in the same way that other Serbian saints from St Simeon to St Sava had been canonized. That spontaneous and sublime act, inspired by God, points towards another, if not the most important moment, the potential of the whole of the Serbian nation for revitalization and as

> such it provides further proof of its spiritual values. ("Kandilo pred ikonom," 1987, p. 26)

In an interview published shortly after the informal canonization, Archimandrite Atanasije Jevtić reiterated these sentiment when he argued confidently that "one thing which is not disputed, and should not be disputed, is the holiness of the person of Nikolaj Velimirović." He defended the controversial act by the diocese of Šabac and Valjevo (in which he and other nationalist clerics played no small part) as being "consistent with the centuries long tradition of the Orthodox Church" (Jevtić, 1987b, p. 31). In invoking the ancient Christian tradition, Jevtić and the editors of *Glas Crkve* were alluding to the customs of Early Christendom, especially in the period between the 4th and 11th century, when canonization throughout the Christian world was the prerogative of lesser church authorities, namely of local bishops (Freze, 1991; Woodward, 1991).

While the legitimacy of the informal canonization remained the topic of some dispute, the event had a notable practical and political objective. It helped to promote, institutionalize, and in some sense reify the alleged cult surrounding Velimirović's name. Albeit unauthorized by the synod or the Assembly of Bishops, the canonization legitimized the emerging practices of referring to Velimirović as the "Holy Bishop," the production of religious icons bearing his image, and even the building of chapels and churches in his honor. Also, this contentious decision by the clergy of a single diocese was flagged as the "first step on the road to [full] canonization" (J. Velimirović, 1991, p. 22). Thus, the events of March 1987 can be said to have been not just a spontaneous act of reverence, but also a calculated attempt to put pressure on the higher church authorities to consider what was identified as the "will of the people" and formally declare Bishop Nikolaj a national saint.

Canonization in the Orthodox Church and the need for divine confirmation of sanctity

Two years after the informal canonization in the diocese of Šabac and Valjevo, the Serbian Orthodox bishop of Western Europe, Lavrentije Trifunović, submitted a formal request to the Assembly of Bishops of the Serbian Orthodox Church in which he appealed to the highest ecclesiastical authority to "examine whether necessary conditions have been met for this great bishop of the Serbian Church [Nikolaj Velimirović] to be canonized as a saint" (cited in Janković, 2003, p. 491). Predictably, the wording of the petition echoed the assumption that formal canonization was the means of recognizing popular belief in someone's sanctity. Bishop Lavrentije argued that "a great proportion of the faithful, even whole dioceses, have already declared Nikolaj a saint" and that his "image is already represented with a halo, and even temples are being erected in his name." Trifunović's petition also cautioned that the failure by the church to recognize the widespread belief in Velimirović's sanctity would "create an insurmountable gap between our people and the highest authorities of the Serbian Church" (Janković, 2003, p. 491).

Velimirović's followers within the church seemed confident in the success of the petition. A few days after addressing the Assembly of Bishops with the request for Velimirović's canonization, Lavrentije Trifunović was instated as the bishop in Velimirović's native diocese of Šabac and Valjevo. One of Trifunović's first projects in the new diocese was to erect a monastery dedicated to Velimirović near the ancient settlement of Soko. The great urgency with which this complex and expensive building venture was embarked upon was justified on the grounds that "the Holy Synod will canonize this monk of the Orthodox spirit [Velimirović] in the very near future" (cited in Janković, 2003, p. 582).

A year later, however, on November 29, 1990, a commission tasked with investigating the issue of Velimirović's sanctity, headed by the newly elected Patriarch Pavle, rejected the request for canonization. Without dismissing outright Bishop Lavrentije's basic premise concerning Velimirović's reputation among the faithful, Patriarch Pavle called for patience and argued that the matter should not be "forced" or "rushed" (cited in Janković, 2003, p. 558). The cautious approach to Velimirović's status as a saint was justified on theological grounds, but also revealed reservations that were of a political nature.

Patriarch Pavle argued that Velimirović's canonization must come about for the right reasons. It must not be merely an act of vengeance for the injustice done to Velimirović by the communist authorities after the war. The report implicitly rejected the argument, often put forward by Velimirović's supporters, that canonization ought to be the church's response to the "blasphemies, stupidities, and political manipulations regarding [Velimirović's] name" ("Kandilo pred ikonom," 1987, p. 26). Similarly, the patriarch saw through the political motives behind the call for canonization, instigated by nationalists within the church. He argued that "we must wait for this crisis to pass, and wait for a time when reason and canonical principles will once again take over from emotions and badly-conceived national interests" (Janković, 2003, p. 559).

In voicing his commitment to "canonical principles," the patriarch was effectively reminding the Assembly that, contrary to popular belief, canonization in the Orthodox Church was more than the ratification of a religious cult. Patriarch Pavle pointed out that prior to canonization, a candidate's reputation of sanctity must be shown to be faultless. He noted that, Velimirović had displayed "certain human weaknesses" which undermined his status as a saint (Janković, 2003, p. 558). The report did not elaborate on the nature of the weaknesses, but according to a popular anecdote frequently recounted in religious circles, the patriarch's comments alluded to Velimirović's smoking habit for which he was well-known among his contemporaries. It is indicative that a relatively minor vice such as smoking was considered the biggest blemish on Velimirović's saintly reputation. The fact that the patriarch did not mention the far more controversial antisemitic political opinions as a relevant flaw is illustrative of the way in which the controversy surrounding the bishop's politics is repressed within the Serbian Church.

And yet, the patriarch's response to the petition did not maintain that Velimirović's "human weaknesses" disqualified him from sainthood indefinitely. He noted that "various weaknesses which [Nikolaj Velimirović's] had as a man, but which he cast aside through spiritual enlightenment, are still visible, like the morning mist. And just as the rising sun dispels the fog and becomes brighter and brighter, so the sanctity of the Holy grows with the passage of time. One should allow time to dispel the mist, and wait for calmer times when with God's blessing, the Saint's holiness will be confirmed" (Janković, 2003, p. 558).

Therefore, the head of the Serbian Church proposed that canonization be postponed until positive aspects of the bishop's life had eradicated the "weaknesses" from popular memory. Significantly, he also mentioned that Velimirović had already divested himself of most of his sins during his lifetime through "spiritual enlightenment." In that sense, the patriarch's doubts about the bishop's virtues appear somewhat equivocal and can be said to have been part of the broader argument against "hasty decisions" regarding the canonization and in favor of "patience."

More importantly for the present discussion, the patriarch's report also argued that prior to formal canonization a future saint's alleged holiness must be shown to have received "divine confirmation." "Divine confirmation" of sanctity would constitute proof that the alleged popular veneration of Nikolaj Velimirović existed for the right reasons, reasons that were not of man's but of God's making. A sign from God would provide a "stamp of approval" on the life and virtues of a servant of God, and provide "proof" of the saint's intercessory powers (Freze, 1991).

The often-neglected requirement for divine proof of sanctity, invoked by the patriarch on this occasion, is rooted in the Orthodox canonical tradition. The authoritative *Canons of the Orthodox Church* written in 1905 by the Serbian Bishop Nikodim Milaš (1845–1915) states that a saint can be declared only "if marks of prophecy and miracle-making were apparent in the deeds of this person, or if their body after death gave out signs of sanctity" (Milaš, 1999). In a book published in 1998, Patriarch Pavle also listed the criteria for sainthood as including "that they suffered as martyrs for the Christian faith, that their life was irreproachable, that their intercession was confirmed with known miracles which occurred during their lifetime or after death" (Patriarch Pavle, 1998, p. 128). Thus, before Velimirović could be canonized, it had to be demonstrated either that the bishop acted posthumously as an intercessor before God, or that during his lifetime the Lord had graced him with supernatural gifts.

Although in the late 1980s Velimirović's supporters placed relatively little attention to miracles associated with the bishop—compared to the emphasis on his widespread cult following and personal evangelical virtues—this is not to say that they were oblivious to this canonical requirement. During the official sermon delivered on the occasion on Velimirović's informal canonization in 1987—in which he was effectively making a case for Bishop Nikolaj's assumed sanctity—Bishop Amfilohije Radović revealed that he and Atanasije Jevtić had personally witnessed one such miracle, in the United States in the 1970s:

> I would like to confess and testify with great joy about something that happened to me sixteen years ago. In 1970 I visited, in the company of Father Atanasije, who is here with us today, our monastery of St Sava in Libertyville in America. Together with our school friend Father Dragoljub Malić, we drove a thousand kilometers to get to Libertyville with the sole purpose of worshipping Nikolaj's tomb, which holds his holy remains—the wonderful gift to the American continent—and to hold a brief service by the grave. We arrived early in the morning, it was quite misty, a quiet dew was forming. Father Atanasije led the service, the two of us sang. No one else was there—in the monastery or around it. The monastery was shut, there was complete silence. And while we sang, from somewhere a soothing melody could be heard. It was as if a strange choir was singing. The melody reached us in waves, I was unsure whether from the monastery or from elsewhere. This lasted for the duration of the service at Bishop Nikolaj's grave. I asked myself: "Is this for real or am I imagining it?" However, under the impression of the melody, which had been angelic rather than human, delight and a wonderful unique happiness took over my soul. Suddenly I thought: "You see, the gracious Holy Bishop wants to reward our small effort and the fact that we traveled from afar to pay him this visit." [...] However, I said nothing about this to the others. It was only on our journey back, somewhere half way, that our driver, Father Dragoljub said: "Fathers, did you hear anything while we held the service at the bishop's grave?" We asked him "What?" —"I swear that a choir sang at the grave, one like I have never experienced before." Then I said: "You know, I was afraid to say anything , but I heard and felt the same thing during the service." Many years have passed since then, but today I feel with my whole being that this was a wonderful divine gift to me and my sinful soul, a gift from Bishop Nikolaj, whom I loved from the very first encounter with his written word. Clearly, the new Serbian educator wanted to comfort me and make me happy. (A. Radović, 1987, p. 33)

In considering Bishop Lavrentije's petition three years later, the patriarch of the Serbian Church evidently chose to ignore Radović's and Jevtić's mystical experience in Libertyville, or at least did not regard it as sufficient justification for formal canonization. There are several possible reasons for this. Firstly, the patriarch may have regarded the two clerics as too involved in the campaign to constitute reliable witnesses to a genuine miracle. Secondly, he may have chosen to ignore it because doing so suited his overall political reservation regarding the canonization. Finally, the miracle itself does not rate very highly in the hierarchy of miracles in Orthodox hagiology. In the Orthodox world, the most highly regarded miracles are associated with the incorruptibility of a saint's remains, or miracles associated with religious icons such as the leaking of holy oil from images of saints. Nonetheless, the event in Libertyville in 1970 continues to be invoked in the discourse surrounding Velimirović's sanctity. For instance, in a statement to the weekly news magazine *NIN* in May 2003, art historian and member of the Serbian Academy of Arts and Sciences Dejan Medaković explained that "miracles are often linked with Saints" and that "we know of some miracles on Nikolaj's grave" (Andrejević, 2003).

Finding the "right" miracle: Incorruptibility of remains and miraculous icons

Because the Orthodox Church does not have formalized procedures associated with the verification of miracles, the requirement for divine proof of sanctity is potentially problematic and often controversial. In the Russian Church, for example, there have been instances when, once the need for miracles had been voiced, what followed was an abundance of unsubstantiated claims. Recent calls for the canonization of the imperial family of Tsar Nikolai Romanov were accompanied by an "industry of miracles" with almost 2,000 unconfirmed instances recorded between 1997 and 2000 (Krivulyin, 2001, p. 20). In the case of Nikolaj Velimirović, the patriarch's reference to the requirement for divine confirmation of sanctity did not result in an epidemic of miracles of the scale described by Krivulyin. Nonetheless, some miraculous events have been reported since 1990, including those referring to the incorruptibility of Velimirović's posthumous remains and miracles associated with icons representing his image.

According to the Orthodox canonical law, the incorruptibility of the holy remains (or *mošti*) and the presence of an unusual, pleasant scent emanating from the corpse are seen as a divine "sign," which confirms the Holy status of the venerated Man of God. For this reason, in the Orthodox world, the holy remains of saints are often displayed in monasteries, partially draped, in open caskets to be worshiped by pilgrims. The strength of belief in the incorruptibility of holy remains is reflected in fact that (according to a story told to me by deacon Radoš Mladenović) when Velimirović's remains were brought from Libertyville in 1991, and were taken to the monastery in Žiča, monks secretly broke the locks on the sealed coffin, in order to discover whether Velimirović's body had decomposed. Although they found no sign of incorruptibility, Velimirović's *mošti* (including the finger kept behind the altar in the chapel in Kraljevo, see Chapter 2) are venerated by the Orthodox faithful as saintly. Furthermore, some followers have reported that the remains emit the saintly scent. Milan Bates, leader of the St. Justin the Philosopher Association of Students, mentioned the following experience during the interview:

> I was in Lelić; it was when the Holy remains of Bishop Nikolaj were brought there from Libertyville. I attended a liturgy, and they usually say that the remains of a saint which are [...] they say they are *mirotočive*, they release a scent which is inexplicable, which emanates from [the remains] which are incorruptible. I can only speak from my own experience, simply that every time during the liturgy—because I was there, right next to the remains of Bishop Nikolaj—every time the *tropar*, that is the prayer for the bishop, was sung, the remains released a scent of sweet basil, incense, of that holy chrism which does not exist and cannot be manufactured. It is a miracle that proves God's presence in the world...

A miraculous event of a different kind was reported in 1999 in the religious journal *Sv. Knez Lazar*, published by the diocese of Raška and Prizren. The miracle, which allegedly occurred in the Monastery of St Archangel in Prizren, in Kosovo, shortly after the arrival of NATO troops in June 1999 was described in a short testimony by the local bishop Artemije Radosavljević. The account of the miracle, published under the title "The miracle of Bishop Nikolaj" was originally conveyed to Radosavljević by a novice from the monastery, named Dobrivoje, who witnessed the following event:

> One day I was sitting on the balcony with two KFOR guards, (Germans by nationality). One of them said he believed in God, the other

> stated that he did not [...] Several days later, the one "who did not believe" asked me to come to the chapel and sing something because he "liked to listen." I sang a hymn to the Mother of God. When I had finished, I looked at the soldier, and he seemed all hysterical, and anxious. I asked him what was going on. He said "He looked at me!" "Who did?" I asked. "*Him*," he answered and pointed at the icon of Bishop Nikolaj on the iconostasis. "How?" I asked. "While you were singing he turned his eyes towards me, and then turned them back to how they are now." When he had regained his composure he said: "Until now I did not believe, but from now on, when I go back home, I will regularly go to church." God really is beautiful when seen through his Saints. (A. Radosavljević, 1999, p. 14)

Although these and similar stories of miracles are part of the overall discourse surrounding Velimirović's sanctity, they were relatively peripheral to the actual cause for the bishop's canonization. As we are about to see, the key miracle cited in the charter which formally declared Nikolaj a saint was not related so much to posthumous miraculous deeds, but to the mystical aspects of Velimirović's earthly existence, which emphasized his qualities as a confessor and Man of God. These refer to what are said to be the bishop's "special charisms" or divine capabilities—namely epiphany, prophecy, and healing.

The bishop who came "face to face with the living God": Velimirović and the miracle of epiphany

The inclusion of Nikolaj Velimirović in the roll call of Serbian saints in May 2003 was preceded by a successful petition, signed in January of that year, by a group of senior Orthodox clerics, including nine bishops. As in 1990, the petition appealed to the custom within the Orthodox Church to honor and celebrate those "who had already been chosen by the faithful as intercessors before the throne of the Almighty." Canonization would be little more than "a proclamation of something that already exists in the life and practice of the faithful" (cited in Jevtić, 2003a, p. 306). On the other hand, the new petition also reflected on the requirement for divine confirmation. The signatories noted that Velimirović had been celebrated among the faithful as "one chosen by God and a Saint, especially since the days of his suffering for Christ in

German prisons and camps, where, according to testimonies of numerous reliable witnesses, he experienced epiphany and the mercy of a visit from God Alive and True" (ibid.). This claim appears to have been accepted by the Assembly of Bishops, which recognized in the formal Canonization Charter that the new saint "had been celebrated by God through splendid omens" (Janković, 2003, p. 589).

Although the act of canonization was accompanied by the acknowledgment that Velimirović's sanctity had received divine confirmation, it would be naive to assume that Bishop Nikolaj's status as a saint hinged entirely on this matter of canonical law. Given the political aspect of his rehabilitation in the 1980s, Velimirović's canonization was always going to be a matter of ecclesiastical politics rather than one of strictly canonical considerations, and the debate over what constitutes the "right" miracle. Even in 1990, the patriarch's recommendation concerning the requirement for a miracle was as much a theological point as the rationalization of his political reservations. Therefore, the success of the petition for canonization filed in 2003 needs to be examined primarily in the context of the ideological warfare between the Church and the liberal public over the memory of Bishop Nikolaj, which intensified after 2000. Deacon Radoš Mladenović, who helped organize the symposium during which the petition was drafted, mentioned several times during our conversation in the summer of 2003 that canonization was a gesture of defiance, in the face of rising tide of criticism: "They attacked him, and we responded with canonization." Importantly however, as the patriarch's reasoning in 1990 revealed, in affairs of the church, political points must be presented as theologically justified, and in the case of canonization as acts of God. Branislav Skrobonja, editor of the magazine *Glas Kosova i Metohije*, explained in an article published in *Danas* in 2002 that "people can declare someone anything they like, but only God, he who forgives and who punishes, can declare someone a saint." Skrobonja argued that in Orthodox Christianity (unlike in Roman Catholicism) sanctity is not decided by "congregations and ministries," but by "miracles associated with holy remains or miracles that follow prayers" (Skrobonja, 2002). Also, in the Orthodox Church, the declaration of saints—which usually takes place during the meeting of the Assembly of Bishops—is preceded by the act of Epiclesis, or the invocation of the Holy Spirit, to whose divine influence any decision is ultimately attributed. Thus, part of the canonization process involves the "theologization" of arguments, and the construction of an inherently *political* decision as emanating from God and the Holy Spirit. At the same time, as will become apparent, irrespective of the political struggles and goings-on behind the scenes which ultimately led to the decision to canonize Velimirović, the public representations of sanctity advanced in the context of the cause for his canonization are themselves revealing. The "theologization" of the decision taken by the Assembly of Bishops in May 2003 carries significant ideological implications with regards to the controversy surrounding Velimirović's work.

Bishop Nikolaj's alleged experience of epiphany during the imprisonment at Dachau, which was invoked as a "splendid omen," is a reference to an event when, in the words of his followers, the bishop "came face to face with God." "Testimonies of numerous reliable witnesses" mentioned in the petition refer above all to a second-hand account provided in the 1950s by a Russian nun, Milica (sometimes also referred to as Sofija) Zernov, who befriended Velimirović during his years in exile in the United States. It is interesting that Velimirović himself alluded to the mystical experience at Dachau when he told the *Chicago Herald American* in April 1946 that he "discovered God in the Nazi Hell-camp of Dachau" ("Bishop Reveals Persecution of Church under Tito Regime," 1946, p. 30). The Anglican bishop of Chichester, George Bell, also mentions in his diaries that when speaking of "his years of imprisonment in concentration camps [*sic*], [Velimirović] spoke of God's presence with him in prison, of the angels, and of his real experience of God's care and love" (cited in Heppell, 2001, p. 92). However, over the past twenty years, it is Zernov's recollection of Velimirović's interpretation of the epiphany that has taken centre stage in the narrative of Velimirović's encounter with God. It has been published numerous times in religious publications and continues to be mentioned in speeches and sermons devoted to Bishop Nikolaj (see Jevtić, 2003a, pp. 306–307; A. Radosavljević, 1986). For instance, in a sermon delivered in 1987, Bishop Amfilohije Radović explained the following:

> In the most tragic moment, not only of his personal life, but also the life of many European peoples including his own—during his internment at Dachau—[Nikolaj's] eyes met the living God himself. When a wonderful and devout soul, Sofija Zernov, asked him after the war

> about his time at Dachau, he was to say: "In the camp it was like this: you sit in the corner and repeat to yourself—I am dust and ashes. Lord, take my soul away! Your soul then rises towards heaven and you see God face to face. But you cannot bear it and you say: I am not ready, I can't, take me back! Then you sit for hours and repeat to yourself: I am dust and ashes. Lord, take my soul away! Your soul then rises towards heaven again..."; and he added to this miraculous testimony: "I would give all that is left of my life on earth for one hour at Dachau." Sister Sofija also said that she could not endure the gaze of the bishop's eyes, the eyes of a man who had encountered God. (A. Radović, 1987, p. 33)

Traditionally, Christian mysticism views such experiences where "the soul is momentarily caught up in the divine presence, oblivious to his or her natural surroundings" and when "God infuses superior knowledge into the mind and soul" and "reveals divine mysteries" as manifestations of a "special charisma"—an unusual gift that provides evidence that the beneficiary had been touched by the hand of God (Freze, 1991, p. 51). As such, it is seen as a "mark of credentials" of saintly figures. Crucially however, in early accounts of Velimirović's mystical experience in Dachau, including the above quotation, the epiphany was not invoked as evidence that divine grace had been bestowed upon the Serbian bishop. Instead, it was used to portray Velimirović as a believer who desired and relished the prospect of a life of adversity, hardship, and suffering and whose virtues of patience, fortitude, faith, and courage were immune to the trials and tribulations of earthly existence. The account by sister Zernov was part of the overall narrative of Velimirović's martyrdom at Dachau, examined in Chapter 3.

In the context of the campaign for canonization, however, and especially in the aftermath of the patriarch's call for the divine confirmation of Bishop Nikolaj's sanctity, the epiphany gradually came to be used specifically to build the bishop's credibility as the beneficiary of divine intervention. The alleged encounter with the Almighty at Dachau emerged in hagiographic narratives as a central life event that transformed Velimirović into a true mystic, miracle-maker, and a Man of God. This is not surprising, given that, within the Christian world, heavenly visions and apparitions of the kind described by Zernov are widely believed to occur for a purpose, as a prelude to further divine intercessions which "serve to convert, inspire, instruct or reaffirm the faithful about God's active presence in their midst" (Freze, 1991, p. 60).

In some accounts, the epiphany was said to have turned Velimirović into a healer. In 1988, in a speech in which he pleaded for Velimirović's canonization, Bishop Jovan of Šabac and Valjevo alluded to his uncle's special power, and linked it to the event in Dachau: "After the war, he used to say that he had never been closer to God than [at Dachau], that he had never felt the presence of God more strongly and that such happiness had never been repeated. This is why he regretted not staying in Dachau for the rest of his life. After Dachau, during his stay in Vienna, the bishop blessed a seriously ill woman at the local church and wished her to recover, and the patient did recover, after many years of illness." (J. Velimirović, 1991, p. 25).

In the same speech, Bishop Jovan reiterated his belief in Velimirović's powers of miracle-making when he noted that even posthumously "numerous pious men and women in our country prayed to Bishop Nikolaj and in turn witnessed instances of healing" (p. 22). In a recent book, Protopresbyter Milan Janković suggested that "there is written evidence of a number of miraculous healings associated with his saintly prayers" (Janković, 2004, p. 42; a number of accounts of healing can be found in Janković, 2003, p. 576). During the interview for this book, Deacon Radoš Mladenović also alluded to the healing properties of Bishop Nikolaj's remains. Mladenović explained, how in 1991, following the transportation of Velimirović's remains back to Serbia, a group of nuns was tasked with the washing of the body with red wine, as required by protocol. The nuns are said to have packed the dust from the coffin "into small parcels," which they distributed to the sick and the disabled "as a blessing for healing."

The miracle mentioned by Bishop Jovan, about the events in Vienna, was first chronicled in 1969, in a little-known book by Stefan Čakić, a Serbian priest from the Austrian city of Graz. Čakić recounted the anecdote in an article in *Glas Crkve* in 1986, and again in 1987, thereby reviving Velimirović's image as a healer. Čakić explained:

> The event took place in Vienna, in the Orthodox Church of St Sava, in the autumn of 1944, when, under heavy German guard, Bishop Nikolaj, together with patriarch Gavrilo Dožić, was being taken to Dachau. Nikolaj was brought to the Church to say a prayer to God and St Sava

> for his oppressed people. The woman's name was Natalija Stanić, and she was a sexton and a singer at the church. Bishop Nikolaj placed his cross above her, rubbed in some holy oil, and said, "May it be according to your faith, and the prayers for the Holy Father St Nicholas." He cured her of her illness, something that not even doctors had been able to do [...] Yes, yes, our great Bishop Nikolaj was not only our most respected theologian and writer and unsurpassed orator, our most famous church dignitary, but also a miracle maker and a healer, and only Saints can do that, those ordained with Saintly halos. (Čakić 1987, pp. 76–77; the original testimony published in 1986, which contains identical claims, appears in Janković, 2003; p. 577)

Since the reappearance of Čakić's claim in 1986, the instance of healing has been recounted many times in Church publications. However, among the various and often very detailed versions of the story, some discrepancy has arisen regarding the nature of the woman's predicament (that is, whether it was a physical or a mental illness), and more importantly regarding the date of the miracle's occurrence. Čakić's original testimony places the event in "the autumn of 1944," when Velimirović and Dožić were being taken to Dachau. Most subsequent accounts, including that told by Bishop Jovan in 1988, place the event *after* the spell at the camp. According to Deacon Ljubomir Ranković, for instance, Velimirović "cured a seriously ill woman" in Vienna in "early 1945" (Ranković, 2003a). During the interview, Ranković described it as taking place "on the way back from Dachau." The reason why the event appears to have been "relocated" to after the spell at the camp is because, in the context of the construction of the bishop's saintly credentials, the account of healing became assimilated into the story of the epiphany. As in the aforementioned speech by Bishop Jovan, the two events were incorporated into a coherent causal narrative: Velimirović became a healer because he saw God in Dachau.

Velimirović as a "prophet": The construction of the "Serbian Jeremiah"

The tale of Velimirović's encounter with God in Dachau and the alleged miracle-making which is so often causally linked to the epiphany, highlighted the importance of this period of the bishop's life and gave it a pronounced mystical dimension. Significantly, belief in the authenticity of the epiphany also affected the perception of the bishop's writing at the camp, namely the notorious *Words to the Serbian People Through the Dungeon Window*. As was noted in earlier chapters, the principal message of Velimirović's notes from Dachau is that World War II was the inevitable consequence of the secularization of "godless Europe." In the book, first published in Germany in 1985 by the then Bishop of Western Europe, Lavrentije Trifunović, Velimirović also attributed the tragic fate of Serbs during the war to their betrayal of God and Christian traditions in favor of the much-maligned European culture.

Following its publication, *Words to the Serbian People Through the Dungeon Window* instantly captured the imagination of Velimirović's supporters in Serbia. This was primarily because the book's anticommunist and anti-Western overtones appealed to nationalists within the church. The text was widely perceived as a prophetic work, in which the author "forewarned us about the country we now live in [...] about Yugoslavia, a state that despises God and the rights of man and a country devoid of any sense of honor and self-respect" (Komnenić, 1991, p. 49). In 1993, an article published in *Glas Crkve* referred to "the Bishop's prophecies," which contained a "warning about the sinfulness of Western civilization and of the Serbian people should they remain tied to it" (Marković, 1993, p. 26).

Because of the assumed prophetic nature of the book, Velimirović was compared with the Old Testament prophet Jeremiah, who warned the children of Israel about the catastrophic consequences that rejection of God would bring about on the Jewish people. In a speech delivered at the commemoration in Lelić in 1989, Vuk Drašković articulated the comparison as follows:

> I would like to focus today on Nikolaj the accuser. On what one might call his Jeremiah's lamentation in the Nazi concentration camp at Dachau, when the prisoner from Lelić, painfully engrossed in the tragedy and destruction of his people, asked himself: Are Serbs responsible for the apocalypse that has befallen us... We have schools without faith, politics without honesty, army without the unity of spirit, state without God's blessing—so accuses our Berdyaev, our Jeremiah. (Drasković, 1989, p. 71).

Similarly, theologian Radovan Bigović notes that "at moments, [Velimirović] reminds us of the Old Testament prophet Jeremiah, who yells in the spiritual desert and unmistakably prophesies and predicts what will happen to Europe and its people if they do not change" (Bigović, 1993, p. 45). Atanasije Jevtić referred to Velimirović as "a genuine patriot, but also a prophet, akin to what Moses or Jeremiah were to the Jewish people" (Jevtić, 1988, p. 19; also Jevtić, 1986a, p. 12). Đorđe Janić (1994) notes that "even without knowing of all the crimes against Serbs which had taken place during World War II, in Dachau he was writing down his thoughts which resemble Jeremiah's grieving over the fate of the Jewish people" (p. 31).

The claims about Velimirović's prophetic gift were not confined to his writing at Dachau. George Bell made a reference to Velimirović's status as prophet at a memorial service held in September 1956 at the Church of St Sava in London. Bishop Bell concluded his tribute with the following words: "A marvellous man, yes. A great patriot, yes. But he was more than that. He was a prophet of God, not only of God's mercy, but of God's judgment" (cited in Heppell, 2001, p. 93). In a recent booklet on Nikolaj Velimirović, Protopresbyter Milan Janković (2004) justifies the bishop's inclusion into the Diptych of Serbian Saints by citing his "prophetic words" uttered shortly before his death in 1956, in which Velimirović predicts that the fall of communism would lead to a civil war in which Serbs would experience "a terrible tragedy" because of the absence of a clear national program. The atrocities would be perpetrated by Croats, who would receive support from the Vatican while the Pope would once again "silence the friendly Anglo-Saxons and give his blessing to the slaughter of Serbs" (p. 42). This "warning to Serbian patriots" had already received some publicity in 1992, at the time of the war in Croatia, when it was also hailed as "prophetic" and published on the front page of the magazine *Pravoslavlje* ("Proročka reč Vladike Nikolaja: Opomena Srbima rodoljubima," 1992). The editors of *Pravoslavlje* saw the "warning"—which was marked "confidential" by its author—as especially relevant, given that it revealed that "Serbia is once again under threat from all four corners of the world."

The references to Velimirović's power of prophecy, and the resulting comparison with Jeremiah, were for the most part metaphorical.

Velimirović was said to have been "akin" to Jeremiah, to "resemble" the Old Testament prophet, and "remind us" of him. And yet some Church dignitaries and commentators interpreted the bishop's words as being "prophetic" in the original Biblical sense. This is because the explanation of Velimirović's gift of prophecy became integrated into the widely available story of the epiphany at Dachau. Just as Jeremiah is said to have acquired his gift when "the Lord reached out his hand" (Jer. 1:8) and graced him with the divine ability to foresee the future, Velimirović's power of prophesy, manifested above all in his most controversial book, was also believed to have resulted from the visitation from God in Dachau. In 1991, Bishop Amfilohije Radović offered the following account of Velimirović's prison writing:

> No one has ever written about Europe what Nikolaj wrote behind the windows of Dachau. His book was written on toilet paper. Nikolaj wrote that text, which is moving, apocalyptic, and relevant both for our times and for those when it was written. That text will only gain importance with the passage of time. Especially because it was written in Dachau, where the bishop saw the Living God. That is what is most important to Bishop Nikolaj. In Dachau, after that vision, he lived like a prophet from both the Old Testament and the Gospels. He described and discovered the internal forces which move events on the continent of Europe and the whole world, and showed his people the way. Every letter written in Dachau is a letter written to every Serbian mother, every Serbian youth, every Serbian girl, every Serbian child, every Serbian sage, Serbian philosopher, poet, and statesman.
>
> Because what happened at Dachau? [...] There he experienced the dust and the ashes. And God raised him and conveyed to him untold secrets. He said to God: "I can't bear it—take me back..." At Dachau, Bishop Nikolaj saw the Living God. He is one of the most important witnesses to the encounter with God. [...] His deepest suffering, his most profound crucifixion was also the source of his most profound enlightenment. [...] There he pronounced the words uttered by Christ on the Golgotha: "My God, My God, why hast Thou forsaken me?" But that is when his soul and everything else became clear to him. And he became a witness to this and will remain so until the end of the world. (A. Radović, 1991, p. 43)

In the same sermon, Radović referred to Velimirović as the "witness to God, the seer of God, the knower of the Secrets and of Nature" (p. 44).

The reputed divine origins of Velimirović's gift reinforced his image as "God's prophet." The aforementioned article published in *Glas Crkve* in 1993 noted that Bishop Nikolaj was "a prophet of planetary dimensions" not simply because he could "predict the future," but because he was able to "read God's plan, understand the intentions of God's Providence, and, by following divine logic from start to finish, draw the intended conclusions" (Marković, 1993, p. 26). The epiphany at Dachau provided this type of assertion with a supernatural point of origin, and in doing so, reinforced the belief that Velimirović is not venerated merely as a theologian, writer and evangelist, but also as a mystic and an intercessor between Serbs and the Almighty.

Controversially, however, by linking the *Words to the Serbian People Through the Dungeon Window* to the author's "profound enlightenment" in Dachau, the narrative of Velimirović's prophetic gift imbued this controversial work with undeserved value and celestial authority. Historian Bora Karapandžić for instance spoke of *Words to the Serbian People Through the Dungeon Window* as a book "based on God's Revelation" (speech delivered in Cleveland, Ohio in 1987, cited in Janković, 2002b, p. 204).

Until recently, when representatives of the mainstream of Serbian Orthodox culture referred to Velimirović's power of prophecy manifested in the prison writing, they seldom mentioned the antisemitic dimension of the book. In line with the general dynamic of repression, the bishop's contempt for Jews was sidelined. Tributes paid to the prophetic character of *Words to the Serbian People Through the Dungeon Window* were by and large limited to the indictment of European secular culture and the condemnation of the Serbian people whom Velimirović saw as straying from the path of Christianity. As we have seen in the previous chapter, any focus on the controversial passages from this book tended to be dismissed as being taken "out of context."

At the same time, the popularization of Velimirović's prison writing as a prophetic work "relevant to our times" and as a testament to all Serbs inevitably guided the audience towards the original text where antisemitic claims are candidly explicated. Moreover, the above quoted sermon by Amfilohije Radović directed potential readers to what is considered to be the most important message of the book, namely the identity of the "internal forces" behind European civilization which Velimirović, as the "witness of God," exposes in his work. Although these "forces" remained unqualified in Radović's speech, some readers would have inevitably linked the maligned influence of modernity and enlightenment to Jews, whom Velimirović openly cites in the book as the clandestine force responsible for the failures of the Old Continent.

Also, however much mainstream writers sidelined the topic of antisemitism, authors of Serbian right-wing antisemitic literature published over the past two decades endeavored to capitalize on the claims regarding Velimirović's power of prophecy and invoked them directly to support overtly anti-Jewish claims. In the book *Western Ideological and Spiritual Poisoners*, Ratibor Đurđević (1997) argues that what makes *Words to the Serbian People Through the Dungeon Window* such an important work is that at Dachau, "inspired by the insights of the Prophets of Israel, the bishop learned the most profound secret about all the tragic events and suffering: it was God's Judgment over the godless, the traitors, and those who despise Christ the Lord... He considered it his holy duty to reveal God's will to the people" (p. 11). These words echo the rhetoric of Radović's 1991 speech, but are used by Đurđević to promote Velimirović's most reprehensible antisemitic claims, including the assertion that the Holocaust represented divine retribution against the "godless" and "treacherous" Jews.

Whatever differences existed between the ways in which the mainstream Orthodox culture and the wilder reaches of the Christian Right invoked Velimirović's prophetic gift, they all but disappeared around the time of the canonization. In his contribution to the edited book that accompanied the canonization, Bishop Amfilohije Radović made a direct causal link between the antisemitic dimension of *Words to the Serbian People Through the Dungeon Window* and the story of the epiphany, not dissimilar to that which appears in the works of Ratibor Đurđević. Radović substantiated the claim about the "prophetic" nature of Velimirović's "harsh words" addressed to, among others, the "people of Israel" (see previous chapter) by reminding the readers that the new saint spent time in Dachau where he "*saw God*" and became a person who "*knows God*" (A. Radović, 2003, p. 511, original emphasis). These four words were the only ones in the eight-page article that were printed in bold type, suggesting that Radović (or Atanasije

Jevtić who edited the book) considered them as deserving special attention. It is as if they wanted to make it clear that whatever Nikolaj Velimirović wrote in Dachau, even his most controversial message to his people, was the result of his encounter with God, and was therefore beyond dispute. This conclusion was in many ways a logical extension of the rhetoric of interpretative denial examined in the previous chapter. The story of the epiphany gave the assumed "Biblical" nature of Velimirović's antisemitism divine origins. Velimirović's antisemitic diatribes described as "mere repetition" of the words of God, became treated as *literally* the word of God, revealed to Holy Bishop Nikolaj during the mystical experience at Dachau.

The social construction of Bishop Nikolaj's sanctity and the way in which it is represented in contemporary ecclesiastical discourse provides an additional example of the way in which the rhetorics of repression and denial, which have become a fundamental feature of the remembrance of Nikolaj Velimirović, have distorted the boundaries between the mainstream and the extreme in Serbian Orthodox culture. When it comes to the topic of antisemitism, the apologist rhetoric has stripped the ideological position traditionally reserved for the radical Christian Right of negative connotations and has assimilated extremism into the mainstream of Serbian Orthodox culture. Most harmfully, by linking the divine proof of Velimirović's blessedness with his most controversial work, apologetics for antisemitism features not just in narratives of the bishop's life, but also in the routine celebration of his sanctity.

CHAPTER SEVEN

Conclusion

> "The only thing worse than perpetrating a crime is trying to rationalize it. The only thing worse than committing a sin is offering an excuse for it. The only thing worse than doing violence is trying to justify it. The only thing worse than waging war is believing that war can be just. There is nothing for which an individual or a people should be held responsible more readily than the belief that they bare no responsibility." (Radovan Bigović, 1994, p. 11)

The main aim of the present study has been to explore the dynamics of repression and denial constitutive of the rehabilitation of Bishop Nikolaj Velimirović over the past twenty or so years. It has examined a variety of discursive and rhetorical practices of social remembering and forgetting which enabled the favorable representations of the controversial bishop—which had been confined, during the communist period, to the relatively marginal group of nationalist clergy gathered around Father Justin Popović and to the Serbian diaspora in the West—to penetrate the public sphere and come to dominate memorial discourse within mainstream Serbian Orthodox culture. The continuing adulation of Nikolaj Velimirović has been shown to involve routine repression of his antisemitism and a whole host of strategies of denial, the aim of which is to justify, play down, and rationalize his lamentable stance towards Jews.

At first sight, various components of repression and denial explored in this study might seem to be in contradiction with each other, especially as willful forgetting of controversial biographical details often appears virtually side by side with their explicit denial or justification. As the preceding chapters have endeavored to show, the co-existence of the two processes can be attributed to the fact that they are functionally related. Aspects of denial, such as emphatic and out-right rejection of accusations of antisemitism, or the refusal to engage in the debate about Velimirović's contentious views, serve the purpose of shifting attention away from the embarrassing topics, thereby facilitating the repression of controversy. Conversely, one of the principal strengths of the martyrdom myth, which lies at the core of the repression of Velimirović's antisemitism, is that its routine nature provides the rhetorical means for denying antisemitism in response to direct accusations. The compatibility of the two processes is ultimately to be found in their common objective, namely to ensure that Bishop Nikolaj Velimirović is remembered in a favorable and complimentary fashion, free of controversy and debate.

In exploring the different aspects of repression and denial, preceding chapters have demonstrated an important aspect of memorial discourse, namely its variability. Portrayals of Nikolaj Velimirović lack consistency and narrative coherence. In the language of everyday remembrance, the claim that Velimirović spent the whole of World War II in the "dungeons of Nazism" quietly coexists with the allegation that during the same period he rescued a Jewish family from Nazi capture. Velimirović's controversial *Words to the Serbian People Through the Dungeon Window* are said to consist of "mere notes," which the bishop never intended to publish, while virtually simultaneously being praised as his most important work of almost divine significance. This fragmented and disjointed nature of memorial representation reveals that social remembering is not determined by the requirement for narrative constancy and structural unity typical of formal historical accounts, but by the immediate rhetorical and argumentative needs of the memory-maker and the locally contingent demands of moral accountability management.

The overwhelming concern with presenting Nikolaj Velimirović in a positive light, which determines the discourse of his remembrance, reflects the argumentative nature of social memory. As Irwin-Zarecka (1994) notes, the "vicissitudes of remembrance" are contingent upon the interplay between two forces: one which constructs and maintains the "morally purified narratives, both ideologically and practically," and its opposing force, located in rival memories, which demands re-evaluation and calls for "full moral accounting for the past" (p. 129). In the context of the controversy surrounding Velimirović's remembrance, the accounts of his personal history are at the same time accounts for his contentious beliefs. Hence, representation of Nikolaj Velimirović in Orthodox culture is determined by the nature and the content of the ongoing ideological confrontation with liberal public opinion. Remembrance of the bishop in the context of his adulation is not a neutral activity, but a "tool for politically charged intellectual debates" (Irwin-Zarecka, 1994, p. 129).

In focusing on the rhetorical aspect of remembering, the present book also argued that in investigating post-communist rehabilitation of controversial historical figures, inquiry should not be limited to the three-pronged question: "Who wants to remember what and why?" It should also address the issue of how specific memories and visions of the past are constructed and told so as to make them appear acceptable and preferable to alternatives. Study of memory ought to explore how accounts of the past continuously and effectively undermine alternative and competing versions, and shed light on the ways in which specific memories impose themselves upon the audience as the rational, reasonable, morally preferable, and, above all, historically accurate representations of the past.

Furthermore, the role which the creation and maintenance of Velimirović's non-prejudiced image plays in determining the structure and the content of his remembrance points towards an important aspect of prejudice emphasized by discourse analytic research. The language of intolerance and discrimination does not consist simply of negative attitudes towards and stereotypes about minorities, but also includes the argumentation surrounding the expression of prejudiced views and the way in which talk is organized rhetorically to avoid or deny attributions of racism (Billig, 1990; Rapley, 2001; Wetherell & Potter, 1992). For this reason, the study of intolerance should focus not merely on dominant representations of the racial, national, or religious "other," but also on the rhetoric of justification, denial, and rationalization by means of which the label "prejudiced" is evaded when talking about that "other." By exploring the representations of Jews in Serbian Orthodox Christian culture—through the prism of Velimirović's remembrance—the present study looked not only at how Velimirović or his supporters talk about Jews, but also at the multitude of rhetorical strategies which the bishop's admirers, as morally accountable agents, use in the context of his remembrance in order to construct themselves, their hero, and in some cases even the whole of the Serbian Orthodox Church and the Serbian people as being devoid of prejudice. In doing so, the study exposed the broader ideological implications of collective remembering. By legitimizing and normalizing the discredited ideological tradition of anti-Jewish prejudice, denial and repression of Velimirović's antisemitism perpetuate social inequality and reproduce existing power relations, while at the same time protecting the dominant group's ideas, symbols and authority against the detrimental charges of intolerance.

In a recently published essay, the author David Albahari (2004) reflected on the differences between antisemitism in Canada and Serbia. The principal difference, Albahari argued, lies not in the frequency or intensity of anti-Jewish prejudice, but in the fact that in Canada, unlike in Serbia, there are efficient "legal provisions" in place which—although incapable of eradicating antisemitism altogether—at least make politicians and public figures accountable for antisemitic statements or actions. Albahari proposes that in order to create a comparable climate of public accountability in Serbia, the country's elite institutions, above all the Serbian Orthodox Church and the state should respond more decisively to manifestations of intolerance towards Jews. However, in the conclusion to the essay, Albahari also provides advice to the representatives of the Jewish community in Serbia. He advises them to

> [r]ecognise the inevitability of different interpretations (as in the case of antisemitic claims in the work of Bishop Nikolaj) because religion and culture, just like history often have two points of view which, apparently, must coexist. What is good for one side might not be good for the other, but if both sides are aware of what this means for the other side, and respect the differences, then coexistence is possible. And this is what Serbia needs the most: quiet coexistence, marked by mutual respect accompanied by the readiness to understand others so that they would understand us. (Albahari, 2004, p. 95)

Evidently, in order to facilitate "peaceful coexistence" between Christians and Jews in Serbia, Albahari proposes a compromise solution: the

Church should stand up in defense of the Jews in the face of increasing antisemitic attacks, while in return Jews would turn a blind eye to the favorable "interpretation" of Bishop Nikolaj's antisemitic views, and accept it as an intrinsic aspect of Orthodox Christian religious dogma and "culture," which "must" be tolerated in the name of liberal open-mindedness and inter-cultural understanding.

The examination, in this study, of the representations of Nikolaj Velimirović in Serbian Orthodox culture has hopefully demonstrated the impracticality, unfeasibility, and undesirability of this particular "conciliatory" approach to the reduction of antisemitism. The hero-worship of Nikolaj Velimirović and the favorable interpretation of his controversial work within Orthodox culture are not peripheral to the problem of antisemitism and are therefore not something that can be simply overlooked for the sake of mutual respect. Remembrance of Nikolaj Velimirović and his uncritical reverence are the most powerful ideological sources of anti-Jewish prejudice in Serbian culture, from which much of contemporary antisemitism derives legitimacy and authority. In drawing the distinction between the type of antisemitism that the Church ought to condemn as unacceptable and that which the Jewish community ought to accept as inevitable, Albahari failed to recognize the fact that, in reality, no such distinction exists in contemporary Serbia.

Also, the reference, in Albahari's essay, to Christian antisemitism as an immutable aspect of Orthodox Christianity, which Jews must learn to accept and tolerate, illustrates the way in which the problematic definition of Serbian-Jewish relations constructed through the remembrance of Nikolaj Velimirović has become accepted as normal and unavoidable even outside Serbian Orthodox culture. This acceptance of the inevitability of Christian antisemitism is detrimental to interfaith dialogue, above all because it ensures that the re-evaluation of the doctrinal stance towards Jews in Orthodox Christianity remains off the agenda of Christian-Jewish relations.

During our four-hour interview with Deacon Radoš Mladenović in the summer of 2003, which was held on the balcony of the house in Kraljevo once inhabited by Nikolaj Velimirović, the deacon described his recent encounter with the head of the Serbian Church, Patriarch Pavle:

> Pavle, our patriarch and holy man, recently visited the town of Vrnjačka Banja, and I went there to greet him. I asked him: "Your Holiness, how are you?" "Very well," he replied and said to the nuns, "Bring the refreshments, serve the deacon." The nuns from Žiča knew that Bishop Stefan granted me the privilege of one glass of brandy each time I visit him at his cabinet. So they brought in the coffee and asked: "Your holiness, how about a shot of brandy for the deacon?" the patriarch remained silent. "Your Holiness, shall we bring the brandy for the deacon?" Still there was no reply. In order to break the uncomfortable silence, I said: "Your Holiness, in my village they say that a coffee without a brandy is like a dead man without a candle." "That is the point, deacon, my brother," the patriarch then said, "the greatest sin is not when you commit one, but when you seek to justify it!"

This was one of several anecdotes featuring the Serbian patriarch which Mladenović recounted during the interview. Its point was to present the head of the Serbian Church as a devout and saintly figure whose uncomplicated way of thinking reflects the traditional wisdom and wit of the Serbian common man. And yet, the anecdote which was a source of great amusement to the deacon, inadvertently summarized the principal problem associated with the remembrance of Nikolaj Velimirović in Orthodox culture, which was the principal topic of our conversation and of this book.

The "problem" with the persistence of Serbian antisemitism in Orthodox culture does not lie in the "sins" of Bishop Velimirović. Although much of the current public debate between different "memory communities" in Serbia revolves around whether or not Velimirović was an antisemite, this issue is of little practical importance. Velimirović lived and wrote in the first half of the 20th century, reaching the pinnacle of his career in the period between the two World Wars. This was a period when conspiratorial antisemitism was at the peak of its worldwide popularity and anti-Jewish slurs were in Billig's (1987) words the "polite currency of gentile conversation" (p. 250). Also, contempt for Jews was a routine feature of Christian theology, liturgical practice, and Church life throughout Christendom. In 1938, a Vatican encyclical, which, somewhat paradoxically, was critical of the passing of antisemitic laws in Italy, argued that "Jews put to death their Savior and King" and invited upon themselves "the wrath of God" and "divine malediction, dooming them, as it were, to perpetually wander over the face of the earth." The same document accused Jews of promoting revolutionary movements that aim to "destroy society and to obliterate from the minds of men the knowledge, reverence and love of God" (cited in Goldhagen, 2002, p. 85). These words are virtually identical to those that Velimirović wrote six years later in his *Words to the Serbian People Through the Dungeon Window.* He, just like the authors of the encyclical, inhabited the world before the post-Holocaust political morality justifiably imposed limitations on expressions of intolerance and pushed antisemitism onto the margins of political discourse. Thus, the fact that we find the language of antisemitism in Velimirović's writing is not unusual, although it does cast a shadow over his integrity, because a considerable number of his contemporaries, who may not have been as educated, knowledgeable, and eloquent as Nikolaj is said to have been, but who were just as devoted to their religion and their people, adopted a more commendable stance towards Jews, and took a political stand which, in contrast to that of Velimirović, was unequivocally anti-fascist.

The main "problem" with contemporary Christian-Jewish relations in Serbia lies not in what Velimirović was "really" like, but in his remembrance and his uncritical adulation. It is to be found in the attempts to justify and excuse his stance towards Jews and present them as normal, acceptable and even necessary. The reluctance by church authorities to address the controversy surrounding his writing obscures the boundaries between the extreme and the mainstream in Serbian Orthodox culture and in doing so facilitates the promulgation of anti-Jewish prejudice and feeds political extremism. Moreover, because of the large amount of cultural space occupied by the commemoration and celebration of the life and work of Nikolaj Velimirović, the problematic interpretation of Christian-Jewish relations, which has become entrenched in memorial discourse, is no longer a latent aspect of Serbian Orthodox culture. It is not just a dormant characteristic of religious ceremonial concealed in the text of the Holy Liturgy or in esoteric theological writings inaccessible to the majority of the faithful. Justifications, trivializations, and denials of antisemitism, which contribute to its legitimization, have become weaved in the routine of remembrance and entrenched in the commemorative speeches, books, articles, sermons, and everyday talk devoted to Serbia's new saint and the country's most popular religious author and spiritual authority.

By revealing the ideological and rhetorical dynamics behind the collective remembering of Nikolaj Velimirović, the present book attempted to deconstruct the widespread claims that Bishop Nikolaj could not have been an antisemite because "he was in Dachau," because there is "no antisemitism in the Orthodox Church," because he "saved Jews" or because in talking of Jews he "merely quoted the Bible." Through the analysis of the rhetoric used in the preservation of Velimirović's reputation, it has tried to undermine the prevailing myths of remembrance, infuse memorial discourse with subversive meaning, and challenge an objectionable and damaging dimension of contemporary Serbian Orthodox Christian culture.

References

Alakaj, I. (1928). "Priča o vuku i jagnjetu" (Story of the wolf and the lamb). *Vreme*, January 15, p. 3.

Albahari, D. (2004). *Teret* (Burden). Belgrade: Forum Pisaca.

Alexander, S. (1979). *Church and State in Yugoslavia since 1945*. Cambridge: CUP.

Allport, G.W. (1954). *The Nature of Prejudice*. Reading, MA: Addison Wesley.

Andrejević, N. (2003). "(Ne)prihvaćeni svetitelj" ([Un]accepted saint). *NIN*, May 29, 2003. http://www.nin.co.yu/2003-05/29/29092.html (accessed 1 June 2007).

Anon. (2000). *Novi Sveštenomučenici i Mučenici Pravoslavne Crkve* (New Serbian martyrs of the Serbian Orthodox Church). Cetinje: Svetigora.

"Antisemitizam ponovo u porastu" (Antisemitism on the rise again). (2003). *Danas*, March 22–23. http://www.danas.co.yu/20030322/hronika3.htm (accessed 1 June 2007).

Apostolović, D. (2003). "Verstvo i bezverstvo" (Faith and infidelity). *Danas*, May 27. http://danas.co.yu/20030527/dijalog.htm (accessed 1 June 2007).

Augoustinos, M., Lecouteur, A., and Soyland, J. (2002). "Self-sufficient arguments in political rhetoric: constructing reconciliation and apologizing to the Stolen Generations." *Discourse and Society* 13, no. 1, pp. 105–142.

Bartlett, F. (1932). *Remembering: a Study in Experimental and Social Psychology*. Cambridge: CUP.

Baum, G. (1974). "Introduction." In R. Ruether (ed.), *Faith and Fratricide: The Theological Roots of Antisemitism*. New York: Seabury, pp. 1–22.

Bauman, Z. (1991). *Modernity and the Holocaust*. New York: Cornell University Press.

Baćirević, K. (1991). "Povika na Vladiku Nikolaja" (Cries against Bishop Nikolaj). *Pravoslavlje*, June 1, 1991.

Belgrade Centre for Human Rights (2002). *Human Rights in Yugoslavia: legal provisions, practice and legal consciousness in the Federal Republic of Yugoslavia compared to international human rights standards*. Belgrade: Belgrade Centre for Human Rights.

Berben, P. (1975). *Dachau 1933–1945: The Official History*. London: The Norfolk Press.

Bieber, F. (2002). "Nationalist Mobilization and Stories of Serb Suffering." *Rethinking History* 6, no. 1, pp. 95–110.

Bigović, R. (1993). "Hrišćanska filosofija Vladike Nikolaja" (Christian philosophy of Bishop Nikolaj). *Jefimija* 2, nos. 2–3, pp. 45–53.

Bigović, R. (1994). "Od Velikog petka do Uskrsa" (Between Good Friday and Easter). Politika, April 30, p. 11.

Bigović, R. (1998). *Od Svečoveka do Bogočoveka: Hrišćanska filosofija vladike Nikolaja Velimirovića* (From all-man to the man of God: Christian philosophy of Bishop Nikolaj Velimirović). Belgrade: Društvo Raška Škola.

Billig, M. (1982). *Ideology and Social Psychology*. Oxford: Blackwell.

Billig, M. (1987). *Arguing and Thinking: a Rhetorical Approach to Social Psychology*. Cambridge: Cambridge University Press.

Billig, M. (1990). *Ideology and Opinions: Studies in Rhetorical Psychology*. London: Sage.

Billig, M. (1997a). "The dialogic unconscious: psychoanalysis, discursive psychology and the nature of repression." *British Journal of Social Psychology* 36, pp. 139–159.

Billig, M. (1997b). "From codes to utterances: cultural studies, discourse and psychology." In M. Ferguson and P. Golding (eds.), *Cultural Studies in Question*. London: Sage, pp. 205–226.

Billig, M. (1999a). *Freudian Repression: Conversation Creating the Unconscious*. London: Sage.

Billig, M. (1999b). "Commodity fetishism and repression: reflections of Marx, Freud and the psychology of consumer capitalism." *Theory and Psychology* 4, pp. 11–47.

Billig, M., Condor, S., Edwards, D., Gane, M., Middleton, D. and Radley, A.R. (1988). *Ideological Dilemmas: A Social Psychology of Everyday Thinking*. London: Sage.

"Bishop Reveals Persecution of Church under Tito Regime" (1946). *Chicago Herald American*, April 28, p. 30.

Bjelajac, B. (2001). "Yugoslav Jews targeted." *Balkan Crisis Report, Institute for War and Peace Reporting* no. 268, August 6. http://iwpr.net/?p=bcr&s=f&o=248657& apc_state=henibcr200108 (accessed 1 June 2007).

Blackwell Dictionary of Eastern Christianity, The (2001). Oxford: Blackwell Publishers.

Boca, S. (1991). "Najveći Srbin i muž naše savremene istorije" (The greatest Serb and man of our recent past). *Glas Crkve* 3, pp. 33–36.

Bogdanović, M. (1931). *Književne Kritike I* (Literary criticism. Vol. I). Belgrade: Geca Kon.

Borković, M. (1979). *Kontrarevolucija u Srbiji* (The counter-revolution in Serbia). Belgrade: Nolit.

Bower, G.H. (1990). "Awareness, the unconscious and repression." In J.L. Singer (ed.), *Repression and Dissociation*. Chicago: University of Chicago Press, pp. 209–231.

Boyer, P. J. (2004). "The Jesus war: Mel Gibson's obsession." In R. Rosenbaum (ed.), *Those Who Forget The Past: The Question Of Anti-Semitism.* New York: Random House, pp. 311–340.

Bremer, T. (1997). *Vera, Kultura i Politika* (Faith, Culture and Politics). Niš: Gradina/JUNIR.

Bunjak, N. (2003). "Razdor u napaćenoj Srbiji" (Divisions in exhausted Serbia). *Danas,* April 29. http://www.danas.co.yu/20030429/dijalog.htm (accessed 1 June 2007).

Burke, P. (1989). "History as social memory." In T. Butler (ed.), *Memory: History, Culture and the Mind.* New York: Blackwell, pp.93–113.

Burr, V. (2003). *An Introduction to Social Constructionism.* 2nd ed. London: Routledge.

Byford, J. (2002). "Christian Right-Wing Organizations and the Spreading of Antisemitic Prejudice in Post-Milošević Serbia: The Case of the Dignity Patriotic Movement." *East European Jewish Affairs* 33, no. 2, pp. 43–60.

Byford, J. (2003). "Antisemitism and the Christian Right in Post-Milošević Serbia: From Conspiracy Theory to Hate Crime." *Internet Journal of Criminology* 1, pp. 1–27.

Byford, J. (2006). *Teorija zavere: Srbija protiv "novog svetskog poretka"* (Conspiracy theory: Serbia vs. the "New World Order"). Belgrade: Belgrade Centre for Human Rights.

Byford, J. (2007). "When I say 'Holocaust' I mean 'Jasenovac': Remembrance of the Holocaust in contemporary Serbia." *East European Jewish Affairs* 37, no. 1, pp. 51–74.

Byford, J., and Billig, M. (2001). "The Emergence of Antisemitic Conspiracy Theories in Yugoslavia During the War with Nato." *Patterns of Prejudice* 34, no. 4, pp. 51–63.

Čakić, S. (1987). "Prepis pisma upućenog uredništvu *Večernjih Novosti*" (Transcript of a letter sent to the editors of *Večernje Novosti*). *Glas Crkve* 1, pp. 76–77.

Carroll, J. (2002). *Constantine's Sword: The Church and the Jews.* Boston: Houghton Mifflin.

Chesler, P. (2003). *The New Antisemitism: Current crisis and what we must do about it.* San Francisco: Jossey-Bass.

"Čiji si ti mali srpski narode?" (Whose are you little Serbian people?). (1968). *Politika,* July 7, p. 7.

Cohen, S. (2001). *States of Denial: Knowing About Atrocities and Suffering.* Cambridge: Polity Press.

Cohn, N. (1957). *Warrant for Genocide: The Myth of the Jewish World Conspiracy and the Protocols of the Elders of Zion.* London: Secker and Warburg.

Čolović, I. (2002). "Čudni ljudi" (Strange people). *Danas,* February 2–3, p. v.

David, F. (1991). "Vladika—Antisemita" (Bishop—antisemite). *Vreme,* July 29, p. 37.

Đikanović, V. (2006). "Prilog istraživanju istorije Srpske pravoslavne crkve u Sjedinjenim američkim državama od 1919 do 1926" (Contribution to history research of the Serbian Orthodox Church in the United States from 1919 to 1926). *Tokovi Istorije* 1–2, pp. 113–124.

Dillon, G.L (1991). *Contending Rhetorics: Writing in Academic Disciplines*. Bloomington: Indiana University Press.

Dimitrijević, V. (1997). *Pravoslavlje i Sekte* (Orthodoxy and sects). Cetinje: Svetigora.

Dimitrijević, V. (2001). "Srbi i Jevreji" (Serbs and Jews). *Dveri Srpske* 11–12, June issue. http://www.dverisrpske.com/brojevi/11_12.htm/srbiijevreji.htm (accessed 1 June 2007).

Dimitrijević, V. (2004). "Srbi i Jevreji" (Serbs and Jews). *Dveri Srpske* 24, special issue, pp. 74–78.

Dimitrijević, V. (2005). *Put kojim se češće ide: okultizam, magija, veštičarstvo* (The road travelled increasingly frequently: occultism, magic and witchcraft). Čačak: Legenda.

Dimitrijević, V. (2007). *Oklevetani svetac, Sveti vladika Nikolaj i srbofobija* (Libeled saint: Holy Bishop Nikolaj and Serbophobia). Gornji Milanovac: Lio.

Dobrijević, M. (1982). *Bishop Nicholai Velimirovich: Aspects of his 1921 missionary activities in America*. Unpublished Master's thesis. St Vladimir's Orthodox Theological Seminary, Cresswood, New York.

Đonović, S. (1976). "Atentat na budućnost" (Assassination of the future). *Nedeljne Novosti*, May 23, p. 4.

Đorđević, B. (1950). "Nismo protiv arhijereja, već protiv njihovih postupaka" (We are not against the bishops, but against their actions). *Vesnik*, March 15, p. 2.

Đorđević, M. (1996). Povratak Propovednika (Return of the Preacher). *Republika* 8, July issue, pp. 1–10.

Đorđević, M. (1998). *Znaci Vremena* (Sign of the times). Belgrade: In Press.

Đorđević, M. (2002). "Trijumf palanačkog uma" (The triumph of the provincial mind). *Danas*, July 21–22, p. v.

Đorđević, M. (2003). "Srpska Organisticka Misao" (Serbian organic thought). In M. Đorđević (ed.), *Srpska Konzervativna Misao* (Serbian conservative thought). Belgrade: Helsinki Committee for Human Rights, pp. 5–33.

Dostoyevsky, F. (1960 [1880]). "The Pushkin Speech". In F. Dostoyevsky, *The Dream of a Queer Fellow and The Pushkin Speech*. (Translated by S. Koteliansky and J. Middleton Murry.). London: Unwin Books, pp. 43–59.

"Dr Nikolaj Velimirović: episkop Žički" (Dr. Nikolaj Velimirović: Bishop of Žiča). (1940). *Rat i Mir: Pupularni istorijski zabavni list*, pp. 17–23.

Drašković, V. (1987). *Odgovori* (Answers). Belgrade: Vuk Drašković.

Drašković, V. (1989). "Pasoš za Vladiku Nikolaja" (Passport for Bishop Nikolaj). *Glas Crkve* 3, pp. 71–74.

Đurić, A. (2002). "Predgovor: Nevinost bez zaštite" (Preface: unprotected innocence). In S.B. Jović (ed.), *Utamničena Crkva* (Incarcerated church). Belgrade: Pravoslavna misionarska škola pri hramu Svetog Aleksandra Nevskog, pp. 7–10.

Đurđević, R. (1997). *Idejni i Duhovni Trovači sa Zapada* (Western ideological and spiritual poisoners). Belgrade: Ihtus Press.

Đurđević, R. (2002). *Svetosavski nacionalizam u judeo-masonskom okruzenju* (Nationalism of St Sava in Judeomasonic surroundings). Belgrade: Ihtus Press.

Đurđević, R. (2003). *Utemeljitelji Svetosavskog Nacionalizma: Vladika Nikolaj, Ava Justin and Dimitrije Ljotić* (The founders of the nationalism of St Sava: Bishop Nikolaj, Father Justin, and Dimitrije Ljotić). Belgrade: Ihtus Press.

Durković-Jakšić, Lj. (1980). *Učešće Patrijarha Gavrila i Srpske Pravoslavne Crkve u događajima ispred i za vreme 27 marta 1941. i njihovo stradanje u toku rata* (The participation of Patriarch Gavrilo and the Serbian Orthodox Church in the events before and during 27 March 1941 and their suffering during the war). Belgrade: Sveti arhierejski sinod Srpske pravoslavne crkve.

"Dva doktorata" (Two doctorates). (1909). *Vesnik srpske crkve* 9, p. 720.

Džaković, M. (1990). *Memoari Patrijarha Gavrila Dožića* (Memoirs of Patriarch Gavrilo Dožić). Belgrade: Sfairos.

Džomić, V. (2000). *Stradanje srbske crkve od komunista, Prvi Deo: Komunistički zločini nad srbskim sveštenicima* (The suffering of the Serbian Church under communism. Part One: Communist crimes against Serbian clergy). Cetinje: Svetigora.

Džomić, V. (2003). "Prilozi za biografiju Sv. Vladike Nikolaja u II svetskom ratu" (Contribution to the biography of Holy Bishop Nikolaj during World War II). In A. Jevtić (ed.), *Sveti Vladika Nikolaj Ohridski i Žički* (Holy Bishop Nikolaj of Ohrid and Žiča). Kraljevo: Sveti Manastir Žiča, pp. 426–440.

Džomić, V. (2005). "Stradanje Srpske crkve of komunista" (Suffering of the Serbian Church under communism). *Dveri Srpske* 26, pp. 46–51.

Edwards, D. (1997). *Discourse and Cognition.* London: Sage.

Edwards, D. (2000). "Extreme Case Formulations: softeners, investment, and doing nonliteral." *Research on Language and Social Interaction* 33, no. 4, 347–373.

Edwards, D. (2004). "Analysing racial discourse: the discursive psychology of Mind–World relationships." In H. van den Berg, H. Houtcoup, and M. Wetherell (eds.), *Analysing Race Talk.* Cambridge: CUP, pp. 31–48.

"Evropski standardi na balkanski način" (European standards, Balkan style). (2002). *Danas*, December 17. *http://www.danas.co.yu/20021217/dezurna.htm* (accessed 1 June 2007)

Foxman, A.H. (2003). *Never Again? The Threat of New Antisemitism.* San Francisco: Harper.

Freidenreich, H.P. (1979). *The Jews of Yugoslavia: A Quest for Community.* Philadelphia: Jewish Publication Society of America.

Freud, S. (1914). *On the history of the psycho-analytic movement.* Complete Psychological Works of Sigmund Freud (Standard Edition), Vol. 14, pp. 7–66.

Freud, S. (1916). *Introductory lectures on psycho-analysis.* Complete Psychological Works of Sigmund Freud (Standard Edition), Vol. 15, pp. 9–239.

Freud, S. (1933). *New introductory lectures on psycho-analysis*. Complete Psychological Works of Sigmund Freud (Standard Edition), Vol. 22, pp. 5–182.

Freud, S. (1940). *An outline of psycho-analysis*. Complete Psychological Works of Sigmund Freud (Standard Edition), Vol. 23, pp. 144–207.

Freze, M. (1991). *The Making of Saints*. Huntington, Indiana: Our Sunday Visitor.

Gajić, E. B. (1938). *Jugoslavija i "jevrejski problem"*. (Yugoslavia and the "Jewish Problem"). Belgrade: Štamparija D. Gregorića, 1938

Gavrilović, Ž. (1998). "Srpska Jeremijada" (Serbian Jeremiad). In N. Velimirović Poruka (ed.), *Srpskom Narodu Kroz Tamnicki Prozor* (Words to the Serbian people through the dungeon window). Belgrade: Svetosavska Književna Zadruga, pp. 9–16.

Gligorijević, B. (1997). "Ujedinjenje Srpske pravoslavne crkve i uspostavljanje Srpske patrijaršije u Jugoslaviji" (Unification of the Serbian Orthodox Church and the creation of the Serbian Patriarchate in Yugoslavia). *Istorija XX veka* 2, pp. 7–19.

Glišić, N. (1969). "Šta hoće *Pravoslavlje*?" (What does *Pravoslavlje* want?). *Nedeljne Novosti*, October 5, p. 6.

Goffman, E. (1979). "Footing." *Semiotica* 25, pp. 1–25.

Goldhagen, D. (2002). *A Moral Reckoning: The Role of the Catholic Church in the Holocaust and its Unfulfilled Duty of Repair*. New York: Alfred A Knopf.

Gordiejew, P.B. (1999). *Voices of Yugoslav Jewry*. New York: SUNY Press.

Grimstad, W. (2000). *Znamenite ličnosti o Jevrejima* (Famous people on the Jews). Belgrade: Ihtus Press.

Grozdić, B.D. (2001). *Pravoslavlje i rat* (Orthodoxy and war). Belgrade: Vojno-izdavački zavod.

Grozdić, B.D., and Marković, S.M. (2001). *Vojska i vera* (Army and Faith). Belgrade: Vojno-izdavački zavod.

Grujić, J. (2000). "Novi zastupnici pred bogom" (New intercessors before God). *Vreme*, May 27. http://www.vreme.com/arhiva_html/490/27.html (accessed 1 June 2007).

Gurevich, A. (1995). "The Orthodox view of the Jews and Judaism." *Religion, State and Society* 23, no. 1, pp. 53–56.

Gur-Ze'ev, I., and Pappé, I. (2003). "Beyond the destruction of the other's collective memory." *Theory, Culture and Society* 20, no. 1, pp. 93–108.

Hackel, S. (1998). "The relevance of western post-Holocaust theology to the thought and practice of the Russian Orthodox Church." *Sabornost* 20, no. 1, pp. 1–12.

Hellig, J. (2002). *The Holocaust and Antisemtism: A Short History*. Oxford: Oneworld.

Helsinki Committee for Human Rights in Serbia (2001). *Report on Antisemitism*. Belgrade: Helsinki Committee for Human Rights in Serbia.

Helsinki Committee for Human Rights in Serbia (2002). *Ljudska prava u tranziciji: Srbija 2001*. (Human rights in transition: Serbia 2001). Belgrade: Helsinki Committee for Human Rights in Serbia. *http://www.helsinki.*

org.yu/report_contents.php? lang=sr&pgno=2&idpub=34 (accessed 1 June 2007)

Helsinki Committee for Human Rights in Serbia (2003a). *Ljudska prava u senci nacionalizma: Srbija 2002.* (Human rights in the shadow of nationalism: Serbia 2002). Belgrade: Helsinki Committee for Human Rights in Serbia.

Helsinki Committee for Human Rights in Serbia (2003b). *Serbia in the Vicious Circle of Nationalism.* Belgrade: Helsinki Committee for Human Rights in Serbia.

Hentoff, N. (2004). "Who Did Kill Christ?" In R. Rosenbaum (ed.), *Those Who Forget the Past: The Question of Anti-Semitism.* New York: Random House, pp. 307-310.

Heppell, M. (2001). *George Bell and Nikolaj Velimirović: The Story of a Friendship.* Birmingham: Lazarica Press.

Hewitt, J.P., and Stokes, R. (1975). "Disclaimers." *American Sociological Review* 40, pp. 1–11.

Hilberg, R. (1985). *The Destruction of the European Jews.* London: Holmes & Meier.

Hilberg, R. (1993). *Perpetrators, Victims, Bystanders: The Jewish Catastrophe 1933–1945.* New York: Harper Perennial.

"Hitler je lično izao naređenje da se likvidira episkop Nikolaj Velimirović" (Hitler personally ordered the execution of Nikolaj Velimirović). (1987). *Glas Crkve* 2, pp. 35–36.

"Hrabri pastor" (The brave pastor). *Žički Blagovesnik* 2, p. 58.

Hutchby, I., and Wooffitt, R. (1998). *Conversation Analysis: Principles, Practices and Applications.* Cambridge: Polity Press.

Iganski, P., and Kosmin, B. (2003). *The New Antisemitism? Debating Judeophobia in the 21st Century.* London: Profile Books.

Ilić, A. (1938). *Moji doživljaji sa dr Nikolaj Velimirovićem i dr Vojom Janićem* (My experiences with Dr. Nikolaj Velimirović and Dr. Voja Janić). Belgrade: n.p.

Ilić, P. (2006). *Srpska pravoslavna crkva i tajna Dahaua* (Serbian Orthodox Church and the secret of Dahau). Belgrade: author's edition.

Information Service of the Serbian Orthodox Church (2002). "Saopštenje za javnost Svetog arhijerejskog sinoda o antisemitskim izjavama i postupcima" (An announcement to the public by the Holy Archiereic Synod regarding antisemitic statements and actions). February 5. http://www.spc.yu/Vesti-2002/02/5-2-02_c1.html (accessed 1 June 2007).

Information Service of the Serbian Orthodox Church (2003). "Poruka srpskog Patrijarha najvišim zvaničnicima Izraela povodom pedesetogodišnjice postojanja Memorijalnog centra Jad Vašem" (Message of the Serbian patriarch to the highest officials in Israel regarding the fiftieth anniversary of the Yad Vashem Remembrance Authority). September 17. http://www.rastko.org.yu/rastko-iz/istorija/holokaust/vesti/2003-09-17-yad_vashem_l.html (accessed 1 June 2007).

Information Service of the Serbian Orthodox Church (2003b). "Sveti Arhijerejski Sabor, Vanredno saopštenje za javnost" (The Holy Archiereic Assembly, an extraordinary statement to the public). May 19. In M. Janković (ed.), *Sveti Episkop Nikolaj: život, misao i delo, Knjiga III* (Bishop Nikolaj: his life, thought and work. Vol. 3). Valjevo: Eparhija Šabačko-Valjevska, p. 588.

Information Service of the Serbian Orthodox Church (2004a). "Saopštenje za javnost povodom napada na arhijerejskog namesnika sarajevskog, protojereja stavrofora Jeremiju Starovlaha i njegovu porodicu" (A statement to the public regarding the attack on the archiereic representative in Sarajevo, Priest Jeremija Starovlah, and his family). April 5. http://www.spc.org.yu/Vesti-2004/04/05-4-04-c01.html#nam (accessed 1 June 2007).

Information Service of the Serbian Orthodox Church (2004b). "Strašnije of Kristalne noći" (More horrible than the Kristalnacht). March 25. http://www.spc.org.yu/Vesti-2004/03/25-3-04-c01.html#kris (accessed 1 June 2007).

"Ipak, ton i gest šovinistički" (Nonetheless, the tone and the gesture are chauvinist). (1968). *Politika*, July 25, p. 6.

Irwin-Zarecka, I. (1994). *Frames of Remembrance: The Dynamics of Collective Memory*. New Brunswick, NJ: Transaction Books.

Isaac, J. (1964). *The Teaching of Contempt*. New York: Holt, Reinhart, & Winston.

Ivanković, N. (1986). "Što se zbiva u SPC?" (What is going on within the Serbian Orthodox Church?). *Danas*, August 5, pp. 24–25.

Jakšić, Lj. (1981). "Kleronacionalisti protiv vlastitih naroda" (Cleronationalists against their own people). *Oslobođenje*, July 7, p. 3.

Janić, Đ. J. (1994). *Hadžija Večnosti* (The pilgrim of eternity). Belgrade: Hrast.

Janić, Đ. J. (1999). "U pepelu očajan sedeći" (While sitting, desperate, in the ashes). *Sveti Knez Lazar* 7, pp. 109–142.

Janković, M. (2002a). *Episkop Nikolaj: život, misao i delo, Knjiga I* (Bishop Nikolaj: his life, thought and work. Vol. 1). Valjevo: Eparhija Šabačko-Valjevska.

Janković, M. (2002b). *Episkop Nikolaj: život, misao i delo, Knjiga II* (Bishop Nikolaj: his life, thought and work. Vol. 2). Valjevo: Eparhija Šabačko-Valjevska.

Janković, M. (2003). *Sveti Episkop Nikolaj: život, misao i delo, Knjiga III* (BishopNikolaj: his life, thought and work. Vol. 3). Valjevo: Eparhija Šabačko-Valjevska.

Janković, M. (2004). *Sveti Nikolaj Srpski: od rođenja do kanonizacije* (Holy Bishop Nikolaj of Serbia: from birth to canonization). Valjevo: Valjevo Print.

Jedlicki, J. (1999). "Historical memory as a source of conflicts in Eastern Europe." *Communist and Post-Communist Studies* 32, pp. 225–232.

Jelić, R. (1950). "Pred zasedanje svetog Arhijerejskog sabora Srpske pravoslavne crkve" (In expectation of the meeting of the Holy Council of Bishops of the Serbian Orthodox Church). *Vesnik*, May 5, p. 2.

Jerotić, V. (2000). *Vera i Nacija* (Faith and nation). Belgrade: Ars Libri.

"Jevreji ponovo raspinju Hrista" (Jews once again crucify Christ). (1992). *Pravoslavlje*, 15 February, p.2.

Jevtić, A. (1981). "Kome služi uravnilovka?" (Who benefits from a level playing field?). *Pravoslavlje*, August 1, p. 4.

Jevtić, A. (1986a). "Povodom napada na Vladiku Nikolaja" (Regarding the attacks on Bishop Nikolaj). *Pravoslavlje*, September 1, pp. 11–12.

Jevtić, A. (1986b). "Laži i klevete na Hrista i Episkopa Nikolaja" (Lies and slanders against Christ and Bishop Nikolaj). *Pravoslavlje*, October 1, pp. 10–11.

Jevtić, A. (1986c). "Zamena istine novim neistinama" (Substituting the truth with new untruths). *Pravoslavlje*, October 15, pp. 10–11.

Jevtić, A. (1986d). "Još dve reči o Episkopu Nikolaju" (A few more words about Bishop Nikolaj). *Pravoslavlje*, November 1, p. 11.

Jevtić, A. (1986e). "Pogovor" (Postscript). In A. Radosavljević (ed.), *Novi Zlatousti* (The new Chrysostom). Belgrade: Atanasije Jevtić.

Jevtić, A. (1987a). *Od Kosova do Jadovna* (From Kosovo to Jadovno). Valjevo: Glas Crkve.

Jevtić, A. (1987b). "Proleće je burno i vetrovito" (The spring is stormy and windy). *Glas Crkve* 4, pp. 17–32.

Jevtić, A. (1988). "Kosovska misao i opredeljenje Episkopa Nikolaja" (Bishop Nikolaj's Kosovo creed). *Glas Crkve* 3, pp. 19–25.

Jevtić, A. (1991). "Mi smo narod kulta živih" (We are a people of the cult of the living). *Glas Crkve* 3, pp. 28–29.

Jevtić, A. (2003a). *Sveti Vladika Nikolaj Ohridski i Žički*. (Holy Bishop Nikolaj of Ohrid and Žiča). Kraljevo: Sveti Manastir Žiča.

Jevtić, A. (2003b). "Tri kruga napada na vladiku Nikolaja" (Three rounds of attacks on Bishop Nikolaj). In A. Jeftic (ed.), *Sveti Vladika Nikolaj Ohridski i Žički* (Holy Bishop Nikolaj of Ohrid and Žiča). Kraljevo: Sveti Manastir Žiča, pp. 555-570.

Jones, J.M. (1972). *Prejudice and Racism*. Reading, MA: Adison-Wesley.

Jovanović - Stojimirović, M. (2003). "Nikolaj Velimirović (1880–1956)." In V. Dimitrijević and G. Veljković (eds.). *Zlatousti Propovednik Vaskrsloga Hrista* (Golden-mouthed preacher of the resurrected Christ). Kragujevac: Duhovni Lug, pp. 11-64.

Jovanović, M. (2005). "'Sveštenik i društvo—eto parole': Ruska pravoslavna zagranična crkva na Balkanu 1920–1940" ("A priest and society—there's a motto": Russian Church in Exile in the Balkans 1920–1940). *Tokovi Istorije* 3–4, pp. 67–100.

Jović, S.B. (2002). *Utamničena Crkva* (Incarcerated Church). Belgrade: Pravoslavna misionarska škola pri hramu Svetog Aleksandra Nevskog.

Judah, T. (2000). *The Serbs: History, Myth and the Destruction of Yugoslavia*. New Haven: Yale University Press.

"Justin je fino mirisao" (Justin smelt good). (2004). *Vreme*, 22 April. http://www.vreme.com/cms/view.php?id=375301 (accessed 1 June 2007).

"Kako je Gerstenmajer vrbovao Nikolaja Žičkog" (How Gerstenmeier wooed Nikolaj of Žiča). (1969). *Politika*, January 16, p. 4.

"Kandilo pred ikonom" (Vigil lamp before an icon). (1987). *Glas Crkve* 3, pp. 26–28.

Kansteiner, W. (2002). "Finding meaning in memory: a methodological critique of collective memory studies." *History and Theory* 41, pp. 179–197.

Klimon, W.M. 1994. "Chesterton, Kossovo of the Serbians and the vocation of the Christian Nation." *The Chesterton Review* 20, February issue, pp. 41–53.

"Kome ne ide u račun da Srpska pravoslavna crkva nađe svoj pravi put?" (Who benefits if the Serbian Orthodox Church fails to find the right path?). (1950). *Vesnik*, June 25, p. 4.

Komnenić, M. (1988). "Setno slovo o vladici Nikolaju" (A pensive word on Bishop Nikolaj). *Glas Crkve* 3, pp. 27–33.

Komnenić, M. (1991). "Sva nam je zemlja Lelić" (Our whole land is Lelić). *Glas Crkve* 3, pp. 48–50.

Konstantinović, M. (1998). *Politika sporazuma. Dnevničke beleške 1939–1941. Londonske beleške 1944–1945* (Politics of agreement: diaries 1939–1941). Novi Sad: Prometej.

Kordić, M. (2001). "Jevreji brane Srbe od antisemitizma" (Jews defend Serbs from accusations of antisemitism). *Glas Javnosti*, August 6. http://arhiva.glas-javnosti.co.yu/arhiva/2001/08/06/srpski/X01080501.shtml (accessed 1 June 2007).

Kosidowski, Z. (1998). *Priče Evanđelista* (Tales of the Evangelists). Belgrade: IP Book Marso.

Kostić, B. (1991). *Za Istoriju Naših Dana: Odlomci iz zapisa za vreme okupacije* (For the history of our days: extracts from a diary in the time of occupation). Belgrade: Nova Iskra.

Kostić, V. (2003). *Episkop Vasilije Banjalučki i Žički.* (Bishop Vasilije of Banja Luka and Žiča). Kraljevo: Episkopija Žička.

Kostić, Ž. (1948). "Onima koji žele da našu veru stave u službu imperijalizma" (To those who want to place our faith in the service of imperialism). *Vesnik*, May15, p. 3.

Kozar, Đ. (1981). "Pokušaji zloupotrebe pravoslavlja" (Attempted abuse of Orthodoxy). *Oslobođenje*, September 18–21, p. 7.

Krivulyin, V. (2001). "Mučenici, strastotrpci i borci" (Martyrs, Passion-Bearers and Fighters). *Republika* 13, January issue, p. 20.

Krstić, N. (2002), *Pobediti ili Nestati* (To win or to perish). Belgrade: Rivel Co.

"Krvave Osnove ili Protokoli sionskih mudraca" (Bloody foundations or the Protocols of the elders of Zion). (1926). *Hrišćanska Zajednica* 5, no. 2–3, pp. 6–9.

Kuburović, M. (2003). "Srpski Zlatousti" (Serbian Chrysostom). *Politika*, May 26, p. 21.

Kuljić, T. (2002). "Historiographic revisionism in post-socialist regimes." In S. Biserko (ed.), *The Balkans Rachomon* [Helsinki Files no. 11]. Belgrade:

Helsinki Committee for Human Rights in Serbia, pp. 1–35. *http://www.helsinki.org.yu/doc/pubs/files/eng/*files11.zip. (accessed 1 June 2007)

Lang G.E., and Lang, K.L. (1988). "Recognition and renown: the survival of artistic reputation." *American Journal of Sociology* 94, no. 1, pp. 78–109.

Latourette, K.S. (1973). *Christianity in a Revolutionary Age: A History of Christianity in the 19th and 20th Centuries. Volume IV: The Twentieth Century in Europe. The Roman Catholic, Protestant and Eastern Churches.* Westport, CN: Greenwood Press.

Lawler, M. (2004). "Sectarian Catholicism and Mel Gibson." *Journal of Religion and Society* 6, http://moses.creighton.edu/JRS/toc/2004.html (accessed 1 June 2007).

Lazarević, Đ. (2003). "Predanjski karakter molbe Svetom arhijerejskom saboru SPC za saborno proslavljanje Sv. Nikolaja Žičkog" (Historical character of the appeal to the Holy Assembly of Bishops of the Serbian Orthodox Church for the collective celebration of Holy Bishop Nikolaj). *Logos*, no. 1, pp. 237–242.

Lebl, A. (2002). "Najogavniji antisemitizam" (The most despicable kind of antisemitism). *Danas*, July 27–28, p. iv.

Lebl, A. (2003). "Slast oca đavola" (The pleasure of the father, the devil). *Danas*, April 29. http://www.danas.co.yu/20030521/dijalog.htm (accessed 1 June 2007).

Lebl, Ž. (2001). *Do "konačnog rešenja": Jevreji u Beogradu, 1521–1942.* (Until the "Final Solution": Jews in Belgrade 1521–1942). Belgrade: Čigoja.

LeCouteur, A., and Augoustinos, M. (2001). "The Language of Prejudice and Racism." In M. M. Augoustinos and K.J. Reynolds (eds.). *Understanding Prejudice, Racism and Social Conflict.* London: Sage, pp. 215–230.

Lilly, C.S. (1991). *Partisan persuasions: Communist ideology and the transformation of Yugoslav culture, 1944–1948.* Unpublished PhD thesis. Yale University.

"Linčuju i mene i crkvu" (They are lynching both me and the church). (2003). *Nedeljni Telegraf*, May 28, p. 1.

Ljotić, D. (1940a). *Drama savremenog čovečanstva* (The drama of contemporary humanity). Belgrade: JNP Zbor.

Ljotić, D. (1940b). *Ko i zašto goni Zbor?* (Who is persecuting Zbor and why?). Belgrade: JNP Zbor.

Maier, C.S. (1997). *The Unmasterable Past: History, Holocaust and German National Identity.* Cambridge, MA: Harvard University Press.

Marcuse, H. (2001). *Legacies of Dachau: Uses and Abuses of a Concentration Camp 1945–2001.* Cambridge, CUP.

Marjanović, B. (1990a). "Izdajnik, a u Dahau!" (A traitor, yet in Dachau). *Ilustrovana Politika*, October 16, pp. 45–47.

Marjanović, B. (1990b). "Vladika—izdajnik ili rodoljub" (Bishop—traitor or patriot). *Ilustrovana Politika*, October 9, pp. 45–47.

Marković, M. (1993). "Pustinjak Ohridski" (Hermit from Ohrid). *Glas Crkve* 2, pp. 19–29.

Martić, M. (1980). "Dimitrije Ljotić and the Yugoslav National Movement Zbor, 1935–1945." *East European Quarterly* 16, no. 2, pp. 219–239.

Middleton, D., and Edwards, D. (1990). *Collective Remembering*. London: Sage.
Milaš, N. (1999). *Pravoslavno crkveno pravo* (Orthodox canonical law). Cetinje: Conteco.
Miletić, V. (1972). "Politički tamjan" (Political insense). *Nin*, October 8, pp. 31–35.
Mileusnić, S. (2003). *Sveti Srbi* (Holy Serbs). Birmingham: Lazarica Press.
Milosavljević, O. (2002). *U tradiciji nacionalizma*. (In the tradition of nationalism). Belgrade: Helsinki Committee for Human Rights in Serbia.
Milošević, K. (2006). "Stradalnik bez krivice" (Blameless martyr). *Odbrana*, December 15, pp. 74–75.
Milošević, M. (1999). "Filozofska misao Vladike Nikolaja Velimirovića o ratu i Evropi" (Philosophical thought of Bishop Nikolaj Velimirović on war and Europe). *Vojno Delo* 5–6, pp. 167–184.
Milošević, N. (1991). "Žrtva nacizma i komunizma" (A victim of Nazism and communism). *Glas Crkve* 3, pp. 47–48.
Mišović, M. (1983). *Srpska crkva i konkordatska kriza* (The Serbian Church and the Concordat crisis). Belgrade: Sloboda.
Misztal, B.A. (2003). *Theories of Social Remembering*. Milton Keynes: Open University Press.
Mladenović, R., and Dimitrijević, V. (2002). "Kroz tamnički prozor" (Through the dungeon window). *Danas*, August 19, p. 8.
"Mnogosvećnjak—Vladika Nikolaj" (The great priest—Bishop Nikolaj). (1987). *Glas Crkve* 2, pp. 19–21.
Muller, J.-W. (2002). *Memory and War in Post-War Europe: Studies in the Present of the Past*. Cambridge: CUP.
Najdanović, D. (2001). *U Senci Vladike Nikolaja*. (In the shadow of Bishop Nikolaj). Belgrade: Arho.
"Neprijatelji Hrišćanstva po Henri-u Ford-u" (Enemies of Christ according to Henry Ford). (1927). *Hrišćanska Zajednica* 6, 1–2, p. 7.
Novick, P. (2001). *The Holocaust and Collective Memory*. London: Bloomsbury Press.
O'Dwyer, T. (1998). "The Vatican's Struggle to Save the Church's Soul." *The Jerusalem Post*, March 23, p. 14.
Obradović, B. (2004). "Šta vole mladi" (What young people like). *Vreme*, November 4. http://www.vreme.com/cms/view.php?id=395506 (accessed 1 June 2007).
Olick, J.K., and Robbins, J. (1998). "Social Memory Studies: From 'Collective Memory' to the Historical Sociology of Mnemonic Practices." *Annual Review of Sociology* 24, pp. 105–40.
Olick, J.K. (1999). "Collective memory: the two cultures." *Sociological Theory* 17, pp. 332–348.
"Osnovan je savez udruženja pravoslavnog sveštenstva FNRJ" (Inauguration of the Union of Associations of Orthodox Priests). (1949). *Vesnik*, April 1, p. 1.
"Osvećena kapela Sv. Nikolaja Srpskog" (The chapel of St Nikolaj of Serbia consecrated). (1989). *Glas Crkve* 2, pp. 16–18.

Parežanin, R. (1971). *Drugi svetski rat i Dimitrije V. Ljotić* (World War II and Dimitrije V. Ljotic). Munich: Iskra.

Pašić. M.K. (1936). "S.O.S." *Pregled crkve eparhije žičke* 11, pp. 3–6.

Pavle, Patriarch of the Serbian Orthodox Church (1998). *Neka pitanja naše vere* (Some questions of our faith). Belgrade: Izdavački fond Arhiepiskopije Beogradsko-Karlovačke.

Pavlowitch, S.K. (1988). *The Improbable Survivor: Yugoslavia and its problems 1918–1988*. London: Hurst & Co.

Pawlikowski, J.T. (2004). "Christian Antisemitism: Past History, Present Challenges." *Journal of Religion and Society* 6, http://moses.creighton.edu/JRS/toc/2004.html (accessed 1 June 2007).

"Pedesetogošnji jubilej njegove Svetosti Patrijarha Srpskog Gospodina Gavrila" (Fiftieth jubilee of his Holiness the Serbian Patriarch Mr Gavrilo). (1950). *Glasnik Srpske Parvoslavne Crkve*, no. 2–3, pp. 18–27.

Peleh, M.S. (1923). "Golota Rusije" (Russian Golgotha). *Pregled Crkve Eparhije Žičke* 5–6, pp. 71–73; 7–8, pp. 103–107; 9–10, pp. 122–127.

Perica, V. (2002). *Balkan Idols: Religion and Nationalism in Yugoslav States*. Oxford: OUP.

Petranović, B. (1983). *Revolucija i Kontrarevolucija u Jugoslaviji: 1941–1945* (Revolution and counter-revolution in Yugoslavia: 1941–1945). Belgrade: Narodna Knjiga.

Petrović, M. (1993). "Za čitanje Vladike Nikolaja" (Reading Bishop Nikolaj). *Jefimija* 2, nos. 2–3, pp. 111–113.

Pipes, D (1998). *Conspiracy: How the Paranoid Style Flourishes and Where it Comes From*. New York: The Free Press.

Poliakov, L. (1974). *The History of Antisemitism*. 4 vols. London: Routledge & Kegan Paul.

Poliakov, L. (1987). "The topic of the Jewish conspiracy in Russia (1905–1920), and international consequences." In C.F. Graumann and S. Moscovici (eds.), *Changing Conceptions of Conspiracy*. New York: Springer-Verlag, pp. 151–165.

Pomerantz, A. (1986). "Extreme case formulations: A way of legitimizing claims." *Human Studies* 9, pp. 219–229.

Popov, N. (1993). "Srpski populizam od marginalne do dominantne pojave" (Serbian populism from a marginal to a dominant phenomenon). *Vreme*, May 24. pp. 1–35.

Popović, D. (1989). "Sinan-Paše u srpskoj istoriji" (Sinan Pashas in Serbian history). *Glas Crkve* 2, pp. 20–26.

Popović, J. (1998). *Besede na parastosu Vladici Nikolaju Lelićkom*. (Commemorative sermons devoted to Bishop Nikolaj of Lelić). Valjevo: Manastir Ćelije.

Popović, M. (2005). "Đeneral Draža Mihailović od mučenika do Svetitelja" (General Draža Mihailović from martyr to Saint). *Dveri* 26, pp. 54–55.

Popper, K.R. (1972). *Conjectures and Refutations: the growth of scientific knowledge*. 4th ed. London: Routledge and Kegan Paul.

Potter, J. (1996). *Representing Reality: discourse, rhetoric and social construction*. London: Sage.

"Priziv za zaštitu ličnosti i dela Vladike Nikolaja Žičkog" (Call for the protection of the person and the legacy of Bishop Nikolaj of Žiča). (1987). *Glas Crkve* 3, pp. 19–20.

"Posle dve godine" (After two years). (1987). *Glas Crkve* 1, pp. 71–72.

"Povratak Njegove Svetosti Patrijarha Srpskog G. Gavrila u Otadžbinu" (The return to his fatherland of his Holiness the Serbian Patriarch Mr Gavrilo). (1946). *Glasnik Srpske Pravoslavne Crkve,* no. 10–12, pp. 210–212.

"Predlog srpskog crkvenonacionalnog programa" (Proposal for an ecclesiastical and national programme). (1989). *Glas Crkve* 3, pp. 3–11.

"Proročka reč Vladike Nikolaja: opomena Srbima rodoljubima" (Prophetic words of Bishop Nikolaj: a warning to Serbian patriots). (1992). *Pravoslavlje,* February 1, p. 1.

Protić P. (1993). "Teški dani srpskog naroda i Vladika Nikolaj Velimirović" (The hardest days for the Serbian people and Bishop Nikolaj Velimirović). *Jefimija* 2, nos. 2–3, pp. 25–31.

"Protiv greha u nama samima" (Against the sin in us all). (2002). *Dnevnik,* January 5. http://www.dnevnik.co.yu/arhiva/05-01-2002/Strane/dogadjaji.htm (accessed 1 June 2007).

Radić, R. (1997). "Srpska pravoslavna crkva i pravoslavlje u Čehoslovačkoj" (Serbian Orthodox Church and Orthodoxy in Czechoslovakia). *Tokovi Istorije* 1–2, pp. 93–121.

Radić, R. (2002a). *Država i verske zajednice 1945–1970,* (The state and religious communities between 1945. and 1970). Belgrade: Institut za Noviju Istoriju Srbije.

Radić, R. (2002b). "Crkva i 'srpsko pitanje'" (The Church and the "Serbian Question"). In N. Popov (ed.), *Srpska Strana Rata* (The road to war in Serbia). Belgrade: Samizdat, pp. 310–339.

Radić, R. (2003). "Verska elita i modernizacija—teškoće pronalaženja odgovora" (Religious elite and modernisation – the difficult quest for response). In L. Perović (ed.), *Srbija u modernizacijskim procesima 19. i 20. veka: 3. Uloga elita* (Serbia in the 19th and 20th Century modernizing processes: 3. The role of elites). Belgrade: Authors' edition, pp. 153–190.

Radosavljević, A. (1986). *Novi Zlatousti* (The new Chrysostom). Belgrade: Atanasije Jeftić.

Radosavljević, A. (1993). "Vladika Nikolaj kao duhovnik" (Bishop Nikolaj as a spiritual guide). *Jefimija* 2, nos. 2–3, pp. 9–15.

Radosavljević, A. (1999). "Čudo svetog Vladike Nikolaja" (The miracle of the Holy Bishop Nikolaj). *Sv Knez Lazar* 3, p. 14.

Radosavljević, A. (2003). "Životopis Svetog Vladike Nikolaja" (Hagiography of Holy Bishop Nikolaj). In A. Jevtić (ed.), *Sveti Vladika Nikolaj Ohridski i Žički* (Holy Bishop Nikolaj of Ohrid and Žiča). Kraljevo: Sveti Manastir Žiča, pp. 329–340.

Radosavljević, J. (2003). *Život i Stradanje Žiče i Studenice pred rat, pod okupacijom i posle rata (1938–1945)* (Life and suffering of Žiča and Studenica before, during, and after the occupation, 1938–1945). Novi Sad: Beseda.

Radović, A. (1987). "Beseda episkopa banatskog Amfilohija Radovića" (The speech by the Bishop of Banat Amfilohije Radović). *Glas Crkve* 3, pp. 29–34.

Radović, A. (1991). "Bogoljubac i narodoljubac" (Lover of God and lover of his people). *Glas Crkve* 3, pp. 39–44.

Radović, A. (2003) "Bogočovječanski etos Vladike Nikolaja" (Bishop Nikolaj's ethics of deihumanity). In A. Jevtić (ed.), *Sveti Vladika Nikolaj Ohridski i Žički* (Holy Bishop Nikolaj of Ohrid and Žiča), Kraljevo: Sveti Manastir Žiča, pp. 504–511.

Radović, J. (1950). "Iz diskusije po izveštaju" (From the discussion following the report). *Vesnik*, January 1, p. 9.

Ramet, S.P. (1999). *The Radical Right in Central and Eastern Europe Since 1989*. University Park, PA: Pennsylvania State University Press.

Ramet, S.P. (2002). *Balkan Babel: The Disintegration of Yugoslavia from the Death of Tito to the Fall of Milošević*. Cambridge, MA: Westview Press.

Ranković, Lj. (1991). "Vladika Nikolaj u službi bogu i rodu" (Bishop Nikolaj in the service of God and his people). *Glas Crkve* 3, pp. 1–9.

Ranković, Lj. (2003a). "Mučenik logora Dahau" (A martyr of camp Dachau). *Večernje Novosti*, June 19. http://www.novosti.co.yu/code/ navigate. php?Id=16&status= jedna&datum=2003-06-19&feljton=3653 (accessed 1 June 2007).

Ranković, Lj. (2003b). "Zvona zvone Vladici" (Bells toll for the bishop). *Večernje Novosti*, June 21. http://www.novosti.co.yu/code/navigate.php?Id =16&status=jedna& datum=2003-06-21&feljton=3655 (accessed 1 June 2007).

Ranković, Lj. (2003c). "Pred izazovima vremena" (Facing the challenges of his time). *Vreme*, May 29. http://www.vreme.com/cms/view.php?id=341695 (accessed 1 June 2007).

Ranković, Lj. (2003d). "Novi srpski zlatousti" (New Serbian Chrysostom). *Glas Javnosti*, May 26. http://arhiva.glas-javnosti.co.yu/arhiva/2003/05/26/ srpski/DO03052501.shtml (accessed 1 June 2007).

Rapley, M. (2001). "'How to do X without doing Y': Accomplishing discrimination without 'being racist'—'doing equity'." In M. Augoustinos and K.J. Reynolds (eds.), *Understanding Prejudice, Racism and Social Conflict*. London: Sage, pp. 231–250.

Ravitch, N. (1982). "The problem of Christian antisemitism." *Commentary* 73, no.4 , pp. 41–52.

Reeves, F. (1983). *British Racial Discourse*. Cambridge: CUP.

Ristović, M. (2000). "Treći Rajh i pravoslavne crkve na Balkanu u Drugom svetskom ratu" (Third Reich and Balkan Orthodox Churches in World War II). *Dijalog povjesničara—istoričara* 2, pp. 551–568. http://www.cpi. hr/download/links/7950.pdf (accessed 1 June 2007).

"Rodoljublje nije mržnja" (Patriotism is not hatred). (2003). *Večernje Novosti*, April 1, p. 3.

Roediger, H.L., McDermott, K.B., and Goff, L.M. (1997). "Recovery of true and false memories: paradoxical effects of repeated testing." In M.A.

Conway (ed.), *Recovered Memories and False Memories*. Oxford: OUP, pp. 118–149.

Rogich, D. (1994). *Serbian Patericon*. Forestville, CA: St. Paisius Abbey Press.

Rosenbaum, R. (2004). *Those Who Forget the Past: The Question of Anti-Semitism*. New York: Random House.

Rousso H. (1991). *The Vichy Syndrome: History and Memory in France since 1944*. Cambridge, MA: Harvard University Press.

Rubenstein, R.L. (1966). *After Auschwitz: Radical Theology and Contemporary Judaism*. Indianapolis: Bobbs-Merrill.

Rudnev, A. (1995). "Conditions for dialogue between Jews and Christians in Russia." *Religion, State and Society* 23, no. 1, pp. 11–18.

Ruether, R. (1974). *Faith and Fratricide: The Theological Roots of Antisemitism*. New York: Seabury.

"Sa skupštine sveštenstva NR Srbije" (From the conference of clergy of the People's Republic of Serbia). (1949). *Vesnik*, October 15, p. 2.

Samardžić, P. (2004). *Episkop Nikolaj i Novi Zavet o Jevrejima* (Bishop Nikolaj and the New Testament on the Jews). Belgrade: Hrišćanska Misao.

Saramandić, Z. (2003). "Veličanstveni besednik" (Magnificent preacher). *Glas Javnosti*, July 31, p. 17.

Saramandić, Z. (2004). *Sveti Velikomučenik Vladika Nikolaj Žički* (Holy Martyr Bishop Nikolaj of Žiča). Belgrade: Tetratron.

Schacter, D.L. (1995). "Memory distortion: history and current status." In D.L. Schacter (ed.), *Memory Distortion: How Minds, Brains and Societies Reconstruct the Past*. Cambridge, MA: Harvard University Press.

Schudson, M. (1989). "The present in the past versus the past in the present." *Communication* 11, pp. 105–113.

Sekelj, L. (1995). *Vreme beščašća* (The age of dishonor). Belgrade: Akademija Nova.

Sekelj, L. (1997). "Antisemitism and Jewish identity in Serbia after the 1991 Collapse of the Yugoslav State." *Analysis of Current Trends in Antisemitism* 12. Vidal Sassoon International Centre for the Study of Antisemitism, Hebrew University, Jerusalem.

Sereny, G. (2000). *The German Trauma: Experiences and Reflections 1933–2001*. London: Penguin.

Shafir, M. (2002). "Between Denial and 'Comparative Trivialization': Holocaust Negationism in Post-Communist East Central Europe." *Analysis of Current Trends in Antisemitism* 19. Vidal Sassoon International Centre for the Study of Antisemitism, Hebrew University, Jerusalem.

Shweder, R.A., and Much, N.C. (1987). "Determination and meaning: discourse and moral socialisation." In W.M. Kurtines and J.L. Gewirtz (eds.), *Moral Development through Social Interaction*. New York: John Wiley, pp. 197–244.

Simić, P. (1986a). "Izdaja pod indigom" (Carbon copied treason). *Večernje Novosti*, September 21, p. 8.

Simić, P. (1986b). "Duhovnik iz mraka" (Cleric out of darkness). *Večernje Novosti*, September 22, p. 8.

Simić, P. (1986c). "Ljotićevci i Nikolajevci stari i novi" (Followers of Ljotić, old and new). *Večernje Novosti*, October 6, p. 8.

Simić, P. (1986d). "Suze za izdajom" (Shedding tears for treason). *Večernje Novosti*, October 7, p. 8.

Simić, Z. (1986). "Oreol vladike Nikolaja" (Bishop Nikolaj's halo). *Intervju*, October 10, pp. 23–25.

Skerlić, J. 1923. *Pisci i knjige IV* (Writers and books. Vol. 4). Belgrade: Geca Kon.

Skrobonja, B. (2002). "Poveli ste se mišljenjem Filipa Koena" (You went along with the views of Philip Cohen). *Danas*, October 12–13, p. vi.

Slijepčević, Đ. (1991). *Istorija srpske pravoslavne crkve. Knj. 3, Za vreme Drugog svetskog rata i posle njega* (History of the Serbian Orthodox Church. Vol. 3: During and after World War II). Belgrade: Beogradski Izdavačko-Grafički Zavod.

"Slobodom ponosni-jedinstvom snažni" (Proud of our freedom—strengthened by unity). (1981). *Oslobođenje*, July 5, p. 3.

Stanišić, M.M. (1977). *Nikolaj: Kratak osvrt na životni put i filosofiju Vladike Nikolaja Žičkog* (Nikolaj: a brief reflection on the life and philosophy of Bishop Nikolaj of Žiča). West Lafayette, IN: Stanišić.

Stefanović, M. (1984). *Zbor Dimitrija Ljotica, 1934–1945* (Dimitrije Ljotić's Zbor, 1934–1945). Belgrade: Narodna Knjiga.

Stojanović, Lj. (2003). "Veliki događaji i velike rasprave" (Great events and big discussions). *Pravoslavlje*, July 15, pp. 26–27.

Stokes, G. 1980. "The Role of the Yugoslav Committee in the Formation of Yugoslavia." In D. Djordjevic, D. (ed.). *The Creation of Yugoslavia, 1914–1918*. Santa Barbara CA: Clio Books, pp. 51–71.

Subotić, D. (1993). "Pravoslavlje između Istoka i Zapada u bogoslovnoj misli Nikolaja Velimirovića i Justina Popovića" (Orthodoxy between the East and the West in the religious thought of Nikolaj Velimirović and Justin Popović). In G. Živković (ed.), *Čovek i crkva u vrtlogu krize: Šta nam nudi pravoslavlje danas?* (Man and Church in the vortex of crisis: what can Orthodoxy offer us today?). Valjevo: Glas Crkve, pp. 111–126.

Subotić, D. (1996). *Episkop Nikolaj i Pravoslavni bogomoljački pokret* (Bishop Nikolaj and the Orthodox devotionalist movement). Belgrade: Nova Iskra.

Subotić, D. (2004). *Srpska desnica u 20. veku* (The Serbian Right in the 20th century). Belgrade: Institut za političke studije.

"'Svetac' protiv Jevreja" ("Saint" against Jews). (1996). *Bilten Saveza jevrejskih opština Jugoslavije* 6, June, p. 16.

Synod of the Serbian Orthodox Church (1971). *Srpska Pravoslavna Crkva 1920–1970: Spomenica o 50-godišnjici vaspostavljanja Srpske patrijaršije* (Serbian Orthodox Church 1920–1970: commemorative volume marking the 50th anniversary of the inauguration of the Serbian patriarchate). Belgrade: Holy Synod of the Serbian Orthodox Church.

Synod of the Serbian Orthodox Church (1992). "Saopštenje povodom napisa 'Jevreji ponovo raspinju hrista'" (Anouncement regarding the article "Jews once again crucify Christ"). *Pravoslavlje*, 1 February, p. 3.

"Šta je u emigraciji govorio i radio Episkop Nikolaj" (What was Nikolaj saying and doing in exile). (1968). *Politika*, August 4, p. 8.

"Šešelju prija Hag" (Šešelj is enjoying The Hague). (2003). *Kurir*, August 5, p. 5.

Tabak, Y. (2000). "Relations Between the Russian Orthodox Church and Judaism: Past and Present." *Jewish Christian Relations*. http://www.jcrelations.net/en/?id=787 (accessed 1 June 2007).

Taylor, G. (1996). *Cultural Selection*. New York: Basic Books.

Terdiman, R. (1993). *Present Past: Modernity and the Memory Crisis* (Ithaca, NY: Cornell University Press.

Terzić, D. (1991). "Svedok istine" (A witness of truth). *Glas Crkve* 3, pp. 51–52.

Thelen, D. (1989). *Memory and American History*. Bloomington: Indiana University Press.

Thompson, J.B. (1984). *Studies in the Theory of Ideology*. Cambridge: Polity Press.

Timotijević, M. (forthcoming). "'Dunuli su vihorni vetrovi': stavovi episkopa Nikolaja Velimirovića o Jevrejima, liberalizmu, komunizmu i nacizmu u štampi Žičke eparhije pred Drugi svetski rat" ("The stormy winds have started to blow": the stance of Bishop Nikolaj Velimirović towards Jews, liberalism, communism, and Nazism in the press of the diocese of Žiča before World War II).

Todorova, M. (2004). *Balkan Identities: Nation and Memory*. New York: New York University Press.

Tomanić, M. (2001). *Srpska Crkva u ratu i ratovi u njoj* (The Serbian Church during the war and the wars within it). Belgrade: Medijska Knjižara Krug.

Tomanić, M. (2003). "Falsifikat sa blagoslovom episkopa" (A forgery with the blessing of a bishop). *Danas*, March 15–16. http://danas.co.yu/20030315/vikend4.htm (accessed 1 June 2007).

Torov, I. (1994). "Izdaja ili podeljene uloge" (Treason or divided roles). *Borba*, February 23, 11.

Trachtenberg, J. (1983). *The Devil and the Jews*. Philadelphia: The Jewish Publication Society.

Trgovčević, Lj. (2003). "South Slav intellectuals and the creation of Yugoslavia." In D. Đokić (ed.), *Yugoslavism: Histories of a Failed Idea 1918–1992*. London: Hurst & Company, pp. 222–237.

Trifunović, L. (1998 [1985]). "Pregovor prvom izdanju" (Preface to the first edition). In N. Velimirović, *Poruka Srpskom Narodu Kroz Tamnički Prozor* (Words to the Serbian people through the dungeon window). Beograd: Svetosavska Književna Zajednica, pp. 5–7.

Trifunović, L. (1991). "Oprosti što smo te vređali" (Forgive us for our insults). *Pravoslavlje*, June 1, p. 3.

Trifunović, L. (2002). "Uvodna reč" (A word of introduction). In M. Janković (ed.), *Vladika Nikolaj: život, misao i delo, Knjiga I* (Bishop Nikolaj: his life, thought and work. Vol. 1). Valjevo: Eparhija Šabačko-Valjevska, pp. v–xi.

Trifunović, L. (2003). "Umesto predgovora" (In the place of a preface). In M. Janković (ed.), *Vladika Nikolaj: život, misao i delo, Knjiga III* (Bishop Nikolaj: his life, thought and work. Vol. 3). Valjevo: Eparhija Šabačko-Valjevska, pp. v–vi.

United States Conference of Catholic Bishops (2004). *The Bible, the Jews, and the Death of Jesus.* Washington: United States Conference of Catholic Bishops Publishing.

van Dartel, G. (1984). *Ćirilometodska ideja i Svetosavlje* (Cyrillo-Methodian idea and the teachings of St Sava). Zagreb: Kršćanska sadašnjost.

van Dijk, T. (1992). "Discourse and the denial of racism." *Discourse and Society* 3, pp. 87–118.

van Dijk, T. (1993). *Elite Discourse and Racism.* London: Sage.

van Dijk, T. (1984). *Prejudice in Discourse.* Benjamins: Amsterdam.

van Dijk, T. (1987). *Communicating Racism: Ethnic Prejudice in Thought and Talk.* Sage: Newbury Park.

Vasiljević, D. (1993). "Povratak Vladike Nikolaja" (The return of Bishop Nikolaj). *Glas Crkve* 2, pp. 30–31.

Veković, M. (1991). "Čovek vijeka i večnosti" (The man of the century and of eternity). *Glas Crkve* 3, pp. 53–57.

Velimirović, J. (1991). "Crtice iz života Vladike Nikolaja" (Notes on the life of Bishop Nikolaj). *Glas Crkve* 2, pp. 21–25.

Velimirović, N. (1902a). "Stara bogoslovija i đačka sirotinja" (The old seminary and students paupers). *Hrišćanski vesnik* 6, pp. 362–365.

Velimirović, N. (1902b). "Ekspedicija na Sever" (Expedition to the North). *Hrišćanski vesnik* 10, pp. 590–592.

Velimirović, N. (1904). *Uspomene iz Boke* (Souvenirs from Boka). Herceg Novi: J. Sekulović.

Velimirović, N. (1908). *Der Glaube an die Auferstehung Christi als Grunddogma der apostolischen Kirche* (Faith in the resurrection of Christ as the foundation of the dogma of the apostolic church). Unpublished doctoral thesis. Department of Old Catholic Theology, University of Berne, Switzerland.

Velimirović, N. (1910). *Französisch-slavische Kämpfe in der Bocca di Cattaro 1806–1814* (French–Slavic battles in the Bay of Cattaro 1806–1814). Unpublished doctoral thesis. Faculty of Philosophy, University of Berne, Switzerland.

Velimirović, N. (1911). *Religija Njegoševa* (Njegoš"s religion). Belgrade: Štamparija Sveti Sava.

Velimirović, N. (1912a). *Besede pod gorom* (Sermons under the mount). Belgrade: n.p.

Velimirović, N. (1912b). "Niče i Dostojevski" (Nietzsche and Dostoyevsky). *Izveštaj bogoslovije Sv. Save* 12, pp. 3–19.

Velimirović, N. (1914). *Iznad greha i smrti* (Above sin and death). Belgrade: S.B. Cvijanović.

Velimirović, N. (1915). *Religion and Nationality in Serbia.* London: Nisbet & Co. Ltd.

Velimirović, N. (1916a). *The Soul of Serbia.* London: The Faith Press.

Velimirović, N. (1916b). *Serbia in Light and Darkness*. London: Longmans, Green & Co.
Velimirović, N. (1917). *The Agony of the Church*. London: Student Christian Movement.
Velimirović, N. (1920). *Reči o Svečoveku* (Words on the All-man). Belgrade: Publisher unkown.
Velimirović, N. (1921). "Ne odbacujte ih—jedna napomena sveštenicima" (Don't reject them—a note to the clergy). *Glasnik Srpske Pravoslavne Crkve* 17, pp. 273–274.
Velimirović, N. (1922). *Molitve na jezeru* (Prayers by the lake). Belgrade: n.p.
Velimirović, N. (1925). *Omilije* (Homilies). Sremski Karlovci: n.p.
Velimirović, N. (1926). "Društvo naroda" (The League of Nations). *Bratstvo* 4, pp. 77–78.
Velimirović, N. (1928a). *Ohridski prolog* (Ohrid prologue). Niš: Štamparija Sv. Car Konstantin.
Velimirović, N. (1928b). "Priča o vuku i jagnjetu" (A story about the wolf and the lamb). *Pregled crkve eparhije žičke* 1, pp. 6–9.
Velimirović, N. (1928c). "Povodom priče o vuku i jagnjetu" (With regard to the story about the wolf and the lamb). *Vesnik Srpske crkve* 1, pp. 42–52.
Velimirović, N. (1935). *Nacionalizam Svetog Save* (Nationalism of St Sava). Belgrade: Knjižnica Pravoslavlje.
Velimirović, N. (1939). No title. *Žički Blagovesnik,* back cover.
Velimirović, N. (1940). "Poslanica omladini Eparhije žičke" (Epistle to the youth of the diocese of Žiča). *Žički Blagovesnik* 1, pp. 2–7.
Velimirović, N. (1977 [n.d]). "Iznad istoka i zapada" (Above east and west). In N. Velimirović, *Sabrana Dela, tom V.* (Collected works. Vol. V). Himmelsthur: Zapadnoevropska eparhija Srpske pravoslavne crkve, pp. 794–810.
Velimirović, N. (1983). "Pismo episkopu Dionisiju Milivojeviću" (Letter to Bishop Dionisije Milivojević) *Sabrana Dela, tom X.* (Collected works. Vol. X). Himmelsthur: Zapadnoevropska eparhija Srpske pravoslavne crkve, p. 704.
Velimirović, N. (1998 [1985]). *Poruka Srpskom Narodu Kroz Tamnički Prozor* (Words to the Serbian people through the dungeon window). Belgrade: Svetosavska Književna Zadruga.
Velimirović, N. (2000 [n.d.]). *Indijska Pisma* (Indian letters). Belgrade: Evro.
Velimirović, N. (2001 [n.d.]). *San o Slovenskoj Religiji* (Dreaming of a Slav religion). Belgrade: Slobodna Knjiga.
Velimirović, N. (2003 [n.d.]). *Srpski Narod kao Teodul* (The Serbian people as a theodule). Belgrade: Hrišćanska misao.
Velimirović, N. (2005 [n.d.]). *Misionarska Pisma* (Missionary letters). Vrnjačka Banja: Bratstvo Sv. Simeona Mirotočivog.
Verdery, K. (1999). *Political Lives of Dead Bodies: Reburial and Postcolonial Change*. New York: Columbia University Press.
"Verozakonsko učenje Talmuda ili Ogledalo Čivutskog poštenja" (Laws of the Talmudic faith, or the mirror of Kyke honesty). (1926). *Hrišćanska Zajednica* 5, no. 4, pp. 8–11.

Vojinović, H. (1971). "Narodna hrišćanska zajednica" (National Christian Association). In Synod of the Serbian Orthodox Church, *Srpska Pravoslavna Crkva 1920–1970: Spomenica o 50-godišnjici vaspostavljanja Srpske patrijaršije* (Serbian Orthodox Church 1920–1970: Commemorative volume marking the 50th anniversary of the inauguration of the Serbian patriarchate). Belgrade: Holy Synod of the Serbian Orthodox Church, pp. 347–362.

Volovici, L. (1994). "Antisemitism in post-communist Eastern Europe: a marginal or central issue?" *Analysis of Current Trends in Antisemitism* 5. Vidal Sassoon International Centre for the Study of Antisemitism, Hebrew University, Jerusalem.

Wachtel, A.B. (1998). *Making a Nation, Breaking a Nation: Literature and cultural politics in Yugoslavia.* Stanford, CA: Stanford University Press

Wertsch, J.V. (2002). *Voices of Collective Remembering.* Cambridge: CUP

West, R. (1994). *Black Lamb and Grey Falcon: A Journey Through Yugoslavia.* London: Penguin Books.

Wetherell, M., and Potter, J. (1992). *Mapping the Language of Racism: Discourse and the Legitimation of Exploitation.* London: Harvester Wheatsheaf.

White, L. (2000). "Telling lies: lies secrets and history." *History and Theory* 39, pp. 11–22.

Wistrich, R.S. (1991). *Antisemitism: The Longest Hatred.* London: Mandarin.

Wodak, R. (1991). "Turning the tables: antisemitic discourse in post-war Austria." *Discourse and Society* 2, no. 1, pp. 65–83.

Wood, N. (1999). *Vectors of Memory: Legacies of Trauma in Post-War Europe.* Oxford: Berg.

Woodward, K. (1991). *Making Saints.* London: Chatto & Windus.

Wooffitt, R. (1992). *Telling Tales of the Unexpected: The Organization of Factual Discourse.* Hemel Hempstead: Harvester Wheatsheaf.

Woolgar, S. (1988). *Science: The Very Idea.* London: Tavistock.

Yates, F. A. (1966). *The Art of Memory.* Chicago: University of Chicago Press.

"Zapisnik XVII redovne skupštine sveštenstva Eparhije žičke oržane na dan 16/3 jula u manastiru Žiči" (Minutes of the 17th regular meeting of the clergy of the diocese of Žiča held in Žiča Monastery on 16th/3rd July). (1936). *Pregled crkve eparhije žičke* 11, p. 23.

Zeljajić, Đ. (1988). "Poslednje godine Vladike Nikolaja u Americi" (The final years of Bishop Nikolaj in America). *Glas Crkve* 2, pp. 23–25.

Živković, M. (2000). "The Wish to Be a Jew: The Power of the Jewish Trope in the Yugoslav Conflict." *Cahiers de l'URMIS* 6, pp. 69–84.

Živojinović, D.R. (1998). *Srpska pravoslavna crkva i nova vlast 1944–1950* (The Serbian Orthodox Church and the new government 1944–1950). Belgrade: Hrišćanska Misao.

"Znaci zla kao simboli vremena" (Signs of evil as symbols of our time). (2002). *BH Dani*, August 9. http://www.bhdani.com/arhiva/269/t26902.shtml (accessed 1 June 2007).

"Žurnalistika—ili ????" (Journalism—or ????). (1987). *Glas Crkve* 1, pp. 73–74.

Index